Arguing for Socialism

Arguing for Socialism

Theoretical Considerations

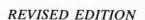

ANDREW LEVINE

REVISED EDITION

VERSO

London · New York

First published in 1984 by Routledge & Kegan Paul plc
This edition published by Verso 1988
© Andrew Levine 1984, 1988
All rights reserved

Verso
UK: 6 Meard Street, London W1V 3HR
USA: 29 West 35th Street, New York, NY 10001–2291

Verso is the imprint of New Left Books

British Library Cataloguing in Publication Data

Levine, Andrew, *1944–*
  Arguing for socialism: theoretical
  considerations.—Rev. ed.
  1. Socialism
  I. Title
  335

  ISBN 0–86091–918–8

US Library of Congress Cataloging in Publication Data

Levin, Andrew, 1944–
  Arguing for socialism: theoretical considerations / Andrew
  Levine.—Rev. ed.
     p.   cm.
  Bibliography: p.
  ISBN 0–86091–918–8 (pbk.) : £9.95 ($16.95 U.S.)
  1. Communism. 2. Socialism. 3. Capitalism. I. Title.
  HX73.L46 1988
  335.43—dc19

Printed in Great Britain by Biddles Ltd, Guildford.

Contents

Preface to the Paperback Edition

When I wrote *Arguing for Socialism* in 1982 and 1983, it was still possible to suppose, from on the scene, that it was a peculiarly American foible to hold socialism in disrepute. Within just a few years, this sense of things, like so much else American, has gained ground in Europe, too – and indeed throughout the world. In part, blame must be ascribed to the evident shortcomings of political forces – in and out of power – that if socialist at all in anything more than name, have been woefully insufficiently so. But the continuing ascendancy of the Right in the United States, in Britain and elsewhere has also contributed to this change in intellectual fashion. In the age of Reagan, Thatcher, et al., political culture and political theory have shifted palpably rightward – to the detriment of socialism's reputation. Arguing for capitalism and against socialism has become an increasingly prominent motif of mainstream political theory, and many of the arguments I originally set out to debunk have gained in influence accordingly. To argue for socialism today is more than ever to cry in the wilderness. But there is consolation in the fact that times can also change for the better; and that even now it is reasonable sometimes to expect the better argument to prevail.

What follows compares socialism and capitalism in light of prevailing standards drawn from mainstream social, political and moral philosophy. Given the intellectual climate of the past few years, my account of some of these standards may already seem anachronistic. In particular, the egalitarianism of the view of justice I endorse, and the dismissive stance I take towards rights, will strike some readers as unwarranted. In thinking about justice, I took – and still take – John Rawls's account in *A Theory of Justice* as a point of departure; and, with regard to rights, I accepted – and still accept – the assessment of the classical utilitarians. Were I to rewrite this book today, it would be necessary to devote more space to alternative, neo-Lockean, conceptions of justice and therefore to take rights talk more seriously. Much might be gained by addressing these and other challenges to the views which I defend. But I remain convinced that these positions are false starts, and that to consider them would not in any fundamental way alter what I go on to claim. Still, I do concede that in the few years that have elapsed since *Arguing for Socialism* first appeared, it has become more difficult to represent what I say about justice and rights as *the* consensus view. Nevertheless, I am content to let what I wrote pass unchanged. Indeed, I would venture that, before long, the inegalitarian and individualistic ideas that have recently become influential will themselves seem anachronistic, while the views that follow here will remain timely.

I am confident that the recent eclipse of socialism too shall pass. However it has become clear in the present crisis that socialism must be rethought. To this end, it is worth calling attention to two aspects of my argument here:

- the role accorded *democracy*, not just in the transition from capitalism to socialism, but above all in the development of *desirable* forms of socialism; and

- the claim that it is the *deprivatization* of real ownership of alienable productive assets that distinguishes socialism from capitalism and that accounts, in turn, for socialism's relative advantages over capitalism (allowing for the considerable indeterminacy that affects comparative assessments at this level of abstraction).

Developing socialist political theory – and elaborating the connection between socialism and democracy – is a priority task for socialists. I have written more on this subject in *The End of the State* (Verso, 1987). But here I would underscore once again a central theme of what follows: the paramount importance of joining the struggle for socialism with the struggle for democracy.

My second point deserves attention, too: the deprivatization of ownership of alienable productive assets is tantamount to ending the control capitalists exercise over investments and disinvestments. Allowing for the futility of moving directly from theoretical considerations to strategic proposals, a practical recommendation suggested by my argument is that socialists again make control over investments a paramount political objective. This emphasis may seem old-fashioned at a time when the energizing forces on the Left come from social movements – for peace, for the rights of women and oppressed minorities, for sound environmental policies – barely concerned with venerable socialist programmes. Old-fashioned, perhaps; but not wrong-headed. The old idea retains an enduring vitality.

In the spirit of this suggestion, I have added an Afterword to this edition, in which I defend a more traditional socialist politics than is nowadays fashionable on the Left. To be sure, the considerations I adduce are largely independent of the arguments advanced in the main text. But not entirely: the theoretical considerations marshalled in the chapters that follow do bear on questions of socialist strategy. Nothing can be concluded definitively. Similarly, neither can anything be concluded definitively at the level of abstraction appropriate for a philosophical investigation of socialism and capitalism. Nevertheless, in arguing among socialists, as in arguing for socialism, ostensibly remote theoretical considerations do have considerable force.

In any case, it is urgent that we socialists again address the perennial question: What is to be done? Through too little fault of our own, the old order is changing. As we emerge from this unhappy decade into a period fraught with dangers – but also offering fresh possibilities – it is crucial that we resume socialist politics on a sound basis, while at the same time continuing to develop socialist theory. These have been dark times for socialists, and perilous times for humankind. But with luck and effort, it is a time from which we shall emerge, disillusioned and chastened, but also strengthened and more capable of waging the fight for what is still humanity's best – and perhaps only – alternative to barbarism and annihilating war.

February 1988

Acknowledgments

This book grew out of a course on capitalism versus socialism, taught at the University of Wisconsin-Madison in 1978 and again in 1981 and 1983. Portions of Chapters 3 and 6 draw on material published in essays written for *Politics and Society*: "Balibar on the Dictatorship of the Proletariat" (vol. 7, no. 1, 1977), a review of Etienne Balibar's *On the Dictatorship of the Proletariat* (London: New Left Books, 1977); and "Toward a Marxian Theory of Justice" (vol. 11, no. 3, 1982), a contribution to a symposium on the work of John Roemer. Chapter 5 draws substantially upon a review essay I wrote with Erik Olin Wright about G.A. Cohen's *Karl Marx's Theory of History: A Defence* (Oxford University Press and Princeton University Press, 1978), published in *New Left Review* (no. 123, 1980).

Of the many students, friends and colleagues whose help has been invaluable, special thanks are due Judith Leavitt, Lewis Leavitt and Julius Sensat. In addition to co-authoring the ancestor to what is now Chapter 5, Erik Wright delayed the final submission of the manuscript for several months, by commenting upon an earlier draft with a degree of rigor and detail that can only be described as heroic. The temptation to blame him for the errors and inaccuracies that remain is overwhelming. Instead, I dedicate this book to him in comradeship.

Introduction

In comparing socialism and capitalism with a view to assessing how well each fares in theory, the first task is to explain how "socialism" and "capitalism" will be understood. The disparate and even conflicting uses of these terms in ongoing political discussion make this task more difficult than might at first appear.

"Socialism" is, at once, deeply contested and highly charged. Nearly everywhere, the United States conspicuously excepted, socialism is very much a political presence. There is, of course, a longstanding socialist tradition even in the United States; but American socialism, since the First World War, has exercised only a marginal impact on American politics. In most other industrialized, capitalist countries, the situation is quite different. Substantial numbers of workers and intellectuals are committed, in varying degrees, to one or another variety of socialism, as are individuals from nearly all social strata. Most important organized labor movements deem themselves socialist. And socialist parties have participated in and even controlled governments, sometimes for many years. While today there exists a widely perceived "crisis" in socialist movements, socialism is still considered by many people throughout the capitalist world to be humanity's best hope and future. In what has come to be called the Third World, the developing countries of Asia, Africa and Latin America, socialism is a nearly universal creed among educated and progressive people, and enjoys at least the passive support of the overwhelming majority of peasants and workers. It has proponents too within many ruling elites; and in some Third World countries, it is even acknowledged as a ruling ideology. In the Communist countries where nearly half of the world's population lives, socialism is, of course, a fundamental component of the

1

"civil religion"; and so, like capitalism in the United States, is accepted doctrine for the large and generally silent majority. There is, to be sure, substantial and (where possible) growing dissent in some of these countries that takes issue with prevailing social and political institutions. But this dissent is seldom expressly anti-socialist and almost never directly pro-capitalist. Socialism has its detractors everywhere, of course; but it is a fair guess that, nearly everywhere outside North America, it is the preferred system of political economy in enlightened public opinion, with broad support among the world's peoples.

But what is "socialism"? It is enough to survey, even at a glance, the range of positions that represent themselves as "socialist" to see that the term is used so variously that, despite the widespread support we find for "socialism" throughout the world, there is virtually no agreement on a definition. If there is something declared socialists share, beyond fidelity to a name, it is a certain hostility, sometimes very attenuated, to capitalism. But anti-capitalism is a slender bond indeed; for many declared socialists, in perfectly good faith, have helped to rule capitalist countries and to pursue policies intended to strengthen their national capitalisms.

There is considerable confusion about "capitalism" too. But it is striking that capitalism, unlike socialism, is very seldom upheld as an ideal to be pursued. What capitalism's defenders prefer to uphold is the euphemism "free enterprise" or even 'freedom" or "democracy" (as though these standards were inextricably linked or even somehow identical with capitalism). This is good public relations, certainly, but bad philosophy, as we will go on to see. Of course, capitalism as such does have its unabashed defenders; and, from time to time, in favorable political circumstances, their views have become prominent. Still, for the most part, even in the most favorable of circumstances, pro-capitalists, with important exceptions, remain characteristically unenthusiastic.

Outside the industrial, capitalist countries, capitalism is even less often defended, except by those who have a plain stake in its continuation. Among peoples recently emerged from traditional societies – and palpably victimized by capitalist expansion – capitalism could hardly have much appeal. In these societies, traditional values and ideologies continue to play an important and sometimes explosive role. Arguably, the resulting turmoil may

2

help, in the end, to strengthen capitalism. But capitalism is hardly a guiding ideology in the Third World today, and still less a goal to be sought after, as socialism is throughout so much of the world. Similarly, in the Soviet Union and China, where capitalism had only begun to be established and to develop before social revolutions wrested these massive territories and populations out of the world capitalist orbit, anti-socialism, where it exists, is more often represented in pre-capitalist ideological forms than in express support for capitalism. The non- or even anti-socialist values affirmed are more often traditional values than specifically capitalist ones.

I think capitalism's generally unattractive image helps to make what its defenders say in its behalf relatively more useful, for clarifying what capitalism is and what can be said for it, than much – but by no means all – of what is said on behalf of socialism. There is less temptation to let "capitalism" stand for whatever, at a particular time and place, is deemed desirable or expedient; less tendency for the term to take on varied and misleading significances. But there is confusion about "capitalism," even so, as the widespread identification of capitalism with freedom and democracy plainly attests.

The situation, in short, is muddled. Ongoing discussion is frequently misleading and confused. And more theoretical treatments of socialism and capitalism too often accede to the prevailing confusion. Suitable definitions of socialism and capitalism can hardly be derived, therefore, by attending just to usage.

I suspect that much of the opposition there is to socialism in the West has less to do with expressly philosophical considerations than with perceptions (sometimes accurate, sometimes fanciful) of the actual functioning of socialist and capitalist societies. It is widely believed that capitalism delivers the goods better, and supports individual freedom and political and civil rights in doing so. Socialism, especially Soviet socialism, appears woefully inefficient, dreary and tyrannical. Existing socialism is capitalism's most effective argument.

Perceptions of this sort are important politically to the extent they shape individual and collective behavior, but they are of little direct philosophical relevance. Even granting that the situation is as widely perceived, and conceding that the Communist countries are correctly described as socialist, the most that follows is that socialist societies can be less attractive, according to prevailing standards, than capitalist societies. *Does* implies *can*; not *must*. Blame for the shortcomings of "actually existing socialism"[1] is, of course, important to locate – above all, for socialists. But that is not the issue here. For socialism to compare favorably to capitalism, it is not necessary to maintain that *any* socialism is preferable to *any* capitalism. What would have to be shown is that in general socialism is superior to capitalism according to acknowledged standards for comparison; and that possible – that is, historically feasible – socialisms can realize this superiority. Even if the Soviet Union or China fare worse, say, than the capitalist countries of North America, Western Europe or Japan with respect to some or all of the pertinent standards for comparison, nothing follows directly on the relative merits of socialism and capitalism, conceived as *theories* of social and economic arrangements. The point here is to compare *visions* of historically feasible social orders, not actual societies – socialist or capitalist – that, for a variety of reasons, fail to fulfill all or even very many of the expectations pro-socialists or pro-capitalists might hold for them.

However, even a comparison of social visions cannot ignore the real worlds of socialism and capitalism. It is fatal to any social vision, no matter how appealing, if it cannot be implemented; or if its implementation is likely to yield undesirable, unintended consequences. Normative theories of society must be sensitive to psychological and historical limitations, to "human nature" and circumstance. Therefore it is crucial to pay attention to the *practicability* of the social visions under consideration here. In this regard, the fate and vicissitudes of actually existing socialism and capitalism plainly are relevant. Precisely what relevance this historical evidence bears, however, cannot be specified in general. It depends on the particular issues under consideration. In all cases, however, it is important not to draw hasty conclusions. Accounts of existing socialist or capitalist societies, whatever their relevance to particular questions, do not in themselves substitute for considered arguments about socialism and capitalism.

Some definitions

In view of the situation just sketched, suitable definitions of "capitalism" and "socialism" cannot be derived just by attending to how these terms are commonly used. Stipulative definitions are unavoidable. However, it is desirable that our definitions connect with and, where possible, reconstruct actual views. For this reason, among others, it is best to define our terms weakly, specifying only very minimal conditions, in order to encompass as much as we can of what, in current discussion, "capitalism" and "socialism" are used to represent.

To this end, let us call political economic arrangements *capitalist* if there are no economically significant juridical or customary relations of bondage or hierarchy (and therefore the possibility of free wage labor exists) and there is *private ownership* of society's principal means of production.[2] Political economic arrangements are *socialist* when private ownership of the means of production is replaced by some form of non-private or public ownership; that is, when ownership of productive capacities is deprivatized or, equivalently (for the present), socialized.

This definition of "capitalism" admits of at least two readings, depending upon how "private ownership" is understood. If understood to imply only rights to *income* derived from owned assets, the resulting view of capitalism is adequate for some purposes – for example, for grasping "capitalist exploitation" (see Chapter 2) – but too weak for a comparative evaluation of socialism and capitalism. We can call political economic systems that satisfy this weak understanding of "private ownership" *minimally capitalist*. Needless to say, it is difficult to imagine a minimal capitalism where those with rights to income derived from owned assets do not also enjoy at least some rights over the movement and disposition of these assets. Indeed, it is natural to understand "private ownership" in this stronger sense, and therefore to define *capitalism* as a political economic system with formal equality and at least some private *control* of productive capacities. We can leave the nature and extent of that control unspecified, except to note, again, that the weaker the final specification – the closer capitalism comes to minimal capitalism – the more encompassing our view of capitalism will be and therefore the better for reconstructing the broad spectrum of actual views. In any case, however, it is finally specified, capitalism is understood to imply minimal capitalism, but not vice versa. Under capitalism, then, there are differential returns to capitalists in virtue of private ownership. Under socialism, this distinctively capitalist mechanism for allocating resources – and generating inequality – is abolished.

Private ownership will typically take the form of *individual* ownership, but it need not. In principle, there can be collective capitalists; groups within society that, in the senses just sketched, own assets. Needless to say, this possibility is unlikely on a large scale. But the theoretical possibility cannot be excluded. If existing capitalist enterprises were somehow transformed into cooperatives with collective ownership of productive capacities – and nothing else changed – the resulting economic order would still count as capitalist. *Public* ownership means ownership by the public; not by some constituent part of it.

The terms "socialism" and "capitalism" will apply to societies, and to enterprises within societies only derivatively. Nationalized firms are publicly owned, according to our definition, even on its weaker reading, because no individual or group less than the state itself, representing the public, has a claim on income derived from their assets. But nationalized firms are not socialist firms, so long as they operate in societies where the principal means of production remain privately owned. I will not discuss here whether socialism might be achieved through successive nationalizations of private enterprises, nor whether, if it could, the result would be likely to fulfill socialists' hopes, except to register skepticism on both counts. Characteristically, nationalized firms resemble capitalist firms in their internal organization, wage differentials and authority structures. But it is not in virtue of these characteristics that they fail to count as socialist. They are not socialist firms because they operate in capitalist societies. Publicly owned firms in capitalist societies are, in effect, capitalist firms without capitalists – firms where the state assumes the capitalist's role.[3]

Socialism is defined here in relation to capitalism. It supposes capitalism's already substantial victory over political economic arrangements based on the division of society into economically significant estates. Capitalism requires formal equality of persons – to the extent that persons must be able to become wage laborers and, more generally, to enter into contractual relations. Socialism takes over the formal equality capitalism has secured, while radically altering capitalism's other distinctive feature: the private ownership of society's principal means of production. Socialism is post-capitalism; capitalism without private property in means of production.[4]

The abolition of private property in means of production is part of what all, or very nearly all, socialists intend in speaking of socialism. Many socialists, of course, intend more as well: the more equal distribution of social goods, the absence of relations of domination between individuals and groups, the democratization of decision-making processes, and so on. However, it is well to distinguish values socialists hope to realize under socialism – values generally shared with pro-capitalists – from socialism itself. For this reason too, it is best to define socialism weakly; and to see how well it fares, thus defined, with respect to widely shared standards of assessment.

Our question, then, is: is it better in general that there be private or public ownership of society's principal means of production? As already noted, this question admits of no determinate and sure answer, though I will argue that the weight of considered speculation does incline in socialism's favor. At this level of abstraction from concrete institutional specifications, nothing definitive can be concluded. But a plausible case, based on reasonable speculations, can be constructed.

In the chapters to follow, however, it will emerge that at least one form of socialism – the form Soviet society approximates, where capitalist property relations are supplanted by state, bureaucratic domination – very likely does *not* fare better than capitalism with respect to many of our theoretical standards. I will call this form of socialism the *state bureaucratic model*. It will be distinguished principally from what, for now, we may call the *democratic model*. In the democratic model, what replaces private ownership is collective control, exercised democratically, by the direct producers themselves. In Part Two, the democratic model will be examined in light of specifically Marxian theoretical commitments. Its historical possibility and desirability will be investigated and, so far as is possible in theory, defended. In doing so, a number of hesitations about socialism in the sense of post-capitalism – a sense broad enough to include the state bureaucratic model – will be addressed.

The term "model" is used to emphasize that it is theories of political economic arrangements, not actually existing societies, that are in question. To distinguish models of socialism is to diminish somewhat the level of abstraction by specifying something of the character of administrative institutions. But we are still at considerable remove from actually existing social orders that acknowledge and even, to some degree, approximate these theoretical forms.

Since it is my intent here to argue for socialism, it is tempting to distinguish among possible socialisms (post-capitalisms) and to reserve the honorific title of "socialism" just for what I have called the democratic model. I would thereby relieve myself of the doubtful task of defending state bureaucratic socialism; and would be able to launch a far more decisive case against capitalism than I otherwise might. There are two principal reasons why I have chosen to resist this temptation. The first and most obvious is that to do so would be to deviate too far from common usage. Whatever else actually existing socialism may be, it is surely, by nearly all accounts, socialist. The second, more theoretical reason is just that I think socialism, even in the sense of post-capitalism, is defensible, albeit weakly; and that it is of considerable interest to investigate how far, at this level of abstraction, that defense can proceed.

I should add, finally, that, in my view, state bureaucratic socialism need not be nearly so bad as actually existing socialism appears to be. Defenders of socialism today find themselves in something like the situation pro-capitalists might, if the only existing capitalist societies were, say, Botha's South Africa, Pinochet's Chile or Hitler's Germany. Plainly, capitalism is compatible with despotic political and social arrangements; and so is socialism. It is important and even urgent to account for the emergence and persistence of such forms, with or without private property in means of production. The fact that, to date, despotic social and political arrangements have been nearly universal under socialism, but not under capitalism, may indeed be of some moment for the comparative assessment of socialism and capitalism as normative theories. This suggestion will be explored in Part Two. For now, I would simply assert that the dismal fate of actually existing state bureaucratic socialism, however embarrassing for pro-socialists, is not an insurmountable obstacle in the way of defending socialism (post-capitalism), including even state bureaucratic socialism. Blame for existing socialism lies much less with its political economic arrangements than with conjunctural historical and political circumstances. I would venture too that despotic forms of capitalist society may be explained similarly.

Markets are systems of exchange in which goods, services or money are transferred through voluntary, bilateral transactions. Where there are markets, coordination is achieved, as it were, without a coordinator; without any structure of command (as in central planning). Neither custom nor law determines market allocations (though, of course, custom and law may regulate market arrangements substantially). Allocations result just from the voluntary transactions of individuals or firms. Markets are *free* if the voluntary, bilateral transactions that constitute them are such that market participants are "price takers," unable by themselves to determine the terms of trade. This requirement speaks as much against monopolistic concentrations of resources as it does against direct state interference with market allocations. Plainly, few if any extant capitalist markets are free in this sense.

Capitalism characteristically relies substantially on markets – in labor and produced goods and also, of course, in capital itself. A reliance on markets is, at least to some degree, unavoidable under capitalism. Still, capitalism should not be identified with market arrangements. The common euphemism for capitalism, "free enterprise," is actually an amalgam of two distinct notions: free markets and private enterprise. Free markets, though not markets in general, have little role in actual capitalism. Nor are *free* markets essential for capitalism in theory. What distinguishes capitalism is private enterprise – private ownership of society's principal means of production.

Socialist societies can rely on markets too; at least for the allocation of labor resources and for produced goods, though more directly authoritative systems of allocation have tended to predominate not only in actually existing socialist societies (Yugoslavia partially excepted), but also in socialist theory. Market socialism is, to date, largely a speculative program. But a substantial reliance on markets under socialism is conceivable in principle. What socialism cannot support, even in principle, are market arrangements that effectively constitute (or reconstitute) private (presumably group, not individual) ownership of means of production. Thus capital markets are impossible under socialism, according to our definition; for they are incompatible with public ownership in our sense.[5]

Similarly, capitalism can support substantially more planning than actually existing capitalist societies yet have. But there is a limit to how much planning capitalism can support – the obverse of that limit confronted by market socialism. Planning cannot intrude to the point that it undoes private ownership of the means of production. Where private ownership is understood to mean just rights to income derived from assets, then of course no amount of planning need undo private ownership. Full-fledged social planning, including social direction of investment decisions, is compatible in principle with minimal capitalism; however historically improbable it may be. But if private ownership is understood to mean rights to the control of assets, then there is a limit to how far planning can proceed. It cannot proceed to the point where these rights are infringed. Capitalism, unlike strictly minimal capitalism, cannot dispense with markets altogether.

There is, therefore, a connection between socialism and planning and capitalism and markets. But it is a very weak connection and an entirely contingent one. Socialism cannot dispense with planning altogether, just because the historically feasible alternative to planning, markets, if introduced beyond a certain point, would undo social ownership of the means of production. And capitalism cannot dispense with markets altogether, because the alternative to market arrangements, central planning, if introduced beyond a certain point, would undo private ownership of the means of production. Still, socialism should not be identified with planning nor capitalism with markets. To a point, "market socialism" and "non-market capitalism" are possible. And, in any case, the dependence of socialism on planning and of capitalism on markets, follows from a lack of alternative, feasible means for allocating resources and coordinating activities, not from the nature of socialism and capitalism themselves.

Note, finally, that just as socialism, as defined here, need not imply workers' power (as some, but hardly all, socialists would have it), neither need capitalism imply capitalists' power, as many

Marxists would insist. Indeed, capitalism, in the very weak sense of our definition, can exist even when owners of capital are themselves direct producers; and where there is therefore, strictly speaking, no capitalist class, and no class of non-capitalists for capitalists to dominate. Thus Adam Smith's "early and rude state of society" would count as capitalist according to our definition. In the early and rude state of society, each person or household owns its own means of production; and products of labor that are not directly consumed (by their immediate producers) are exchanged in markets. There are no economically significant social divisions; and there is full freedom of contract. But there is no market in labor; for, by hypothesis, direct producers own the means of production with which they labor. There is free wage labor in principle, then; but in fact there is no wage labor. Strictly, then, there are neither capitalists nor proletarians. Still, means of production are privately owned both in the sense that individuals derive income from owned assets and in the sense that individuals control the assets from which they derive income. Thus, according to our definition, on both understandings of "private ownership," the early and rude state of society would count as capitalist.

In short, the proposed definitions of "socialism" and "capitalism" do not make reference to the class character of the societies in which private ownership does or does not exist. In Part Two, it will be necessary, in some contexts, to retreat from these very abstract definitions, and to consider forms of class domination. Even in Part Two, however, except where otherwise indicated, the difference between "socialism" and "capitalism" should be understood just in terms of the abolition or continuation of private property in means of production.

An overview

It will be helpful at the outset of an extended argument that touches on so many issues to state clearly what the overall position is. The general problem, again, is to determine how well socialism and capitalism fare with respect to important and widely shared theoretical standards. I have already remarked that no clear and unequivocal answer can be provided at this level of abstraction. However, a weak case for socialism can be sustained. Part One aims to support this contention.

Introduction

We will find that what replaces private property in means of production – state bureaucratic domination or direct democratic control – matters tremendously in comparisons of socialism and capitalism. If this question is left open, there is a weak case to be made for socialism over capitalism. But despite that result, for at least some pertinent standards, capitalism does seem to fare better than state bureaucratic socialism, though there is more to be said in favor of state bureaucratic socialism than might at first appear. On the other hand, a far stronger and less tentative case can be made for democratic socialism over capitalism and, of course, over non- or less democratic forms of socialism. In Part One, that case will be largely implicit, awaiting a fuller discussion – in Part Two – of the possibility and desirability of democratic socialism.

Part Two investigates and defends socialism in general and democratic socialism in particular, from a specifically Marxian vantage point. I will argue that Marxian views of history and politics together provide good reasons for supporting socialism over capitalism, and also for thinking democratic socialism both possible and desirable. Marxism provides good reasons for supporting the conclusions reached in Part One. However, even Marxism cannot provide a decisive case for socialism at this degree of remove from particular institutional specifications and historical considerations. The best that can be expected, still, is a case for socialism in theory.

Providing such a case is of moment not only for the immediate political task it (very partially) serves, but also for the critical examination of the standards against which socialism and capitalism are compared. Assessing the relative merits of socialism and capitalism is an unconventional but instructive way to do social and political philosophy. In what follows, standards for assessing socialism and capitalism will be as much under investigation as socialism and capitalism themselves. The question of socialism provides some purchase on these standards, individually and together. Socialism is not only a *political* ideal of paramount importance. It is also a notion of *philosophical* significance.

Part One

Part One

Introduction to Part One

In the next four chapters, I investigate socialism and capitalism in relation to concepts of freedom, equality and justice, social welfare and efficiency, democracy and respect for individuals' rights. I assume throughout what follows that there is a rough consensus on these and related values, and will speak, accordingly, of a *dominant tradition* in social and political philosophy.

This dominant tradition has emerged in the course of the past several centuries, particularly (but by no means exclusively) in the English-speaking world. The character of the dominant tradition, as it bears on arguments for and against socialism and capitalism, will emerge in the chapters to follow. For now, a very schematic account will help to provide bearings. What I would call *liberal democratic theory*, the specifically political theory of the dominant political culture, provides a convenient point of entry.

Liberal democratic theory is that genre of political argument that articulates, at once, both liberal and democratic judgments on political institutions. Very generally, the liberal judgment holds that there are aspects of persons' lives, including some important range of activities, that ought to be immune from (coercive) societal and, particularly, state interference. The democratic judgment holds that political decisions ought to be determined collectively, and that collective choices should be based upon individuals' choices for the alternatives in contention; though, typically, it is thought best that these choices be made indirectly – through representatives. In general, then, political institutions are justified, for liberal democrats, to the extent that they allow for the realization of these judgments.[1]

I have argued elsewhere[2] that liberal democratic theory rests upon distinctive notions of freedom (construed, roughly, as the

15

absence of coercive restraint in the pursuit of individuals' ends) and interest (where interests are held to be reducible ultimately, though not always directly, to wants); and that these notions of freedom and interest, in turn, rest upon a distinctive notion of practical reason of the sort Hobbes was among the first to articulate, according to which reason is purely instrumental (concerning the adaptation of means to ends) and does not rule substantively on the content of the ends individuals will. I would hazard too that the other, less specifically political notions that comprise what I designate the dominant tradition – equality and justice, welfare and efficiency – also rest upon this distinctive view of practical reason, though I will not attempt to defend that claim here. It will be enough to suggest that there is indeed a constellation of social and political concepts – in effect, a tradition within moral, social and political theory – within which a good deal of contemporary thinking about socialism and capitalism is framed.

Strictly speaking, it need not even be conceded that there is a coherent tradition, but only a general consensus on the particular values in question. In what follows, I will suppose this weaker claim, for each of the standards against which socialism and capitalism will be compared. As in any debate, the more agreement there is on fundamental assumptions, the more constructive discussion is likely to be. Where there is disagreement over what is most fundamental, it is virtually inevitable that those who disagree will end by talking past one another. It may be inevitable in any case that pro-socialists and pro-capitalists will talk past one another, in consequence of overwhelmingly hostile political commitments. But mutual incomprehension and futility of dialogue are at least in principle avoidable, for there is already substantial agreement on fundamental assumptions.

Within the parameters imposed by the dominant tradition, there are, to be sure, shades of difference; and these differences, even when slight in comparison to genuinely alternative ways of thinking about society and politics, can have momentous consequences for what is in question here. Care must be paid to these shades of difference and their implications. However, in no case are they so great as to undermine the possibility of constructive dialogue. Where there are significant shades of difference, the tendentially pro-socialist notions are generally more defensible than their tendentially pro-capitalist rivals.

The dominant tradition, while dominant, is not quite exclusive. There exists, I think, a distinctive idealist rival tradition, emerging in the works of such writers as Rousseau, Kant, Fichte, Hegel, the British Idealists and their successors. This alternative tradition supposes a different view of freedom (as autonomy or self-direction, with or without externally imposed, coercive restraint) and interest (irreducible, even in the final analysis, to wants; but conceived instead in an ideal-regarding sense). These notions, in turn, rest on a conception of practical reason, according to which reason *does* rule substantively on the content of our ends.[3] However, even in this alternative and largely incompatible tradition, ideas and theoretical formulations proper to the dominant tradition have penetrated extensively. In any case, idealism in moral and political theory has not fared well. Ideas proper to this tradition are of continuing importance, not least for defending the possibility of genuinely democratic socialism (see Chapter 6). But strictly idealist political theory is today virtually defunct. In a word, the dominant tradition dominates.

In comparing socialism and capitalism, reference will of course be made, from time to time, to Marxian arguments. But in Part One, no indispensable role will be played by any distinctively Marxian positions. In Part Two, a number of Marxian theses will be used to defend the possibility and desirability of democratic socialism. But how far, if at all, the Marxian theory of history or other distinctively Marxian positions, supposing they can be sustained, undercut the dominant tradition or idealism will remain moot. If Marx was right to insist, as he does in *The German Ideology*, that consciousness arises out of life and not life out of consciousness, it is unlikely that an elaborated view of social and political arrangements radically different from what we already have could now be elaborated. Existing standards can be criticized and radical alternatives proposed, but developed alternative conceptual frameworks, full-fledged rivals to the dominant tradition (or its subordinate, idealist rival), probably lie for now well beyond our grasp. So long as we remain in the sort of social order in which the dominant tradition and idealism developed, we cannot expect to supersede them, except programmatically and speculatively.

There is, therefore, no Marxian moral philosophy to rival the dominant tradition. It is not even clear what it would mean to assess dominant tradition values from a specifically Marxian point of view. It will be evident, however, that some dominant tradition standards bear a deeper affinity than others to specifically Marxian concerns. Autonomy particularly, but also justice, are important values for Marxists, as they are important throughout the dominant political culture.[4]

Philosophy comes into play less when there is puzzlement over clearly tractable questions than when it is unclear what would dissipate our puzzlement; when we do not know what the right questions to ask are, and what would count as answers. Conceptual quandaries brought on by accumulated challenges to received conceptual frameworks generate philosophical responses. In this sense, philosophy is an historical discipline. The problems it addresses are historically generated – by new knowledge that upsets inherited worldviews and conceptual schemes, and by changing material circumstances that put entrenched values and beliefs into question. Philosophical positions are therefore joined to the circumstances that elicit them.

For Western philosophy, the most important challenges to inherited conceptual frameworks have come from the sciences. Western philosophy was born in Greek antiquity in response to the conceptual challenges posed by the emergence of Greek mathematics. Modern philosophy, from Descartes on, is at least in part a response to the conceptual crisis generated by the new sciences of nature that, since the seventeenth century, have revolutionized human thought and profoundly upset established worldviews. Social and political philosophies have always, to some extent dwelt in the shadow of the epistemological and metaphysical concerns elicited by the challenge these and other cognitive developments have occasioned. But the general philosophical context within which society and politics are conceived is by no means the only, nor even the most important historical condition to be taken into account. Social and political philosophy – and moral philosophy too – occupy, so to speak, a relatively independent space. As one might expect, the theoretical upheavals that have decisively shaped Western thought, and Western philosophy particularly, are of less importance for shaping the dominant tradition in moral, social and political theory than are the major social and political upheavals that have transformed Western society. With the demise of European feudalism and the steady growth and consolidation of capitalism, the consequent rise of the bourgeoisie, and then the development of organized popular and especially working-class institutions, received views of society and politics have been put in perpetual crisis for at least three centuries. Without in any way detracting from the theoretical integrity and internal dynamic of philosophical discussion, we must pay heed to these real world conditions that have shaped the dominant tradition, if we are to grasp its character and understand its implications.

The ideas of freedom, equality and justice, welfare and efficiency, democracy and rights against which socialism and capitalism are to be compared are all linked historically to the emergence, development and continuation of bourgeois society. Each of these concepts, of course, has ancient roots. But in the precise senses that will figure here, each may be viewed as of relatively recent – that is, post-seventeenth century – origin. There is no reason to expect these notions, in their present senses, to endure perpetually into the future. The dominant tradition will be the last tradition only if civilization itself comes to an end or if fundamental historical change is somehow decisively blocked. However pervasive it may now be, the dominant tradition is ultimately transient. For now, though, its conceptual horizons are virtually inexorable. The dominant tradition is *our* tradition and will remain so, if Marx was right, for as long as bourgeois society continues.

The concepts that comprise what I have called the dominant tradition are sufficiently independent of one another to warrant separate discussions. However, arguments for socialism or capitalism that appeal to these standards are generally more interdependent. For better or worse, it is not possible to discuss everything at once. Particularly at the beginning, therefore, but also throughout the rest of Part One, this interdependence will be very evident. The conclusions drawn at any particular point will often depend upon or anticipate conclusions drawn elsewhere. Much of what follows is therefore very provisional. However, the tentative character of the positions I shall advance will diminish considerably if Part One is considered in its totality, as an extended discussion of distinct, but related, facets of our question.

1
Freedom

Before the English revolutions of the seventeenth century brought *freedom* into paramount importance as a political ideal, the term was used primarily to designate a legal status in a hierarchically structured society – of masters and slaves or lords and serfs. Slaves were unfree, while their masters, so long as they were not themselves also slaves, were free; and similarly for lords and serfs, despite their different juridical status. What was crucial was not mastery *per se*, but the absence of juridical domination. Thus throughout most of Europe, before capitalism and the full achievement of formal equality, coexisting with masters and bondsmen were free peasants and townsmen; deemed free precisely because there was no one to whom they were juridically bound. The absence of legally recognized domination is the core idea behind "freedom" in its earliest uses.

In traditional societies, where bonds of social solidarity took precedence over relations between individuals, the entities recognized as free or unfree might more often be households, villages or even entire political communities rather than individuals. Even today a state is called free if it is not subject to legally recognized domination by other political entities. This usage is a residue of the pre-seventeenth century use of the term.

In its post-seventeenth century uses, freedom is no longer an exclusively legal category; and it is not even any more a strictly political designation. It is widely appreciated how, with the emergence of bourgeois society, a singular and radical separation of the political from the social, of politics from society, has come into being.[1] Today, the idea of a non-political "civil society" and of politics existing in a realm apart from society, removed from ordinary social life, has become so commonplace that it requires

20

sustained intellectual effort even to conceive of society interpene-
trated and structured by politics, as most traditional political
philosophy, including important strains of idealist political theory,
conceived it to be.[2] In the dominant tradition, politics is distinct
from and subordinate to society. Its role is to maintain society, the
sphere of non-political individual and group activity. Political
institutions are praised or faulted by liberal democrats not so much
for their own sake, as they were for Aristotle or Rousseau, but for
their role in fostering (non-political) civil society and preventing its
dissolution. Against this background, as the importance and range
of application of freedom as a political ideal has expanded, its
theoretical significance has changed accordingly. Individuals or
groups are not free or unfree only with respect to states (or other
political entities), but with respect to others generally. Freedom is,
still, the absence of domination, but no longer only in relation to
the law. What was once a strictly juridical designation has become
a full-fledged social category.

Senses of freedom

Since the seventeenth century, freedom has taken on a number of
related, but conceptually distinct senses. In each case, the absence
of domination, the core idea of freedom in its earlier uses, may be
viewed as the underlying principle, however attenuated the link to
freedom in its pre-seventeenth century sense may have become. It
will be convenient to distinguish the following senses:

> *Freedom 1* (F1): the absence of political and social
> interference in the pursuit of one's ends;
> *Freedom 2* (F2): the ability – so far as this ability is socially
> conditioned – to pursue one's ends; and
> *Freedom 3* (F3): the ability – again, so far as this ability is
> socially conditioned – to set (achievable) ends before
> oneself; to be self-determining.

Freedom (F1) captures what is usually intended by "negative
freedom"; and freedom (F2) at least part of what is intended by
"positive freedom." However, that familiar distinction can
obscure the difference between idealist views of freedom and
freedom as conceived within the dominant tradition. Accounts of

21

"positive freedom" typically straddle these distinct senses.[3] It is therefore best to avoid the familiar terminology. In what follows, I will call freedom (F1) *liberty* and freedom (F2) *capacity-freedom*. Although "liberty" is sometimes used synonymously with "freedom," those who are inclined to prefer "liberty," libertarians particularly, tend to view freedom primarily, if not exclusively, as freedom (F1). The usage I propose is therefore more or less in line with common usage, at the same time that it is suggestive of what is intended by these distinctions. Freedom (F3) may be called *autonomy*, though with a reservation to be noted presently.

We are free (F2) to do X only if we are free (F1) to do it. Capacity-freedom presupposes liberty. But liberty does not presuppose capacity-freedom. We may be free (F1) to do X without being free (F2) to do it. Likewise, freedom (F3) supposes capacity-freedom (and therefore also liberty), but not vice versa. We may be free to do things we have not freely chosen to do; but we cannot freely choose to do things we are not able to do. Freedom (F3) captures what is normally intended by *autonomy*, in a sense compatible with dominant tradition views of practical reason. Idealists, supposing that reason rules substantively on the content of our ends, conceive autonomy as rational self-determination, determination by practical reason as such. Idealist autonomy is compatible with the denial of liberty. Reason may require that those who are recalcitrant to its requirements be "forced to be free."[4] But idealist autonomy has virtually nothing to do with ongoing debates over socialism and capitalism; and can be overlooked here in any case, since the intent is to compare socialism and capitalism against values posed in the dominant tradition, not its rivals. Accordingly, autonomy will be understood to presuppose capacity-freedom and therefore also liberty.

Freedom in each of its senses is a social category. What restricts freedom is therefore always imposed by others (whether or not through specifically political mechanisms). Circumstances of nature, in so far as they can be distinguished from social constraints, do not restrict liberty. And neither do physical inabilities restrict capacity-freedom. Likewise, cognitive limitations or shortcomings in individuals' capacities for judgment, in so far as these incapacities are strictly natural, do not restrict autonomy.

Distinguishing these senses of freedom will help, I think, to clarify the dominant view and also to cut through the imprecision and confusion that afflicts much current thinking about socialism and capitalism. The discussion to follow will be organized around these distinctions. I will show first that there is a case for capitalism with respect to liberty, but that its appeal depends on two mistaken assumptions: that freedom is *only* liberty; and that capitalist property relations are effectively beyond critical scrutiny. On these assumptions, an *a priori* argument for capitalism can be constructed, but the argument is unconvincing because the assumptions upon which it depends are unacceptable. Capitalist property is no more ineluctable than socialist property or indeed any system of property whatsoever. And the considerations that support our viewing freedom as liberty incline us also to view freedom as capacity-freedom and even as autonomy – senses of freedom for which pro-capitalist conclusions become increasingly untenable.

Our question may be put as follows: with respect to freedom, is it better or not that there be private property in means of production? We shall find that in general it *is* better that there *not* be private property in means of production. Thus socialism fares better than capitalism with respect to freedom, despite what is widely supposed. However, when we distinguish democratic from state bureaucratic socialism, our general conclusion will require qualification. It will be evident that the case for socialism with respect to freedom can be supported more easily for the former model than the latter. Indeed, we shall find that state bureaucratic socialism does not fare better than capitalism at all.

Again, it will not be possible to conclude anything definitively – in part because comparative assessments depend on empirical speculations that cannot be established with complete assurance, particularly at this degree of abstraction from concrete institutional specifications; and in part because what can be said at this point for socialism and against capitalism depends, to some extent, upon how well socialism and capitalism fare with respect to values to be considered subsequently. What follows, therefore, can only be indeterminate and also tentative. Nevertheless, there is a plausible case for socialism and against capitalism to be made.

Part One

Liberty and its rationale

For Hobbes, who was among the first to articulate a notion of liberty, freedom was conceived in systematic accord with a materialist metaphysics. In Hobbes's view, fundamental reality, matter, consists of atoms in (inertial) motion. These atoms bear only "external relations" to one another; the existence and character of any particular atom is logically independent of the existence and character of any and all others. Through their motions, atoms affect one another, of course; but no atom depends essentially upon any other. The world is a collection of these atoms, the fundamental constituents of reality. It is decomposable, therefore, into radically independent, fundamental units. Society, in the Hobbesian scheme, is then conceived by analogy with the world of matter.[5] Atomic individuals, bearing only external relations to one another, pursue their interests, just as physical atoms follow their inertial motions. In an enclosed territory, under conditions of scarcity, where there is general competition for the same, relatively scarce resources, "collisions" will result. If uncontrolled, these collisions can have disastrous consequences. Individuals' "motions" will be thwarted; interests will generally fail to be realized. But, so far as possible, we ought to encourage the realization of individuals' interests, for their pursuit is "natural," as the analogy with the inertial motions of atoms in physical space suggests. Ideally, institutions should be so constituted that collisions that cannot be eliminated will be accommodated – in the interests of the atomic individuals who comprise society. Essentially, individuals, like atoms in motion, are "free" (F1). Actual constraints are always contingent, arising in the main from the "motions" of other "atoms." So far as possible, then, these constraints ought to be removed. But even if some constraint is unavoidable, as Hobbes thought, no constraint is ever essential for determining our nature. We are essentially – and radically – free (F1). From its inception, then, liberty was part of a systematic vision in which the absence of constraint is pictured as a fundamental aspect of the natural order; and by parity of imagery, as a fundamental normative value. Hobbesian freedom, liberty, is a systematic part of an atomistic materialism that, in the view of Hobbes and his co-thinkers, gave definitive expression to a new scientific view of the world.

More important still for shaping our conception of liberty and bringing it into prominence is its evident historical pertinence; its connection with the profound social transformations of the seventeenth and succeeding centuries. Even for those who are skeptical of such associations, it is hard not to see in the concept of liberty a representation of the dissolution of feudal society, of the shattering of traditional bonds of social solidarity, and a glorification of atomized market relations. The call for liberty is a call against the old, traditional order, and for the new. It is a call for the radical independence of the individual. It represents a positive valorization of the fragmentation of feudal society and the emergence of atomizing capitalism.

At its origin, then, liberty was a forward-looking value – both for its role in articulating a new, scientific vision of reality, but even more for supporting the demise of feudalism and for encouraging capitalism, its historic successor.

Where liberty is a value, other things being equal, we should seek to have as much of it as possible. We should therefore aim at optimal levels of liberty; or, equivalently, minimal social or political interference with individuals' lives and behaviors.

Other things being equal, advocates of liberty should therefore support the traditional political liberties central to the liberal tradition – freedom of speech, assembly, religion and so on. In principle, of course, other things might not be equal. Political liberties might conflict with rival values, necessitating trade-offs. Or restricting political liberties might be necessary for optimizing liberty, for rendering persons more free (F1) in other domains. Conflicts with other values are unlikely, but not inconceivable. On the other hand, it is difficult even to imagine circumstances where political liberties need be restricted for the sake of liberty. It is therefore fair to conclude that other things generally will be equal; and that advocates of liberty should support the traditional political liberties.

But what of the "economic liberties" that make capitalist market relations possible – not just the freedom to buy and sell products of labor, but also the freedom to buy and sell labor itself, and to buy and sell capital (claims on real assets)? At first blush, it would seem that the argument for supporting political liberties should apply here as well. Individuals should be as free (F1) as possible to do as they please with their property, just as they should be as free (F1) as possible in matters of speech, assembly and religion. Thus it seems that the case against restricting political liberties carries over to the economic liberties. Traditional liberalism, epitomized in John Stuart Mill's *Principles of Political Economy*, was emphatic on this point. *Laissez faire* was Mill's prescribed policy in both domains.

Of course, even for traditional liberals, it is conceivable that, in the economic domain, other things might not be equal. It might be deemed expedient, for example, to deviate from strict *laissez faire*, for the sake of justice or welfare or to promote equality. Traditional liberalism could countenance these trade-offs, even if it was disinclined to make them. But in the traditional view, there is as little likelihood that economic freedoms need be restricted for the sake of liberty, as that political freedoms need be restricted on these grounds. If in contemporary mainstream liberal theory and practice, economic liberties are not quite so sacrosanct as political liberties are, it is because of perceived incompatibilities with other values. But if there is not quite the incontrovertible case for economic liberties that there is for political liberties, there remains, for all the heirs of traditional liberalism, a powerful presumption favouring these freedoms (F1). Contemporary libertarians are simply the most extreme in their advocacy. They faithfully continue the policy provisions of the intellectual ancestors of contemporary liberalism.

There is therefore an *a priori* case for capitalism where liberty is a value; a case that has weight to the extent liberty has priority over other values. It follows *a priori* – from a description of the system alone, in advance of any empirical speculations – that capitalism must be preferable to any alternative that is like it in other respects, but that proscribes capitalist market relations. For if only the economic liberties are considered – and all else held "constant" – any non-capitalist alternative must be less free (F1) than capitalism for proscribing what capitalism allows. But socialism is precisely like capitalism, but for the proscription of distinctively capitalist economic freedoms. Therefore, in this view, socialism proscribes more; and is less free.

To assess this pro-capitalist argument, it will be well to begin by reflecting why, for those who value liberty, liberty need ever be restricted. At first glance, it would seem that there ought to be no restrictions at all. However, advocates of liberty, virtually without exception, are also advocates of states. And states, by promulgating laws and imposing sanctions on disobedients, necessarily restrict liberty.

There plainly are circumstances in which some liberties need to be restricted, strictly, for liberty's sake. The liberty of those who would dominate others, or otherwise coercively restrain them from the pursuit of their ends, cannot be given free rein by those who would optimize liberty. But it is not only citizens' behaviors that may be in need of constraint. As traditional liberals were wont to insist, above all, citizens need protection from state officials. Laws promulgated in states are instrumental for these purposes, for establishing a framework within which individuals can freely (F1) pursue ends, without threatening the liberties of others. But this consideration by no means exhausts the liberal rationale for states.

A coherent and traditional case for states can be reconstructed as an argument for optimizing freedom (F2) by restricting liberty. It is instructive to make this case, both for underscoring how arbitrary it is to construe freedom *just* as liberty, and also to begin to question the apparent parity of the case for political and economic freedoms. An indispensable point of reference is the perspicacious and seminal account of the establishment of sovereignty in Hobbes's *Leviathan*.

Hobbes argued that the liberty of the state of nature, unrestrained by any public coercive force, is literally self-defeating, and requires restrictions – achieved through the institution of sovereignty – for its full realization. The argument is familiar and can be briefly resumed. In the state of nature – that is, in the absence of political institutions – where people coexist in the same territory and make conflicting demands on the same (relatively) scarce resources; and where people are sufficiently equal in mental and physical endowments that they are able, individually or collectively, to harm one another; and where individuals are moved, as Hobbes would have it, by "diffidence," "vainglory" and the desire to accumulate resources ceaselessly and without limit – everyone is in mortal competition with everyone for everything. The state of nature is therefore, in Hobbes's apt expression, "a war of all against all." In these circumstances, individuals' ends are generally unrealizable, and individuals' liberties are consequently in vain. The absolute liberty of the state of nature, it seems, diminishes freedom. This result might seem paradoxical; but the paradox is not fatal. The problem lies with our viewing freedom only as liberty, and Hobbes's clear account of the self-defeating character of absolute liberty reveals this error and suggests a remedy.

What Hobbes's account shows is that the rationale for viewing freedom as liberty requires that we view freedom as capacity-freedom as well. If the absence of (coercive) restraint is prized, then we ought also to value the socially conditioned capacity to do what we want. For what is the point of being free (F1) except to achieve our ends? Absolute liberty diminishes freedom (F2); but except in so far as liberty is deemed good in itself (as it may well be, but for what reason?), capacity-freedom is what makes liberty worth having. Hobbes therefore urges proponents of freedom to move away from absolute liberty; to institute restraints sufficient for insuring a common framework for regulating competition and conflict – *for capacity-freedom's sake*. In Hobbes's account, the establishment of sovereignty is the means by which individuals in the state of nature achieve this end. The sovereign establishes a political community with enforceable rules. In doing so, the absolute freedom (F1) of the state of nature is ended. Liberty is diminished. But this diminution of liberty is the price paid for a substantial gain in capacity-freedom. Limiting liberty, in the Hobbesian view, is indispensable for maximizing capacity-freedom.

Proponents of liberty ought, therefore, to advocate states, though states necessarily restrict liberty – but only minimal states. The best state is the state that governs least; that restricts liberty only to the extent necessary to insure optimal levels of liberty – and, above all, to maximize capacity-freedom. Any greater state would restrict liberty unnecessarily, and therefore diminish freedom in general.

If we follow Hobbes in granting that there is more to freedom than liberty, we see that there is no reason in principle why a minimal state might not proscribe capitalist property relations. To this end, it need only be shown that capacity-freedom is maximized by doing so. The issue is ultimately an empirical one, for which reasoned speculation, but not *a priori* argument is decisive. Needless to say, proponents of minimal states have shown a remarkable reluctance to put capitalist property relations in question. Historically, the minimal state suggested by the Hobbesian argument has been the "nightwatchman state" depicted by Locke and his followers. It is a state that exists mainly to support the acquisition and accumulation of capital. It provides sanctions against criminal behavior (where crime is conceived largely as crime against property), enforces contracts, and generally does all and only those things – like establishing a uniform monetary system and controlling the supply of money – that make capitalist markets function well. Proponents of minimal states usually will grant that the state should provide for "public goods" like defense, but they are reluctant to include much of what others ordinarily suppose to be public goods (roads, schools, means of communication) in this category. Most importantly, in the Lockean tradition, the minimal state does not transfer wealth from those who gain through market arrangements to those who lose; and still less does it proscribe the economic liberties that constitute capitalist property relations. But, again, there is no reason in principle why the minimal state must have the character commonly ascribed to it. A state that redistributes what the market has allocated or even one that bans "capitalist relations between consenting adults" altogether[6] could be a minimal state – should such prohibitions turn out to maximize capacity-freedom.

In the liberal tradition, following Locke, this possibility is ruled out in advance because prevailing property relations are taken as given (or, as for Locke himself, viewed as uniquely legitimate and therefore morally unalterable). If we are committed to capitalist private property come what may, then we are of course cut off from seeking to increase capacity-freedom by tampering with, or radically overturning, capitalist private property. But there is no warrant for regarding prevailing property relations as given. Capitalist private property is a human institution, of changeable character and transient duration. It is hardly "natural" or immutable. Nor is it supported by any sustainable normative theory of property rights. But once capitalist property relations are in question, the appeal of an *a priori* case for capitalism with respect to liberty collapses. There is of course still a *prima facie* case for the economic liberties, in the sense that *any* restrictions on freedom (F1) require justification. But there is no longer a clear parity between political and economic freedoms. No general reason, of even moderate plausibility, can be given for restricting political freedoms for freedom's sake, except perhaps for marginal categories of persons whose use of liberty might diminish the freedom (F1) of others. A case against traditional political freedoms, if it can be made at all, would have to appeal to values other than freedom. But it is quite different with the freedom to engage in capitalist relations. Commitment to liberty does imply commitment to a minimal state in the sense of the Hobbesian argument. But that state will be a Lockean minimal state only if, in fact, capacity-freedom is best served under such arrangements.

In comparing political economic arrangements, it is precisely systems of property that are in question. All systems of property restrict liberty. We are unfree (F1) to violate property rights, whatever they may be. If an asset is privately owned, as means of production are under capitalism, no one but the owner is free (F1) to use it, exchange it, or destroy it, except of course with the owner's permission. And even owners of property are not entirely free (F1) to do as they please with what they own. They cannot violate the law with it; nor can they infringe other people's rights, including their property rights. In short, private ownership restricts everyone's liberty somewhat, though non-owners are generally much more severely restricted than owners. In modern capitalist societies, private ownership is often severely regulated too; and hardly anyone, except perhaps the most ardent libertarians, would dispute the right of political communities, say, to pass zoning regulations or to regulate income derived from such forms of (private) property as patents or licenses. Thus the system of property relations in force in actually existing capitalist societies, like any system of property conceivable – including what would follow from the abolition of private property in means of production – restricts liberty, in varying degrees, for everybody. To declare property in or over anything is to declare a system of rules regulating access and use. These rules, in so far as they are recognized and enforced, limit liberty.

Thus to claim, as some libertarians do, that freedom consists in being unrestrained from doing what one wants with what one *owns*, is to ignore the respect in which what one owns is itself in question in assessing how free one is. Philosophical analysis alone will not settle the question. It is necessary to consider the likely consequences of living under different systems of property relations or, what comes to the same thing, under different sorts of restrictions on liberty. How capacity-free we are likely to be under socialism or capitalism is the pertinent question; and commitment to liberty, in and of itself, leaves this question emphatically open.

So long as we recognize that property is in question, it can be argued that under socialism, the loss of freedom for owners of property in means of production is offset by gains in capacity-freedom for others; so that freedom throughout society is increased. There can therefore be no automatic case for capitalism. Freedom supports capitalism directly and unequivocally only for those so wedded to the prevailing order that they effectively remove capitalist private property from critical scrutiny.

Whenever capitalist property is accorded some privileged status, there is, as we would expect, a bias in capitalism's favor. For it is natural to conclude, even if it is not strictly implied, that society is freest (F2) when owners of property are freest (F1) to do as they please with what they own; and capitalism is precisely the political economic system that accords the greatest degree of such liberty to owners of property. However, the question is not: given capitalist property, does socialism or capitalism best advance capacity-freedom? Rather the question is: which system of property relations, which sorts of restrictions on liberty, socialist or capitalist, are optimal for maximizing capacity-freedom? Neither question can be answered definitively, but only the former is even tendentially pro-capitalist. I suspect the widespread inclination to suppose that capitalism and freedom are closely joined follows, in part, from the mistaken view that the former question is the right question to ask.

How well socialism and capitalism fare with respect to liberty is hardly settled by noting that under socialism, but not capitalism, some liberties, the economic liberties, would be proscribed. If capitalism is preferable to socialism, so far as liberty goes, it will not be just in virtue of its allowing what socialism does not. What matters is not how many restrictions there are, but what the impact of allowing or proscribing capitalist relations is likely to be for what provides liberty's *raison d'être* – freedom (F2).

Part One

Capacity-freedom and equality

In showing how unrestricted liberty is self-defeating, Hobbes showed, in effect, how liberty is valuable instrumentally: for promoting the realization of individuals' ends. Liberty is worth having, in so far as it promotes capacity-freedom. This is not to say that capacity-freedom need be viewed as an end-in-itself. What the Hobbesian argument shows, strictly, is that whoever supports liberty as an ideal – including those who would defend capitalism by appeal to liberty – ought also to support capacity-freedom. Even liberty's most ardent defenders should therefore ask whether we are free (F2) under socialist or under capitalist property relations. Under capitalism we are free (F1) to do some things we are not free (F1) to do under socialism.[7] In particular, we are freer (F1) than we would otherwise be to dispose of and to use those productive assets we own. But does this freedom (F1) advance freedom (F2)?

In actual capitalism, productive capacities are not owned by those who labor on them, but by a class of non-laborers, the capitalists. Let us imagine, therefore, a model of capitalism that incorporates this feature of historical capitalisms, the division of society into owners of means of production and direct laborers. A consequence of the unequal distribution of means of production in this model is, of course, a very unequal distribution of income. Workers own nothing except what they are able to acquire through savings – that is, from unconsumed wages. In all likelihood, even if workers are able to command more than a subsistence wage, wages will be low in comparison with returns on owned assets. In this idealized capitalism, direct producers and owners of capital are equally free (F1). But we know that freedom (F1) is pointless and, we might say, merely "formal" for those who are unable to do what they want. The ability to do what one wants depends, in large part, on access to means for doing what one wants; and therefore, for individuals in our idealized capitalism, on income. If income is high enough to provide means for realizing ends, liberty matters substantively. If income is insufficient, liberty is merely formal. In our model, where only capitalists own means of production, it is likely that the liberty of rich capitalists will be substantive and of poor workers merely formal. Let us suppose, finally, that there are few capitalists and many propertyless direct producers.

Liberty is formal if we are free (F1) to do things we are not free (F2) to do. What will in fact render our freedoms (F1) substantive is, of course, historically variable. Formal and substantive liberty are distinguished here simply to indicate rough, qualitative differences in access to means for the realization of ends. What counts as means for realizing ends depends, in large part, on what is historically possible and ultimately, therefore, on a society's level of development. It is fair to assume that there is, as it were, an historically variable norm specifying a degree of access to means for rendering some historically variable repertoire of ends achievable. In so far as individuals have access to means below that norm, their liberty is merely formal. Otherwise it will count as substantive.

In so far as this idealized model reconstructs pertinent features of actual capitalisms, there is a *prima facie* case against capitalism – and therefore for its rival, socialism – with respect to capacity-freedom. Under capitalism, a sizable portion of the population, the direct producers, are relatively unfree (F2), for they do not have access to means sufficient for realizing their ends. Only the relatively few capitalists are genuinely free (F2). It would seem to follow, then, that capacity-freedom would be better served under political economic arrangements in which direct producers might have the consequence of diminishing the capacity-freedom of capitalists. But, for advocates of capacity-freedom, producers might have the consequence of diminishing the capacity-freedom of capitalists. But, for advocates of capacity-freedom, this should be an acceptable price to pay. Capitalists are, by hypothesis, few in number, while direct producers are many. If we count individuals equally in determinations of social well-being, as the dominant political culture would have us do (see Chapter 3), it would follow that freedom (F2) would be advanced by promoting the freedom (F2) of the many, even if need be at the expense of the few. Socialism, in so far as it equalizes access to the means for realizing ends, would have precisely this effect. Therefore, with respect to freedom (F2), socialism seems to fare better than capitalism.

Of course, this is a weak argument, even if we grant its quasi-utilitarian rationale. For it invokes a view of capitalism where workers are very poorly off – at the limit, where they have "nothing to lose but their chains" – and of socialisms that distribute goods and services, so far as possible, with a view to enhancing capacity-freedom. This picture is not unreasonable, but it is hardly incontrovertible. It is far from obvious that distributions under socialism and capitalism need have the character just imputed to them. In principle and in fact, workers under capitalism can have much more than chains to lose; and there is no firm assurance that under capitalism they are bound to do worse than under socialism.[8] Indeed, at this level of generality, nothing definitive can be concluded. For there is no sure correlation between socialism, capitalism and equality, nor for that matter between equality and capacity-freedom. However, the argument is not entirely without merit. For it *is* reasonable to suppose that equality fares better under socialism than under capitalism, though not necessarily in *all* socialisms (see Chapter 2); and it is likely too that freedom, in both the senses so far in question, fares best the more equally scarce resources are distributed – wherever unequal access to the means for realizing ends can be held to blame for rendering freedoms (F1) merely formal.

Under conditions of abundance, where all have access to whatever is needed to realize their ends, this putative connection, between freedom and equality, would be of no account. Indeed, distributional considerations generally would cease to matter (see Chapter 2). But scarcity and abundance too are historically relative notions, varying directly with productive capacities. The more there is, the more it is possible to do; and the more is needed with which to do it. In principle, superabundance, a saturation of means for realizing ends, is conceivable. But I would venture that it is unachievable – that scarcity is unavoidable, and abundance unattainable – so long as gross inequalities persist. In any case, today, scarcity plainly persists; and distributional questions are pertinent. In such circumstances, the view that more egalitarian distributions would help to promote capacity-freedom is clearly plausible. Its plausibility redounds in socialism's favor.

Autonomy

Autonomy is much less often invoked in the dominant tradition, even implicitly, than liberty or capacity-freedom, in large part because it is so easily construed in a way that is foreign to the spirit and letter of that tradition. The ability to shape the ends one pursues sounds very much like the rational self-determination we find in the idealist tradition, and raises the spectre of "totalitarian" usurpations of freedom for freedom's sake.[9] But the dominant tradition can encompass a notion of autonomy; and indeed, I think it must, in so far as it is committed to liberty and therefore also to capacity-freedom. We have seen that capacity-freedom is the point of liberty; the absence of socially imposed constraint is of value in so far as it facilitates our doing what we want. Both liberty and capacity-freedom, in turn, are of little moment, except in so far as the ends of our actions – ultimately, our wants – are themselves self-determined.

If our wants are imposed upon us, what is the advantage, even for those who (initially) value only liberty, in our being free (F1) to pursue them? And what difference does it make how free (F2) we might be to realize these ends? Plainly, there is no point to liberty or to capacity-freedom in such circumstances. We might as well be straightforwardly coerced. Intuitively, if I want X because a desire for X has been somehow instilled in me, say by "brainwashing" or by the administration of mind-altering drugs, my pursuit of X is hardly a free act, however free (F1) I may be to pursue X and however free (F2) I am to obtain it. To this conclusion, any proponent of liberty (and therefore of capacity-freedom) should assent. Then a commitment to at least part of what is intended by "autonomy" – freedom from the deliberate imposition of ends – is unavoidable for advocates of liberty and capacity-freedom.

Attempts at persuasion, in so far as they rely on the presentation of information and rational argument, do not restrict freedom[10]. But control over ends through extra-rational means must be considered differently. At the very least, freedom is undone when ends are manipulated *deliberately*. But if this much of autonomy is conceded, we find ourselves on a slippery slope leading to a full-fledged notion of autonomy as the (socially conditioned) ability to shape the ends we pursue; a slippery slope from which there is no theoretically well-motivated escape. To the degree wants are manipulated, freedom is restricted. When deliberate control over individuals' ends is attempted, freedom is menaced; and when control is achieved, freedom is reduced.

Those who would still resist viewing freedom as autonomy might suggest that what is objectionable in brainwashing and its close approximations is that the shaping of individuals' ends, in these instances, is *deliberate*. If choices are deliberately manipulated, freedom is restricted; otherwise not. Then the slippery slope stops, it might be held, at the peripheries of freedom (F3), and need not carry over into full support for autonomy. Adherents of the dominant view of freedom need concede no more than has already been conceded.

There is no patent incoherence in drawing the line at deliberate manipulation of individuals' ends, just as there is nothing wrong in principle in insisting, as many writers in the dominant tradition do, that only deliberate interferences with individuals' activities restrict liberty. However, this characteristic move is demonstrably arbitrary. The parallel is instructive and bears further consideration.[11]

To hold that only deliberate interferences restrict liberty is to deny that social practices that impede individuals' abilities to do what they want restrict freedom (F1), so long as the impediment is unintended. According to this view, I am unfree (F1) to buy an airplane, if sales of airplanes to private parties are prohibited by law. But if airplane sales are legal and I am simply unable to afford the price, then I am entirely free (F1), though unable, to buy an airplane. That I am unable to buy an airplane in virtue of a nexus of social practices that result in the distribution of wealth and the pricing of commodities is deemed irrelevant. So too is the fact that at least some of these practices, particularly those having to do with property relations, are enforced – deliberately – by law. Property is, we have seen, characteristically assimilated to the natural order of things, and therefore the social practices necessary for its maintenance tend to be overlooked. Strictly speaking, those who would maintain that only deliberate interferences render us unfree (F1) suppose a very limited view of what counts as interference – a view that would be difficult to sustain, except from the tendentiously abstract vantage-point of so much theorizing within the dominant tradition.

It is from this vantage point that workers are free to start their own factories; or that the unemployed are free to find jobs. They are indeed free (F1), if there is no deliberate interference with entrepreneurship or with labor markets. But this freedom (F1) is plainly only formal in most circumstances. For workers generally are not free (F2) to start enterprises, nor are the unemployed usually free (F2) to find jobs. The stipulation that only *deliberate* interferences restrict liberty tendentiously supports a positive assessment of situations where liberty is only formal. It supports the view that, so far as freedom is in question, there is nothing to fault in a situation where workers are free (F1) to start factories or the unemployed to find employment, no matter how unfree (F2) they may be.

There are, I think, two mildly compelling reasons for regarding freedom this way, for insisting that the only constraints acknowledged in discussions of freedom be deliberate constraints. First, it could be held that to count unintended, institutional impediments as restrictions on liberty expands the extent to which social and political practices can be assessed with respect to freedom, thereby closing off evaluations of these practices from the point of view of other, more appropriate standards, like justice or equality.[12] To count institutional impediments as restrictions on liberty risks conflating freedom with other standards of assessment, breeding confusion and, in the end, stultifying social criticism.

The second reason makes a virtue of necessity. To suppose that only deliberate interferences restrict liberty is to assimilate all impedances to freedom (F2), even when they are mainly social in etiology and character, to natural inabilities. I am unable to buy an airplane, in this view, in the way I am unable to fly; but not in the way I am unable, because unfree (F1) to trespass. My inability to fly is plainly not a restriction on my freedom (F2). It is a natural inability. However, most inabilities are not purely natural inabilities. They are, to some extent, socially conditioned. In general, it is difficult, even qualitatively, to distinguish nature from society, and therefore natural from social impediments. But it is relatively easy to pick out cases of overt, deliberate interference, and to distinguish deliberate interferences from inabilities (of whatever sort). Drawing the line at deliberate interferences facilitates sorting cases out neatly. The orthodox view of what renders us unfree can be appealing on this account.

However, neither of these arguments is persuasive. More space, as it were, is indeed opened up for other values, if freedom is restricted in its application as an evaluative standard, but there is no need, even so, to fail to countenance institutional impediments to freedom. As we shall go on to see, even allowing for unintended as well as deliberate interferences with persons doing what they want, there *is* ample room for assessing social and political economic arrangements with respect to justice, equality and other values as well. Assimilating social to natural inabilities may facilitate sorting cases out neatly. But why should this advantage override the case for a full-fledged notion of capacity-freedom? In a world where many of our inabilities to do what we want derive, in large part, though not entirely, from social practices and institutions, a neat and exhaustive distinction of natural from social impediments hardly seems desirable, even were it possible. To be sure, strictly natural impediments and physical inabilities do not limit capacity-freedom. But as we move away from the "nature" side of what we might regard as a nature-society continuum of impedances, it does seem increasingly plausible to speak of restrictions on capacity-freedom. It sounds odd to say to an unemployed worker that she is free to find a job; or to a dissatisfied worker that he is free to start his own factory. There is no good reason, in these cases, to deny our intuitions.

In short, there is no justification for claiming that only deliberate interferences render us unfree (F1). The standard liberal insistence to the contrary is arbitrary. But however unwarranted that insistence may be, it is hardly innocent. If only deliberate interferences count for restricting freedom (F1), much of the social context within which human interactions occur is removed from critical assessment (with respect to freedom). Thus the concept of freedom becomes remarkably – and, I think, objectionably – abstract. Market (voluntary) transactions, for example, could hardly fail to be free, viewed in this light, even if the exchanges that constitute particular markets occur because, for at least some of the parties, there are no feasible alternatives to the choices actually made. If a worker faces the choice of working for a subsistence wage or not having access to the most basic means of life, and therefore chooses the wage, that choice would count as free, in this view, so long as it is made voluntarily – without having been coerced (deliberately). It is as free, say, as the exchange of a bushel of wheat for two bushels of corn by self-sufficient farmers in "the early and rude state of society." The latter exchange arguably is genuinely free and unobjectionable, in so far as we suppose, as the dominant political culture does, that legitimacy is conferred through free choice. The wage bargain, on the other hand, seems something less than a genuinely free exchange. However, through the abstract spectacles of those who would insist that only deliberate interferences render us unfree, the wage bargain, if joined voluntarily, is unimpeachable. That there might be some failure of freedom in the choice – work or starve – is unthinkable, so long as the choice is voluntary. Whatever is voluntary is free, regardless of the nature of the alternatives in contention and the social contexts within which transactions occur.

At this level of abstraction, capacity-freedom is rendered otiose. It collapses into liberty. We are free (F2) just to the extent that we are free (F1). But this result, we know, accords poorly with the dominant tradition's chief, discernible rationale for supporting liberty: its role in promoting capacity-freedom. Insisting that only deliberate interferences restrict liberty is therefore inadmissible, finally, even if it is not strictly incoherent. Construing liberty in this way undermines the rationale for valuing liberty at all.

A parallel consideration applies to the attempt to block the move from capacity-freedom to autonomy – or, more strictly, to a full-fledged notion of autonomy – by insisting that only deliberate manipulations of individuals' ends restrict freedom. That position too is arbitrary and misleadingly abstract. Social life plainly does affect individuals' ends profoundly; not just by shaping preferences for alternatives, but by shaping alternatives themselves. Why should we confine considerations of freedom to individuals' abilities to realize their ends, without considering as well the control they exercise over the formation and character of the ends they seek to realize?

This question admits of no satisfactory response. The slippery slope runs from the absence of (coercive) restraint to autonomy, from freedom (F1) through freedom (F2) to freedom (F3). To deny this progression is both unwarranted and tendentious. We have seen how, where liberty is in question, restricting attention to deliberate interferences with individuals' actions introduces a bias for capitalist market relations; and therefore, under capitalism, for the status quo. Where autonomy is in question, drawing the line at deliberate manipulation of individuals' ends introduces a more subtle bias, but one that is, again, unwarranted and tendentially pro-capitalist.

Thus, it is sometimes said that capitalism is preferable to socialism because it better delivers the goods people want. This argument depends, in part, on comparative assessments of socialism and capitalism with respect to values distinct from freedom (efficiency, particularly), values that will be considered in due course (see Chapter 3). However, this argument also reflects a way of thinking about individuals' choices that effectively shields the goods people want from critical assessment. I think this consequence unfortunate, particularly in so far as we value freedom. For we are free to the extent we control the choices we make. It is therefore pertinent to ask how free (F3) we are in the determination of what we want. Should it be that we are not very free (F3) in that determination, it is plainly a reproach against our institutions, no matter how well they deliver what we actually desire. This charge, wherever it can be sustained, is distinct from the complaint that our desires themselves are somehow irrational, a charge difficult even to formulate within the conceptual parameters of the dominant tradition (see Chapter 3).

With respect to some particular sort of activity, we either are or are not free (F1). Capacity-freedom, however, admits of degrees. So too does autonomy. At the limit perhaps we can be strictly unfree (F3) or very nearly so. But it is not at all clear what it would be to be entirely autonomous. In comparing socialism and capitalism, then, the question is which is more likely to foster autonomy; which can be expected to better expand the range of individual self-determination? The answer will not follow directly just from the concepts of socialism and capitalism themselves. Rather the answer will depend on expectations about the consequences for autonomy of different social practices. Again, a definitive conclusion at this degree of remove from actual institutional specifications is not possible. But as with capacity-freedom, there is a plausible case to be made for socialism. The former case depended upon a likely connection between capacity-freedom and equality, and between equality and socialism. It was posed tentatively, in anticipation of a fuller discussion of the latter issue in Chapter 2. The case for socialism with respect to autonomy depends, similarly, on a plausible connection between autonomy and democracy, and between democracy and socialism. This case too will be posed tentatively, awaiting a fuller discussion of both issues in Chapters 4 and 6.

Irreducible psychological differences apart, how autonomous we are is a function of our institutional arrangements and of their *effects* on us. What difference, if any, does the private or social ownership of society's principal means of production make for fostering or impeding autonomy? What are the consequences of one or the other political economic system for our institutions? It might seem, at first, that there are no direct and sure consequences; and that, so far as autonomy is a value, there is nothing to be said for or against socialism or capitalism. I would hazard, however, that there is a difference that bears on our question, albeit indirectly. This difference follows from plausible views about the connection between autonomy and democratic collective choice.

What I would assert, tentatively for now, but in line with a venerable strain of democratic theory, is that in general the more popular control there is over societal institutions, the more autonomy is fostered throughout society. Political participation *educates*; it develops moral and intellectual capacities for choice. I would assert too that a high level of political participation requires a high degree of actual control over institutions. For what other than popular control can, in the long run, sustain a high level of participation? When our choices and activities have tangible effects, we are more inclined to take responsibility for what we do than when what we do is without recognizable consequences. In nearly all actually existing political communities, changes of government have hardly any impact on ordinary life; and political participation, for most citizens, has little actual effect. Therefore, citizens can afford to be ill-informed, capricious and apathetic. The greater the impact of individuals' choices, however, the more inclined people will be to inform themselves and to act responsibly. This sense of responsibility is, I suggest, instrumental for promoting autonomy; and while it may not be, strictly, necessary for it, it is unlikely that autonomy could be very well promoted in its absence. If this view is right, what promotes active citizenship promotes autonomy. Therefore, if social institutions are arranged so that there is in fact a high degree of collective control – if they are politicized and democratized – individual autonomy will be well-served.

I will argue in Chapter 4 that socialism fares better in general than capitalism with respect to popular, democratic control over societal institutions; that, under capitalism, there are limits to politicization and democratization that need not exist under socialism. And in Chapter 6 I will hold that radically democratic socialism is possible and desirable, not least for its consequences for autonomy. This is not yet the place to argue for these contentions, though it is appropriate to anticipate some of what is to follow. The argument begun here and continued in Chapter 4 will be a principal theme of Part Two. We will find that the connection between socialism, democracy and autonomy is important not only for making a case for socialism with respect to the dominant view of freedom, but also in arguing for socialism from a Marxian perspective. Autonomy is, as it were, the main point of contact between dominant tradition and Marxian valuational commitments.

Unlike socialism, capitalism necessarily depoliticizes at least some questions pertaining to the disposition of means of production. Recall that socialism is here defined negatively in relation to capitalism: it is post-capitalism, capitalism without private ownership of means of production. Private ownership of means of production implies both rights to income derived from assets and, (some) rights over the disposition and use of assets. These rights that are definitive of capitalist property effectively mark off a domain that is not subject to political determination. Therefore, at least some questions concerning the disposition and control of means of production are removed from the political sphere. Socialism, on the other hand, is free of these restrictions. Under socialism, in principle, all matters pertaining to means of production may be politicized. In other words, capitalism but not socialism requires *some* "civil society," some sphere of the private that the state may superintend or guarantee, but cannot rightfully infringe. In socialist societies, the distinction between civil society and the state can be collapsed.

Sometimes this possibility is invoked in defense of capitalism. It is argued that the existence of a realm where politics may not rightfully intrude protects individual freedom. We will consider aspects of this contention in the following section; and the issue will recur in the discussions of socialism and democracy to follow in Chapters 4 and 6. Whatever we finally conclude, it should be noted that in so far as autonomy is in fact promoted by democratic collective choice, the establishment and expansion of civil society works to the detriment of this aspect of freedom. To be sure, this consideration need not weigh very strongly against capitalism, unless there is reason to think that, under capitalism, the sphere of civil society is likely to be so vast that the educative opportunities democratic collective choice can provide are effectively forsaken, and provided too that civil society under capitalism provides no alternative institutions that might equally well form autonomous individuals. I have already suggested that, under capitalism, the sphere of civil society is likely to be considerable, even if it need not be quite so considerable as it characteristically has been in existing capitalist societies. In Chapter 4, I will argue that civil society under capitalism is generally not beneficial for promoting autonomy, despite what is sometimes said in its behalf. Then I will argue that there is good reason to expect the politicization of crucial aspects of social life under socialism. In Chapter 6, I will resume the contention that the politicization we can expect under socialism can – and should – take on a democratic form, and can be expected to advance autonomy and therefore freedom generally.

Freedom and power

What can be said on behalf of socialism in general does not unequivocally carry over to forms of socialism that replace private property in means of production with state bureaucratic domination. Political liberties particularly have fared badly in actually existing socialism, to the detriment, surely, of capacity-freedom; but this shortcoming of existing socialism is, I would hazard, mainly a consequence of conjunctural political and historical factors. With an important reservation to be noted presently, the failure of existing socialist societies to uphold political liberties cannot be ascribed to their socialism.

A more direct challenge to the *model* of state bureaucratic socialism can be made with respect to autonomy. By hypothesis, in state bureaucratic socialism, state bureaucratic domination, not popular democratic control, replaces the domination of capital. There is, as we shall see, no systemic reason to expect state bureaucratic socialism to do well with respect to democracy. It can therefore be less democratic even than capitalism, a possibility actually existing socialism bears out all too well.

What mainly tells against state bureaucratic socialism in comparison with capitalism is a consequence of the likely distribution of effective power in state bureaucratic socialist and capitalist societies, respectively. In socialisms that accord with the state bureaucratic model, power is inordinately concentrated. This problem afflicts state bureaucratic socialism generally, but its effects are particularly acute when freedom is the value against which these rival political economic arrangements are compared.

We have already seen how, under capitalism, there is bound to be some civil society, some sphere where political interference can never be rightful. Thus power will always be at least somewhat diffuse: first, because independent capitalist enterprises, competing capitals, constitute independent centers of power; and second, because the state exists as an institutional apparatus or set of apparatuses distinct from any particular concentrations of capital and from the capitalist class as a whole. Independent capitals and the state therefore act as countervailing powers. In particular circumstances, of course, these powers may not be very independent. There may be enormous concentrations of capital (monopolies, cartels) that centralize power. Or the state may be instrumentally linked to particular capitalist interests or to the capitalist class as a whole, serving directly, as *The Communist Manifesto* would have it, as its "executive committee". Still, under capitalism, there is always at least the juridical possibility of establishing independent enterprises. At the limit, a limit that has never been even remotely approximated for any time in any geographically significant territory, there might be a unique, capitalist employer. But even were this the case, there is solace in the fact that this circumstance could never be fixed permanently – for capitalism requires freedom of contract and therefore, in principle, free ingress to capitalist markets. A unique employer would always find its monopoly position jeopardized. And there would still be a formally independent state. No matter how subordinate to the capitalist class the state might become, and no matter how many economic functions it might assume, it must remain institutionally separate from capital. The state could not entirely assume the capitalists' role, and the system remain capitalist – for capitalism is defined by *private*, not public, control over productive capacities; and state control, so long as it is not merely a juridical fiction, is a form of public control. Countervailing power is intrinsic to capitalist, but not socialist, political economies.

Countervailing powers work to promote freedom. To the extent power is concentrated, individuals find themselves at the mercy of the powers that be. At the limit, were there only one employer, to run afoul of that employer would be to incur trouble indeed; worse trouble by far than where effective power is less concentrated. The less concentrated power is, the easier it is for "troublemakers" and dissidents of all sorts to avoid the effects of "blacklisting" or outright proscription. Thus capacity-freedom and also liberty are advanced by institutional arrangements where countervailing powers exist. Countervailing powers are hedges against tyranny. Capitalism may not provide much of a hedge, particularly if there is a tendency for capital to concentrate and to dominate the state; but some resistance to tyranny is built into the capitalist system in virtue of the "space" capitalism provides for civil society.

On the other hand, under state bureaucratic socialism, the state *is* the sole employer. Economic and political power are concentrated in a single, institutional nexus. The consequences for freedom are evident. In principle, of course, even state bureaucratic socialism could correct for the likely effects of enormous concentrations of power – by establishing and enforcing legal protections analogous to those offered, say, by the U.S. *Bill of Rights*. However, nothing of the sort has ever taken place in practice, though the legal documents of existing socialist societies, particularly the Soviet Union, do proclaim many very advanced measures against tyrannical usurpations of individuals' freedoms. In any case, for state bureaucratic socialism to protect against tyranny is to correct for tendencies inscribed in a political economic system where political and economic power are inextricably joined and concentrated. It is therefore to go *against* the system, to rectify what state bureaucratic socialism in itself tends to promote.

Capitalism too promotes concentrations of power, precisely by according individuals ultimate control over productive assets. Capitalist markets characteristically exacerbate power inequalities by generating substantial material inequalities (see Chapter 2) and by facilitating the formation of monopolies (see Chapter 3). At the same time, capitalism supports the existence of countervailing powers. Even if those tendencies supporting concentration dominate, capitalism, at its worst, can only approach the situation realized systemically in state bureaucratic socialism. For this reason – in conjunction with what has already been noted about the likely prospects for autonomy – it is fair to conclude that with respect to prevailing views of freedom, capitalism – which fares worse than socialism in general – is likely preferable to state bureaucratic socialism.

Dissidents in state bureaucratic socialist societies might, of course, be vulnerable to any sort of persecution; but it is unlikely that those who escape outright incarceration would endure economic hardships worse, say, than those endured by unemployed workers in advanced capitalist countries (with systems of unemployment insurance or other welfare-state measures). Even the most despotic of actually existing socialist regimes maintain relatively high levels of social consumption and provide, wherever possible, minimal means of life for everyone. Despotism menaces at a more directly political level. With all power concentrated in the state, specifically political freedoms – freedoms basic to liberal judgments on political institutions – are prone to abuse. For there is no institutional check on state power. This concern raises a number of issues best dealt with in Part Two. There I shall inquire whether what is attractive in the socialist vision can be realized without incurring unintended and undesirable consequences. For now, it will suffice to comment briefly on some aspects of the question that bear directly on freedom.

When existing socialist countries are blamed for suppressing political freedoms, or when some capitalist countries are praised for promoting them, the term "political freedoms" stands for two, relatively independent notions. On the one hand are specifically political *rights* – the right to vote, to hold office, to fair treatment in courts of law, and so on. Most of these rights have little directly to do with freedom in any of the senses in question here, and are best considered in other contexts (see Chapter 4). On the other hand, the term also designates certain *liberties* or *immunities*, familiar from traditional liberalism: freedom of speech, of religion, and of the press, among others. We have already examined the case for these liberties. Pro-capitalists have made much of the fact that political liberties have grown up under capitalism and, in some cases at least, have flourished under it. Conceding that this historical correlation holds and is not purely coincidental, it is plainly not enough just to note the correlation; something must be said to account for it. It might be, for example, that there is a causal link joining capitalism and traditional political liberties, but that it runs only in the converse of the way usually assumed: that political liberties helped capitalism emerge and flourish, but not vice versa. Then nothing would follow, even hypothetically, about the continuing importance of capitalism for maintaining these freedoms (F1). But even if the standard, pro-capitalist view is right, if capitalism supported and sustained these liberties, still it would not follow that capitalism is necessary for their continuation or development. At most, it would follow that, under the particular historical conditions of late feudal Europe, emerging capitalism contributed to the rise of political liberalism. Such a conclusion would be of some historical interest, certainly; but its relevance for political philosophy – and particularly for assessing the relative merits of socialism and capitalism – would be slight at best. It certainly would not follow that political liberties can survive and flourish only under capitalism. Nor even would it follow that these freedoms can only come into being under capitalism. In short, there is no reason to conclude anything at all about the importance of capitalism for political freedoms, even if the most defensible historical argument is the one pro-capitalists proffer.

It is worth remembering too that while the record of some existing capitalist countries on political liberties is good, capitalism's overall record is not at all uniformly impressive. Nazi Germany was a capitalist society and so are all the fascist and comprador regimes outside the Soviet and Chinese spheres of influence that have terrorized their populations and undone the freedoms of their peoples. It is worth remembering too that many of these regimes were put in place and sustained by the most liberal of the capitalist countries – by Great Britain, France and, particularly in the past four decades, by the United States. From that perspective, capitalism's record on political liberties appears much less sound than it might if one looked just at Britain, France or the United States themselves.

In many capitalist countries of Asia, Africa and Latin America, the record on political liberties is easily as dismal as anywhere in the Soviet bloc. Indeed, for these dependent capitalist economies, it may be that their economic organization or, more strictly, their place in the capitalist world system is to blame, at least in part, for their palpably illiberal character. For in such regimes, typically, a collaborationist minority enriches itself at the expense of large portions of the population who are, in turn, impoverished. Pre-existing social tensions are therefore exacerbated while new antagonisms are formed and the traditional social fabric disintegrates. How but through terror and despotic uses of force could such polities be governed? The political economic pressures supporting despotic usurpations of freedom in the actually existing socialist countries are more difficult to identify, if indeed they exist at all.

In any case, the dreary record of the Communist countries on political liberties proves nothing, except that, like capitalism, socialism – or, at least, state bureaucratic socialism (with its enormous concentrations of power) – is susceptible to despotic political administration. It is not at all clear, though, that countervailing *economic* powers, the specifically capitalist form of civil society, would help very much. In all existing states, socialist or capitalist, liberal or illiberal, authorities can trample individual freedoms. What will protect liberty are appropriate *political* institutions and a vigilant citizenry, not capitalism. The fate of political liberties under socialism and capitalism depends mainly, it seems, on *political will*, not on the political economic organization of society.

Both socialist and capitalist societies can undo or defend political liberties. The Communist countries, without exception, have labored under the most unfortunate of circumstances and, for the most part, in the absence of liberal political traditions. Their leadership has shown a conspicuous failure of will to sustain free institutions and an inclination towards despotism, and their citizenry has been unwilling or unable successfully to resist. In some circumstances, capitalist regimes have fared better; but not in all, and arguably not even in most. It is well to reflect on the historical record of actually existing state bureaucratic socialist regimes, just as it is important to investigate the emergence of political liberalism and the fate of the traditional political liberties in capitalist states. But these are historical questions, of only the most indirect and attenuated relevance for our question. Even with respect to political liberties, there are no grounds for deciding for or against socialism (including state bureaucratic socialism) or capitalism on the basis of the historical record.

But there is still some reason in theory to decide for capitalism over state bureaucratic socialism where freedom is in question: in virtue of the concentration of political and economic power that is systemic in state bureaucratic socialism but not capitalism. State bureaucratic socialist societies need not actually fare worse. In principle, tyranny can be guarded against and egalitarian policies can promote capacity-freedom. Even autonomy can be well served, though not nearly so well as in the democratic socialist model. There is no reason why state bureaucratic socialism need be less democratic than capitalism (see Chapter 4); nor why it cannot foster autonomy equally well. But neither is there any good reason to expect state bureaucratic socialism to do well in these respects. Actually existing socialism, capitalism's best argument, is hardly decisive; but it does attest to dangers, for freedom and for other values too, that, at best, the state bureaucratic model does little, if anything, to overcome.

I will argue that democratic socialism can be counted on to avoid many of these dangers, and to realize socialism's advantages with respect to freedom. However, that argument can only be intimated at this point. For we have still to establish the connection between socialism and democracy, and to argue for the possibility of democratic socialism. The latter claim is intractable within the conceptual parameters of the dominant tradition. The dominant tradition in moral, social and political theory has nothing to say about what is or is not *historically possible*. The question is therefore best deferred until Part Two.

2
Distributional values

Socialism and capitalism may also be compared with respect to distributional values – clustering around notions of equality and justice. Distributional assessments cannot always be made in isolation from other values. What will count, say, as a just distribution may depend, in part, on how much there is of what is to be distributed; that is, on aggregative concerns (to be considered in Chapter 3). Even so, distributional values are distinct enough from aggregative values, and also from freedom and the political values to be considered in Chapter 4, that it is appropriate and feasible to assess socialism and capitalism with respect to them. However, assessments made in light of these standards will unavoidably suppose or anticipate conclusions drawn with regard to other components of the dominant tradition. Whatever determinate conclusions we can draw about socialism and capitalism in theory must therefore be posed provisionally, awaiting discussion of these other values.

Concern with distributive justice goes back to the earliest days of Western philosophy. Justice (including distributive justice) was the supreme moral idea in Plato's *Republic*; and Aristotle, in the *Nicomachean Ethics* and elsewhere, pays rigorous attention to the question of just and equitable distribution. The core pre-philosophical intuition, from the very first, has been *fairness*. Roughly, a just distribution is a fair distribution. What has undergone radical change is not a commitment to fairness as such, but ordinary pre-reflective intuitions as to what counts as fair. Here, again, the dissolution of feudal society and the emergence of atomizing (capitalist) market relations have been decisively influential. For roughly contemporaneous with the emergence of liberty as a value, a concern for *equality*, equality of all members of the political community, began to erupt upon European consciousness. Equality was a new and radical political ideal, unthinkable in the ancient world, despite its concern with justice, and plainly incompatible with any social order divided into juridically or traditionally recognized hierarchies. The concern with equality has, I think, radically transformed our intuitions about fairness, and therefore our conception of justice. In discussing distributional values, with a view to assessing socialism and capitalism with respect to them, it is therefore best to start with equality in its various senses, before turning directly to justice itself. I will argue that the dominant view of justice expresses an emerging consensus in favor of equality, and that, in so far as conclusions can be drawn at this degree of remove from institutional arrangements, socialism (including state bureaucratic socialism) fares better than capitalism in light of that standard.

En route to this conclusion, socialism and capitalism will be compared with respect to a number of related distributional values – to notions of equality, including equality of opportunity, and also exploitation. A case for socialism will emerge from these comparisons. I will suggest, finally, that Rawlsian justice, the position John Rawls elaborates in *A Theory of Justice* and elsewhere,[1] perspicuously and comprehensively articulates the dominant view. Then I will argue, contrary to Rawls's express declaration of neutrality on the choice between socialism and capitalism,[2] that Rawlsian justice supports pro-socialist positions.

Contemporaneous with the view of justice Rawls articulates are a number of non-comparative claims, effectively rival theories of justice, that are sometimes invoked in support of capitalism or, more rarely, socialism. What characterizes these claims is a view of justice as an absolute value, uniquely satisfied by particular – typically capitalist – social relations. Very generally, claims of this sort fall into one of two categories: those that would justify capitalism (or, more rarely, socialism) by appeal to a notion of justice as desert; and those that would make essential use of the notion of property rights. In my view, these non-comparative pro-capitalist and pro-socialist positions are without exception defective. They are also of little relevance for the question at hand – the comparative assessment of socialism and capitalism within the conceptual and valuational framework of the dominant tradition in Western moral and political philosophy. I address some of these claims briefly in the Appendix to this chapter.

Part One

Equality

Egalitarian distribution, where everyone to whom some benefit or burden is to be distributed gets the *same* amount, has been advocated both as a means for some further end and as an end-in-itself. Historically, talk of equality became important in the former sense first,[3] and has only lately come to be defended as an end-in-itself. Today, equality is widely regarded as desirable for its own sake. However, in balancing off the various ends social policy aims to realize, equality is characteristically accorded low priority; and the support there is for achieving equality is typically overwhelmed by other considerations.

It is important to distinguish between equality as a distributional principle and other notions of equality with which it is closely associated, conceptually and historically. There is, first of all, equality as a formal, political category: equality before the law, equality in the determination of collective choices; in short, equality of membership in political communities. Another important sense of equality that will need to be taken into account is equality of opportunity. Several centuries ago, each of these standards was controversial. Today there is virtual consensus on their desirability, though there is still residual disagreement as to what counts as formal equality – and recalcitrance in implementing equal political "rights," particularly for women and minorities – and considerable disagreement concerning what equality of opportunity requires.

Historically, talk of equality came into prominence in the West with political movements directed against feudalism and its political expressions. To be for equality was to be against the hierarchical divisions of feudal society. The claim that all humanity is "created equal" is a claim directed against these hierarchical social divisions and for the formal equality of persons. The political implication of this acknowledgment is precisely a commitment to political equality. Historically, therefore, there was a close connection between partisanship for equality and capitalism. It could even be argued that formal political equality, in the historical conditions of late feudal Europe, was a *precondition* for establishing a class of free wage laborers of the sort European capitalism required for its inception and development. However, this claim, even if sound, is historically limited. Wherever capitalism is the sole, historical rival of feudalism or of other hierarchically divided social orders, to be against hierarchy and for political equality is, of course, to be for capitalism. That was, I think, the situation of seventeenth- and eighteenth-century partisans of equality. But if socialism too is historically possible, there is no reason to conclude for capitalism and against socialism where formal equality is a value. Between pro-socialists and pro-capitalists there is agreement on political equality, in opposition to pro-feudal reactionaries and others who yearn for a juridically or customarily sanctioned, hierarchical social order.[4]

Reactionary anti-capitalist critics of the French Revolution such as Joseph de Maistre or the Vicomte de Bonald, argued that there was a dynamic implicit in the advocacy of equality.[5] To concede anything at all, even on political equality, they maintained, is to open the floodgates that lead to radical, egalitarian social movements of which Babeuf's "conspiracy of equals" is symptomatic. Many pro-socialists hold a similar view of the dynamic implicit in the advocacy of equality. Their idea, roughly, is that capitalism engenders and promotes an ideal of equality that is fully realizable only with the end of capitalism. What follows will endorse this view, subject of course to the reservations that are unavoidable at the level of abstraction at which this investigation is pitched.

In the Republican tradition of progressive and, at times, radical seventeenth- and eighteenth-century politics in England and France, equality was defended primarily for promoting *virtue* – in the sense the Spartans and Romans of the Republican period were believed to have evidenced virtue[6] – and freedom. Virtue in the intended sense requires simplicity of manners and morals (*moeurs*) and abhorrence of luxury and corruption. Freedom requires, as Rousseau would have it, if not strict equality, at least some limits on permissible inequalities.[7] Mediated through Montesquieu and Rousseau, Republicanism found radical expression in Revolutionary France, among the Jacobins and *sans-culottes*, and more moderate expression in the political upheavals that led to the founding of the United States. Even in the American context, though, the impulse towards imposing limits on admissible inequalities remained. There is evidence of it in some of the *Federalist Papers* and in the writings of Thomas Jefferson. In the role assigned (material) equality in promoting virtue, it is held, in effect, that proper political arrangements presuppose something like Adam Smith's "early and rude state of society," where urban artisans and especially yeomen farmers own their own means of production, while producing mainly for their own consumption and only incidentally for "free markets." Rousseau insisted that this political economic system was indispensable too for maintaining freedom.[8] Thus, from the very first, a tension between political equality and capitalism – or, more strictly, between political equality and the class divisions capitalism engenders – was recognized by equality's most ardent proponents. If this acknowledgment faded from importance in the political movements the Republican tradition helped to inspire, it may be because the political economic measures the Republicans advocated were simply utopian in the face of the emerging capitalist organization of Europe.

Following the treatment inaugurated by Aristotle, it will be useful to view egalitarianism as one of a number of substantive principles of justice.[9] Formally, justice requires that like cases be treated alike. This principle is formal because it does not specify what counts as a like case, and what counts as equal treatment. A substantive principle of justice specifies content for each of these formal categories. Egalitarianism, then, is that substantive principle of justice that stipulates that all beings for whom it is appropriate to make distributions in accordance with justice form a single, unique category, and are to get the same amount of whatever is being distributed in accordance with the principle. There are, in other words, no distinguishing characteristics that justify differential distributions among individuals falling within the scope of the principle; everyone is a "like case." And "equal treatment" amounts to treating each of these like cases in the same way.

A commitment to egalitarian distribution – to the substantive principle "to each the same" – does not automatically imply the sort of universal, egalitarian humanism that many adherents of this principle seek to bring about.[10] For universal, egalitarian humanism, we must stipulate in addition that the class of beings for whom the egalitarian principle is to apply should consist of all humanity; or, in a more strictly political context, to all members of a political community. Otherwise, as in political or religious sects or monastic orders or even, in some instances, within feudal estates, egalitarian distribution, so far from furthering a vision of humanity "created equal," might instead promote a sense of in-group solidarity and out-group exclusivity, encouraging a sense of unequal humanity and social division, and conflicting even with the requirements of strict formal equality. With the demise of feudalism and the emerging consensus on formal equality, universal, egalitarian humanism becomes a possible social ideal. Were a vision of a single humanity unthinkable, as it doubtless was under European feudalism and in many other pre-capitalist social orders, a commitment to egalitarian humanism could hardly have arisen. As reactionaries feared, formal equality does indeed set an egalitarian dynamic in motion.

Even were it desirable, the egalitarian principle could not work as a substantive principle of justice for the distribution of *all* benefits and burdens. It is in the nature of some goods and services that they are imperfectly divisible or even indivisible; and much of what there is to distribute is sufficiently scarce that a portion could not be given to everyone. This leads us, in considering the qualities that differentiate one person from another, to distinguish those qualities that might plausibly be counted morally relevant, from those that are plainly irrelevant, for the administration of justice. What principles are appropriate for the distribution of different sorts of benefits and burdens to different kinds of groups? Egalitarianism provides, as it were, a limiting-case answer: everyone is to get exactly the same amount of everything.

Alternative proposals too are raised within the framework of formal justice. No one, I should think, would contend that it is fair to treat like cases differently. Even a feudal reactionary would advocate treating like cases alike, while insisting that sharing a place in the social hierarchy is a necessary condition for counting as a like case. What emerges with capitalism, then, is not a commitment to justice *per se*, but an egalitarian sense of human community. A commitment to justice is as old as Western political thought; but an egalitarian conception of justice – applicable to all of humankind – is a product of the dissolution of social hierarchies and does not predate the emergence of capitalism.

Some rival substantive principles are apparently motivated by a desire to grasp the spirit, if not the letter, of the egalitarian principle. Consider, for example, distribution according to need. "To each according to need," the substantive principle that, in Marx's view, is to regulate distributions under communism,[11] asserts that benefits are to be distributed proportionally to need. Unless needs are strictly equal, as we cannot reasonably expect, distributions under this principle will not be egalitarian. But the reason for distributing according to need, arguably, is precisely to equalize distributions of some higher-order benefit – presumably, happiness or well-being. Suppose, for instance, that the benefit to be distributed is income. Then it could be argued that the more needful require more income to make them as well-off (happy) as the less needful would be with less income. Or if healthcare were to be distributed according to need, it would not be because it is thought that the ill are somehow more deserving of a benefit than the healthy, but rather because it is thought rightful to try, so far as is humanly possible, to bring the ill up to the welfare level of the healthy (by rectifying what, other things being equal, is the source of their lower welfare level – their illness). Then strictly inegalitarian distributions of income or healthcare would be instrumental for realizing egalitarian distributions of happiness. And it would be in order to distribute this higher order benefit equally so that distributions were made according to need.

There are other substantive principles of justice, currently regulating distributions of benefits and burdens, that are non-egalitarian even in the higher-order sense that distributions according to need can be considered egalitarian. "To each according to productive contribution"[12] and "to each according to merit" are examples. In these cases, it is supposed that differences among the class of individuals to whom justice is to be administered – differences in productive contribution or merit – are morally relevant in a way that warrants grouping individuals into categories, or arraying them along a continuum, representing the morally relevant dimension, and treating these individuals differently, according to the category into which they fall, or their place along the continuum. Benefits would then be distributed in direct proportion to the pertinent dimension – the degree of productive contribution or merit. Adoption of such principles is bound to lead to contention, unless there is an agreed upon way to measure degrees of contribution or merit and to distribute benefits accordingly. (Similar contention can afflict distributions according to need.) However, the general strategy is coherent. The formal principle of justice, that like cases be treated alike, is satisfied, even when we utilize a non-egalitarian notion of what constitutes a like case.

However, even in these cases, there is a presumption for equal distributions. Someone must *do* something or *be* something to deserve more than someone else. An egalitarian sentiment underlies virtually all current intuitions about justice, including those expressed in substantive principles of justice that are, strictly speaking, non-egalitarian.

Equality of opportunity

We have seen that substantive principles of justice are either directly egalitarian or indirectly egalitarian (distribution according to need); or simply non-egalitarian (as in distributions according to productive contribution or merit); but that even these non-egalitarian principles do enjoin a *presumption* in favor of material equality. There is, however, a deeper sense in which even non-egalitarian principles represent an emerging consensus on equality. Those who would administer justice according to productive contribution or merit or according to similar criteria generally suppose the resulting distributions fair only if there is equal *opportunity* to compete for the benefits that are distributed according to these principles. In other words, even when distributions themselves are non-egalitarian, there is something prior that must in fairness be distributed equally: opportunity.

What is equality of opportunity? As a first approximation, we might suppose that equality of opportunity requires that a benefit be allocated on a basis that does not categorically exclude anyone who might want it, or that does not weight the selection process in favor of some individuals and not others – on grounds that are inappropriate for excluding individuals or weighting the selection process.[13] If, say, scarce medical school positions are to be allocated competitively, it does seem fair to exclude the less able or those who have done less well than their competitors in prior training, but unfair to exclude individuals on grounds of poverty or race, just because ability (supposing it can somehow be ascertained) and prior educational background are relevant to medical training while poverty and race are not. If we suppose that ability (aptitude) and prior academic success represent merit and effort, and decide that medical school admissions are to be allocated according to these criteria, then, apparently, equality of opportunity is realized if aptitude and prior training are taken as the basis for selection, but not if poverty or race are.

However, to appeal to the appropriateness of grounds for selection or exclusion supposes more consensus that we are generally likely to find. The medical school admissions example works intuitively because there is substantial agreement on what a proper function of medical school is. We can confidently exclude the less able, but not the poor or non-white, if we agree that the point of medical education is to train the most able medical practitioners and researchers. But that may not be the sole or even the principal function of medical schools, despite their self-representations. Medical schools in many parts of the world are part of an educational apparatus that, among other things, reproduces social elites – where elites are drawn overwhelmingly from among the children of the wealthy and the white. It would not be far-fetched, then, were someone to claim that a proper function of medical schools is to perpetuate and promote an aristocracy of wealth and race. Were that objective acknowledged, poverty and race would count as legitimate grounds for exclusion. And it could then be claimed that a system of medical school admissions that discriminates against the poor and the non-white is one that satisfies the ideal of equality of opportunity. But no one, I should think, including those who want medical schools to discriminate in this way, would be happy with the conclusion that, by doing so, equality of opportunity is realized. To defend discrimination is surely to *deny* equality of opportunity. This simple fact can be obfuscated but not, finally, denied. Thus the criterion proposed so far will not quite do for capturing the prevailing notion.

Let us say, therefore, that the grounds for exclusion or selection should be both appropriate for the benefit in question, and also should be such that people throughout society, in all social strata, have an equal chance of satisfying them. Then, as our intuitions require, there would not be equality of opportunity in a competition that discriminated against the poor or non-white. Equality of opportunity requires, instead, an equal chance for individuals, regardless of social position.

There is certainly an emerging consensus on equality of opportunity. Today there are few outright defenders of discrimination. Nearly all pro-socialists and pro-capitalists can agree that social arrangements may be assessed – not definitively perhaps, but importantly – according to how well equality of opportunity is realized. However, there is good reason to expect that, in fact, capitalist societies will be less able to provide equality of opportunity for individuals than socialist societies will, at least if we grant what seems plausible (and will be defended presently): that in general there will be more material inequality under capitalism than under socialism. The causal connection between material equality and equality of opportunity may seem obvious, but it is worth investigating none the less. By doing so, we can discern yet another connection between apparently non-egalitarian distributional principles and egalitarianism, and, at the same time, learn a good deal more about equality itself.

In a socially stratified society, with gross material inequalities, there are groups of individuals that can be identified by *irrelevant* characteristics that turn out to be correlated with, and causally connected to, characteristics that are, by most accounts, legitimate grounds for exclusion or selection in competitions. There is a familiar correlation, for example, between academic promise or disability and family wealth and race. A causal link is easy to discern. Those who are already privileged are able to pass on advantages to their offspring that contribute substantially towards academic achievement. They provide books and leisure, opportunities for cultural enrichment, travel and so on. The underprivileged cannot pass on these advantages, and are very often also immersed in cultural norms that, whatever their other merits, do not foster academic excellence. Suppose these causal connections in fact hold. Suppose, in other words, that *remediable* social conditions – not "natural" abilities and disabilities – account for observable correlations between, in our example, social position and race and qualifications for medical studies. We may then ask: is equality of opportunity realized when admission to medical schools is by unrestricted competition? In unrestricted competitions, we can safely suppose that the privileged will do overwhelmingly better than the underprivileged. But have the underprivileged been denied equality of opportunity?

As with freedom, the different positions one can take on this question depend on how ready one is to abstract from the institutional context in which claims about equality of opportunity are raised. At one extreme are those who hold that equality of opportunity is realized whenever there are no legal or customary impediments to individuals' entering into selection processes. It is fair, I think, to call this pole the "right-wing" view of equality of opportunity, since it is the most supportive of existing arrangements. As does the parallel view of freedom, this view of equality of opportunity effectively supports the status quo by removing much of it from critical scrutiny. Thus, in the medical school admissions case, whatever the causal links between family, wealth, or race and academic ability might be, so long as there are no legal or customary impediments to medical school admissions for the poor or non-white, there is, according to the right-wing view, equality of opportunity. On the other hand, it is possible within the dominant tradition to refuse to ignore the institutional context, and to insist that causal connections, at least if they are remediable in principle, be taken into account. From that perspective, it would be concluded, in all likelihood, that equality of opportunity is not in fact realized if admission to medical schools is awarded *solely* through unrestricted competitions.

Then the point would be to equalize the starting-points for individuals entering competitions. This is one rationale for affirmative action programs or other compensatory measures. "Centrists" might advocate, say, unequal allocation of educational resources for the poor or non-white, in order to compensate for other social disadvantages, but they would object to systems of quotas or "reverse discrimination" designed to correct the results of unrestrained competition. Those who would support such measures comprise, we may say, the "left-wing" of the dominant view on equality of opportunity. Reverse discrimination, in the right-wing view, would blatantly violate equality of opportunity. The left-wing, on the other hand, would support such measures in the hope of redressing existing inequalities and restoring – or, more likely, achieving for the first time – actual equality of opportunity. The presumption, of course, is still against discrimination of any kind. Even the most ardent proponents of reverse discrimination would agree that the measures they propose *would* violate equality of opportunity if that ideal had *already* been achieved. But since equality of opportunity is not already achieved, so far from denying equality of opportunity, reverse discrimination or similar interventions that "correct" the results of formally equal competitions may sometimes be called for precisely to realize what all proponents of equality of opportunity desire.

The right-wing view of equality of opportunity effectively devolves into formal equality – in circumstances where benefits are to be allocated according to non-egalitarian substantive principles of justice. Then to support equality of opportunity is just to oppose legal or customary impediments to individuals competing for benefits. The left-wing view, on the other hand, devolves into egalitarianism, in so far as giving everyone the same is the surest way to equalize starting-points in competitions (once socially remediable handicaps are rectified). To advocate equality of opportunity, in this view, is tantamount just to advocating equality as such. In each case, the point is to distribute opportunity equally. The difference has to do with how much of the institutional context is taken into account in determining what must be done to this end.

What I have called the "centrist" view veers towards the left-wing position. I think this designation fair, both descriptively and conceptually. The left-wing view, though hardly without detractors, is far more plausible than its right-wing rival. It certainly has many adherents within the dominant tradition, even among those who are inclined to take a more abstracted view of other values, such as freedom. For even more than in the analogous dispute over freedom, it seems odd to view equality of opportunity as a formal notion, as a matter just of the absence of discriminatory laws or customs. It is, of course, still possible to insist on the more abstracted understanding. Then the causes for the observed correlation between, say, privileged social status and academic qualifications would be simply irrelevant. To return to our example: no one, one could argue, is excluded from medical school for their social status; nor is anyone selected for it. There is no actual discrimination. Places are allocated competitively. Too bad, if, in general, some social strata do better than others. The fact that the distribution of places can be explained is beside the point. What matters is just that law and custom do not discriminate. But this position is barely plausible. Equality of opportunity is vacuous, if understood as a purely formal standard.

The point of equality of opportunity, after all, is to bring about fair competitions. It is not just to make fair competitions juridically *possible*.

The right-wing view of equality of opportunity renders that notion otiose. The point of equality of opportunity is to render competitions fair. Thus it is relevant, given the causal connection between being poor and lacking appropriate qualifications for admission to medical schools, that the competition *can* be made fair. We can be confident, indeed, that a more egalitarian distribution of income and of other societal benefits would bring about a fairer competition. It is our institutions that are to blame for what is plainly a failure of equality of opportunity. It follows, then, regardless of the absence of legal or customary impediments, that equality of opportunity is not achieved whenever, in fact, some sections of society do significantly worse than others, for reasons that are institutional and that can be remedied in principle by appropriate social action. If there is any point at all to talking of equality of opportunity, the left-wing view of that contested notion – or its less controversial, centrist approximations – is surely more plausible than its right-wing rival.

If I am right about how equality of opportunity is best understood, and if socialism can reasonably be expected to promote material equality better than capitalism, then there is a case for socialism (including state bureaucratic socialism) over capitalism with respect to equality of opportunity. I think this case can be sustained, for it is not difficult to provide good reasons for thinking that socialism is more egalitarian than capitalism.

Socialism, capitalism and material equality

Material equality can be pursued under both socialist and capitalist political economic arrangements. Of course, capitalism has a mechanism for generating material inequalities that socialism lacks: it allocates income differentially in virtue of private ownership of productive assets. But capitalist societies can rectify the resulting inequalities by progressive taxation and redistributive transfers that modify the allocations capitalist market arrangements generate. There is no reason in principle why these allocations might not be modified with a view to promoting material equality. Socialist societies too can rely on redistributive measures to advance equality. However, one would expect them to have less to correct for, inasmuch as the distinctively capitalist mechanism for generating material inequalities is, by definition, absent under socialism.

Of course, there are *other* mechanisms for generating inequalities under socialism. So long as there are differential rewards proportional to productive contributions, so long as scarce and vitally needed skills are rewarded materially, there will be material inequalities. Under state bureaucratic socialism, an additional mechanism can become important: individuals occupying commanding positions in the state and bureaucracy can use their incumbency to extract compensation greater than that accorded to those they dominate.[14] Each of these mechanisms, however, exists under capitalism too, though differential returns based on incumbency of positions will characteristically take different forms than in state bureaucratic socialist societies. Under socialism, then, there is, in effect, one *less* mechanism for generating material inequalities than there is under capitalism. And the mechanism socialism eliminates, differential income arising from ownership of productive capacities, is the principal means for generating inequalities under capitalism.

It is possible, of course, that the elimination of the distinctively capitalist mechanism for generating material inequalities will not actually diminish material inequality, because the mechanisms remaining will, as it were, expand to fill the void left by its absence. The achievement of material equality is, in the end, a *political* struggle that political economic arrangements can facilitate or impede, but not finally determine. All that can be concluded, considering just the question of the relative advantage of private or public ownership of productive capacities, is that socialism enjoys a comparative advantage in theory. For there are fewer systemic pressures under socialism generating material inequalities. Put differently, socialism enjoys a *qualitative* advantage over capitalism with respect to material equality – an advantage that may, however, be overridden in particular historical and political circumstances.

This advantage is enjoyed even under state bureaucratic socialism, where bureaucratic incumbency remains as a major potential source of material inequality. To the degree bureaucratic

63

administration diminishes – the more the democratic model is approximated – we can expect yet a further qualitative advantage for socialism. Indeed, with democratic socialism it is difficult to imagine what *could* generate significant material inequalities. Just as socialism in general, post-capitalism, eliminates the principal culprit under capitalism, democratic socialism eliminates the principal culprit in actually existing socialism.

At this level of abstraction from actual institutional specifications, we can only draw conclusions based on likely expectations of the consequences of political economic arrangements. In actual practice, it seems, *other* factors may be decisive in determining how well material equality is achieved. Chief among these factors, I think, is, again, political *will*. We know that, in most (but not all) actually existing capitalisms, this will is seldom evident. Material equality is not a high priority, though some of its consequences – equality of opportunity, particularly – may be more highly valued. Material equality probably is more highly valued in actually existing socialist societies, even if the consequences of this more positive valuation are disappointing. These observations are to be expected. A desire to distribute societal benefits and burdens more equally is, historically, an important motive of socialists of all sorts, including the leaders of existing socialist countries. No corresponding desire motivates pro-capitalist positions, though some pro-capitalists may in fact value material equality. In any case, in so far as political will is decisive, there is nothing to impugn socialism's advantage in theory. The requisite political will is more likely under socialism than under capitalism, even if it is not always more evident. State bureaucratic socialism is, in this regard as in so many others, more problematic than is the democratic model. But it is not so problematic as to require significant qualification of the general case.

We will find that democratic socialism enjoys an overwhelming advantage over both capitalism and the state bureaucratic model, not only for having fewer mechanisms for generating material inequalities, but also for generating the requisite political will for achieving equality. At this point, however, this claim can only be asserted. Its defense requires an argument *for* the historical possibility of the democratic model, and a more developed account of the democratic model. These issues will be considered in Part Two.

In Chapter 1, we saw how restrictions on the liberty to own productive assets need not restrict overall freedom; indeed, quite the contrary. We saw too how a good reason for restricting economic liberties is precisely to advance material equality – and thereby to advance capacity-freedom and autonomy. Still, it is not clear how far socialists ought to go in restricting "capitalist acts between consenting adults,"[15] since doing so appears to impinge, inadmissibly, on individuals' freedoms. This important question for socialist ethics falls largely beyond the scope of a comparative assessment of socialism and capitalism. However, there is a clarification that bears notice here.

A commitment to socialism by itself does not *imply* commitment to material equality. Therefore measures necessary for achieving material equality – or, more strictly, for aiming towards it – are not *necessarily* enjoined by a commitment to socialism. Socialism does proscribe private property in society's principal means of production, but it need not proscribe all activities of individuals that frustrate or upset egalitarian distributions. It is entirely possible that, in socialist societies, individuals would have rights to dispose of income and other assets in ways that upset egalitarian patterns (though not, of course, in ways that restore capitalist social relations). How socialist societies might implement egalitarian policies is a vexed and complex question requiring considerable investigation; and also, surely, trial by practice. Were it the case that equality could not be achieved, or at least achieved perfectly, without interfering inadmissibly with individuals' liberties, no direct brief against socialism would follow. Socialists are generally moved by the ideal of equality more than capitalists are. But socialists are not egalitarians *per se*, and particularly not strict egalitarians. Moral difficulties in the way of achieving material equality must be confronted by socialists, just as practical difficulties in achieving this end require attention. However, these are problems socialists must explore. They are not, as is sometimes supposed, arguments against socialism.

Exploitation

Exploitation is yet another notion, closely linked to justice – or, more precisely, to injustice. It is not widely acknowledged by writers in the dominant tradition, though, as we shall see, the dominant tradition can support the concept. To recognize exploitation, however, it is usually necessary to look beyond the surface of events to the institutional context and historical background of social life. It is an effect, therefore, of the abstractness of so much social and political theory, as it is done within the dominant tradition, that exploitation is generally not accorded its due. Still, the concept is a viable one; and an important one too for the comparative assessment of socialism (including state bureaucratic socialism) and capitalism.

Exploitation is, of course, a fault to be avoided. Pro-capitalists and pro-socialists would agree that in general the less exploitation the better. However, many in the dominant tradition would deny the pertinence of the concept in comparing socialism and capitalism. And there is scant agreement, in any case, over what exploitation is.

The concept of exploitation has come into prominence largely at the peripheries of the dominant tradition: among socialist writers of various tendencies, of course including Marxists; and in some social and economic theory. The concept has generally not been used with much precision. Care must be taken, then, in comparing socialism and capitalism with respect to exploitation, for we cannot go very far on pre-theoretical intuitions. Once the concept is clarified, it will be evident how, in light of this standard, socialism enjoys an important *prima facie* advantage over capitalism. The argument parallels the case just sketched for material equality. This is to be expected. Exploitation is, in effect, a way of generating material inequalities. It is a way worth considering in its own right, however. From a moral point of view, exploitation is presumably an *unjust* (unfair) way of generating inequalities. Its investigation helps, accordingly, for clarifying our sense of fairness, and, we shall see, for providing some purchase on justice.

As a point of departure, it will be convenient to focus on exploitation in exchange.[16] An exploitative exchange is, first of all, an unequal exchange; an exchange in which the exploited party gets less than the exploiting party, who does better at the exploited party's expense. This is, intuitively, the sense in which exploitative exchanges are unjust (unfair). However, not all unfair exchanges are exploitative. To count as exploitative, a further condition must be satisfied: the exchange must result from social relations of unequal power. The parties to an exploitative exchange do not confront one another as equals. To be sure, under both socialism and capitalism, individuals typically will count as politically equal. Therefore there will also be at least formal equality of opportunity. In consequence, if we view the world through the abstract spectacles of so many in the dominant tradition, we may not be able to *see* the inequality that underlies exploitative exchange. That inequality is an inequality of power, not typically of juridical or customary status. Among equals, unfair exchanges might result from any number of causes: skill in bargaining, luck, or even altruistic leanings on the part of one or both parties to the exchange. These reasons may pertain as well in exchanges among unequal parties. But an exchange is exploitative only if the unequal power relation itself accounts for the net transfer.

John Roemer has shown how to conceive the unequal power relations that underlie exploitative exchanges, and exploitation generally, by specifying the property relations that regulate individuals' control over societal assets.[17] This is essentially the core idea underlying Marx's account of exploitation, though Marxian exploitation, strictly speaking, is only a special case of the more general concept.[18] Following Roemer's analysis, we can conceive of a political economic system as a "game" in which the economic agents are players. The game has rules defined by prevailing property relations. A group of individuals, a "coalition," is exploited in some game if there are withdrawal rules under which that coalition could do better – in the sense of commanding more resources – not playing the game than by continuing to play it; and under which, as well, another coalition, its complement, would be worse off, in virtue of the withdrawal of the exploited coalition. Then those who could do better are *exploited*; and those who benefit from their exploitation are *exploiters*. A coalition is exploited, in short, if prevailing property relations work to its disadvantage, and thereby to the advantage of those who benefit at the exploited coalition's expense.

For example, under feudalism, serfs work their own property a certain number of days and their lord's property the rest of the work week. Or they work a single piece of land, but give over some of the produce of their labor to the lord to whom they are subordinate. If the serfs withdrew from this arrangement, taking the land they work and their other means of production with them, they would surely be better off. For they would then retain all the produce of their labor. Correspondingly, the lords would be worse off, for they would no longer acquire what the serfs produce. Thus the serfs are exploited by the lords; the lords benefit at the serfs' expense, in virtue of the rules of the (feudal) game. Feudal exploitation exists, then, whenever there is a coalition of individuals that could do better if they withdrew from the feudal economy with their personal assets – with the assets they use to produce their own subsistence. If we assume what was generally not strictly true – that serfs *owned* these means of subsistence (the family plot), then we can say that feudal exploitation exists wherever there is a coalition that would be better off if it withdrew with its private property, as private property is understood under capitalism.

Defenders of feudalism might argue that, in fact, the serfs would not be better off by withdrawing from the feudal economy; the lords, even as they draw off some of the serfs' produce, perform indispensable functions – in organizing manor life and in providing military protection – without which, even with all their assets, the serfs would be worse off. This rejoinder is implausible, but it is well directed. Whether or not some coalition can be regarded as feudally exploited depends on whether there are specifiable withdrawal rules under which that coalition would be better off. If serfs would not in fact be better off by leaving the feudal economy, then feudal exploitation does not exist. Put in terms of the conditions for exploitative exchange just stipulated: if the pro-feudal argument is right, then the exchange of produce for the coordination of manor life and the provision of military protection is not, under the circumstances that pertain, an unequal exchange.

A number of comments are in order. First, it should be stressed that withdrawal rules are invoked to capture the *possibility* of doing better by ceasing to play a game in which others benefit at one's expense. Nothing is to be inferred about the actual likelihood of doing better by withdrawing under the specified rules. The fact that feudal lords *do* monopolize military force would certainly make withdrawal difficult and costly. It may be, given the probable costs of withdrawing from the feudal game, that serfs are better off, as it were, continuing to play. But that consideration, though very likely true for most of the history of European feudalism, is beside the point. What matters is just whether, given prevailing social and technological conditions, there is *in principle* a way that serfs could do better than they do under feudalism. In the pro-feudal argument just sketched, it is plainly disingenuous to appeal to the military protection lords provide, if what they offer is just protection from feudal lords. In feudal societies such protection is no doubt important and useful. But what is in question is precisely feudalism itself: a system that, among other things, renders this sort of military protection necessary. In determining whether or not exploitation exists, we ought, so far as possible, to distinguish intra-systemic benefits putative exploiters provide from benefits provided by the system itself. Finally, note that we are talking here about political economic orders, not particular circumstances that may pertain within these orders. A lord who receives feudal tribute and then does not supply the military protection which it is his duty to provide is reprehensible, even by standards internal to feudalism. Very likely even defenders of feudalism would find these circumstances exploitative. But this is not what is intended here by feudal exploitation, nor is it what will be intended by the senses of exploitation that will figure presently in comparative assessments of socialism and capitalism. Exploitation is a charge leveled at political economic arrangements, and only indirectly at particular agents or circumstances. What we want to know is whether or not these arrangements are exploitative, when agents perform their prescribed roles. The assessment of agents who do not perform their prescribed roles is another matter.

Turning to capitalism, we might ask whether there are withdrawal rules under which a coalition of individuals would do better (in terms of the resources it could command) if it withdrew from the game being played, as defined by capitalist property relations. A likely candidate is, of course, the proletariat: that collection of individuals who are direct producers and who do not own means of production.[19] In historical capitalisms, proletarians exchange labor power for a wage in voluntary, market transactions. Were the proletariat to withdraw from the capitalist economy according to the withdrawal rule stipulated for grasping feudal exploitation – were it to withdraw, that is, with its assets as defined by private property relations – it obviously would not be better off. For then the only productive asset each member of this coalition possesses, the capacity to labor, would be rendered unusable. Given private property and its supposed distribution, the wage bargain is plainly advantageous for all parties. Many have concluded, therefore, that there is no exploitation under capitalism – except when proletarians (workers) receive less in wages than their contribution to the production process (measured by the marginal productivity of labor inputs) warrants. This sort of exploitation can occur when there is, say, a buyer's market for labor or when the state interferes, against labor, in the labor market. But even if workers receive less than their "fair" share (less than the marginal productivity of labor inputs), there are still, for workers as for capitalists, gains from trade. This is, after all, why the wage bargain is entered into voluntarily.

That the wage bargain is entered into voluntarily shows only that capitalist exploitation, if it exists, does not, like feudal exploitation, operate through a coercive labor market.[20] However, there is no reason to suppose that a coercive labor market is necessary for exploitation. In principle, exploitation can be entered into voluntarily; and can even, in some sense, be advantageous to the exploited party. To decide for or against capitalist exploitation, what we must determine, following Roemer, is whether there are withdrawal rules such that the putative exploited coalition, the proletariat, would be better off were it to withdraw from the capitalist "game," leaving its putative exploiters, the owners of capital, worse off.

To grasp capitalist exploitation, then, Roemer would have us ask whether there are individuals who would do better were they to withdraw from the capitalist game, taking with them not only their privately owned assets, but their per-capita share of society's alienable assets.[21] Would proletarians, say, do better if they owned their per-capita share of society's means of production? The answer, it seems clear, is unqualifiedly yes. Were the character and distribution of property different from what it is in a private ownership economy, proletarians would, in all likelihood, do better. Thus capitalist exploitation exists. In virtue of the system of private property, owners of capital exploit non-owners who are also, it happens, the direct producers, the workers whose labor power is set to work on means of production owned by others.

Just as feudal reactionaries might have argued that feudal social relations are in fact advantageous for serfs, so too defenders of capitalism might argue that capitalists are necessary for organizing the production process; and that without the exercise of capitalists' entrepreneurial skills, workers would be worse off even with their per-capita share of society's alienable assets than they are under capitalism. As Roemer would have it, the real or "subtle" controversy over the existence of capitalist exploitation turns precisely on the viability of this assertion. Do capitalists exercise vital and indispensable functions or not? If not, then workers would do better without capitalists, and are therefore exploited by capitalists. If so, then workers are doing as well as they can, and are not exploited. The dispute over capitalist exploitation, properly conceived, is therefore a dispute over the role of the capitalist or, more strictly, over the role of capitalists' activities *as* capitalists (since actual capitalists may contribute to the production process in many ways, including even as direct producers). If capitalists draw off social surplus without making *any* productive contribution towards its generation, they are outright exploiters. On the other hand, if capitalists do exercise indispensable functions, then the existence of capitalist exploitation is more problematic. Suppose we had a way to measure productive contribution. Then if the imputed contribution of the capitalist corresponds to the profits capitalists realize, there is no capitalist exploitation. On the other hand, if the contribution of the capitalist is less than capitalists' profits, to that extent capitalists are exploiting workers. We will consider some putative contributions of capitalists as capitalists in the Appendix to this chapter.

In assessing the role of the capitalist, attention should be paid to dynamic, as well as static, contributions. It may be that the role of capitalist is vital, perhaps even indispensable, for accumulation; that without capitalists, accumulation would proceed more slowly or not at all. Then it would be misleading to measure capitalists' productive contributions by focusing just on particular cycles of the production process. In other words, capitalists as capitalists might contribute substantively in the capitalist "game," but only in the long run. In assessing such claims, we should be careful not to assume the indefinite desirability of accumulation and growth. That issue will be broached in Chapter 3 and resumed in Chapter 6, in the context of Marx's theory of history. For now, it may be suggested that the desirabiliy of accumulation and growth is historically variable; that there are, as the experience of existing socialist societies attests, non-capitalist paths to accumulation and growth; and that even under capitalism, the dynamic contributions capitalists make doubtless vary, depending on historically changing social and technical conditions.

The question of the existence of a form of exploitation is closely related to the question of its social utility. In Roemer's view, for particular historical conditions, there may be "socially necessary exploitation." Roughly, a coalition is exploited if it could do better in principle. But even if we abstract from the issue of *withdrawal costs*, we may find that there will be coalitions that could do better in principle, but that would not do better in practice by withdrawing from the game being played. This may be so for both short- and long-run reasons. In the long run, it may be that exploitation is useful for promoting development and is therefore, in so far as development is desirable, in the interest even of the exploited coalition (or its descendants). Roemer calls instances of such exploitation socially necessary exploitation in a *dynamic* sense. In the short run, exploitation may also be socially necessary. For it may be that economic agents are such that without exploitation and the social inequalities that result from it, overall production would decline (to everyone's disadvantage) for want of incentives to produce. Then, to use Roemer's term, exploitation would be socially necessary in a *static* sense. There could be circumstances, in other words, where workers would do better if they were to withdraw from the capitalist game; but only if, contrary to what would then be the case, everyone continued to work just as they had before. In these circumstances, capitalist exploitation would exist, but be useful (given the interests even of the exploited coalition) and, for that reason, socially necessary.

There is plainly no *moral* justification for exploitation that is socially necessary in this sense. To the degree capitalist exploitation is indeed necessary for maintaining production levels, it is in virtue of a motivational structure capitalism promotes, according to which people work mainly for material advantages that are awarded differentially. There is, I should think, no significant strain of thought in the dominant political culture that would consider this situation desirable. However, it is easy to lose sight of the moral *irrelevance* and even *reprehensibility* of what might make capitalist exploitation socially necessary. A conceptual advantage in focusing on exploitation is precisely to underscore the morally problematic character of (short-run or "static") socially necessary exploitation.

Before considering this advantage further, and also other lessons gained by reflecting on exploitation, it is appropriate to draw a tentative comparison of socialism and capitalism with respect to exploitation. This task can be accomplished with dispatch, as the argument parallels what has already been said about material equality.

Socialism eliminates capitalist exploitation. Therefore socialist societies – including state bureaucratic socialisms – have one less form of exploitation than do capitalist societies. Inasmuch as political economies are better the less exploitative they are, there is a case for socialism and against capitalism that follows immediately from the elimination of capitalist exploitation. By eliminating capitalist exploitation, socialism is less exploitative. For this case to be sustained, it must be shown that new forms of exploitation which nullify the gain achieved by eliminating capitalist exploitation do not come into being upon capitalism's demise; and also that without capitalist exploitation, the forms of exploitation that remain do not intensify to a point where the gain registered by the elimination of capitalist exploitation is undone. We must show, in other words, that there is in fact a qualitative advance registered by eliminating capitalist exploitation, and that this advance amounts to a quantitative diminution of exploitation as such.

Apart from substantive views about the nature and direction of human history, nothing can be concluded either in support or in opposition to the claim that the elimination of capitalist exploitation does, in fact, amount to a qualitative diminution of *forms* of exploitation. This issue is therefore best postponed until Part Two, where historical materialist positions are introduced and defended. But even in the absence of an express theory of history, Marxian or otherwise, the dominant political culture certainly disposes us to support the claim our *prima facie* case for socialism supposes. The dominant tradition, as conceived here, is strictly a constellation of moral philosophical notions, not a theory of history. But within the dominant political culture, there are widespread, even commonsensical, *beliefs* about history that tend to support the contention that in fact socialism (post-capitalism) does not introduce *new* forms of exploitation. It is of course possible for these beliefs to be false. For example, slavery, a form of exploitation missing in capitalism, though sometimes coexisting with it, *could* emerge if the means of production were socialized; but, I would hazard that not even the most ardent anti-socialists think it would. Nor is it believed that any other new form of exploitation would emerge. In general, even in the absence of an express theory, socialism *is* understood as *post*-capitalism; as a political economic system free from all the forms of exploitation capitalism is already free from, and free from capitalist exploitation too. This belief is not, strictly, a tenet of the dominant tradition. And it does require justification. But it is a pervasive belief, and one in which most pro-socialists and pro-capitalists are plainly confident.

We have already considered the possibility that mechanisms for generating inequalities – mechanisms we may now identify as forms of exploitation – might intensify upon the elimination of capitalist exploitation to a point where they effectively take the place of capitalist exploitation. We have found the likelihood of realizing this possibility to be slight, though greater for socialisms that approximate the state bureaucratic model than for democratic socialisms. The principal remaining forms of exploitation are, again, the exploitation of the unskilled by the skilled (what Roemer calls "socialist exploitation") and the exploitation of those who are commanded by the state and bureaucratic apparatus by those who occupy commanding positions within these hierarchies ("status exploitation," in Roemer's typology).[22] Presumably, the gravest risks – evident primarily in state bureaucratic socialism – are posed by status exploitation. But whatever the very ambiguous evidence of actually existing socialism, it does not seem likely, in general, that status exploitation should be expected to swell to the point where aggregate exploitation is greater under socialism – that is, under state bureaucratic socialism – than under capitalism. Again, the role of political will in this regard cannot be overestimated. But in so far as there are systemic advantages from one or another political economic arrangement, the advantages are in socialism's favor.

Not all inequalities result from exploitation; but exploitation always, by definition, generates inequalities. The elimination of exploitation may therefore be viewed as part of a broader project to eliminate material inequality. How far can that project be carried out? There are plainly enormous practical and theoretical difficulties in the way of doing so. For the most part, these difficulties revolve around the general problem of motivating and organizing production. Thus, those who would defend capitalist exploitation and the inequalities that result from it could argue that, by eliminating capitalist exploitation, production would suffer unacceptably, for want of incentives to utilize resources efficiently, and of means for organizing production. A task of Chapter 3 is the critical examination of this contention. The issue is plainly pertinent for the comparative assessment of socialism and capitalism. Socialists too might wonder how differential returns to skills might be eliminated, without, at the same time, eliminating scarce skill themselves – that is, without destroying the motivation of individuals to develop and utilize their talents. And they might wonder how administrative and other social tasks involving special responsibilities of one sort or another could be performed well, were there no special rewards for those who performed them. The problem, in general, is that there are tasks to be done that might not get done – or done well – unless individuals are provided appropriate, material incentives. It may be unavoidable, then, that there be trade-offs between equality and other values (like efficiency). These trade-offs are a problem, potentially, for both pro-socialists and pro-capitalists, in so far as equality – and the elimination of exploitation – are values.[23]

Put differently, it may be that some forms of exploitation are unavoidably socially necessary. Pro-capitalists are generally not inclined to acknowledge capitalist exploitation. But they could do so and still defend capitalism, just as defenders of state bureaucratic socialism could acknowledge the evils of status exploitation but still defend the political economic arrangements that support it. The dispute over rival political economies – between socialism and capitalism, between capitalism and state bureaucratic socialism, and even between state bureaucratic and democratic socialism – is therefore, in part, a dispute over what forms of exploitation are and are not socially necessary.

Those who defend the social necessity of one or another form of exploitation generally suppose that, regardless of political economic arrangements, susceptibility to material incentives and the requirements of social organization and work discipline remain largely invariant. The experience of actually existing socialism is sometimes adduced in support of this supposition.[24] To be sure, it is naive to expect the abolition of private property in means of production will in itself transform human motivations or other pertinent aspects of human psychology. But it does not follow from the recognition of this naiveté that "human nature" is immutable or that people must always be, more or less, as they are under capitalism.

In general, socialists, including all but the most abject defenders of actually existing socialism, have made the opposite assumption. They have supposed that human nature is sufficiently plastic that under appropriate social conditions, cooperative and solidary human beings will come to supplant acquisitive and competitive ones. The ideal economic agent, it is believed, is a creature of capitalist society. There is, of course, no way conclusively to prove this claim right. But, in the end, this is the "wager" upon which the socialist project rests. Socialism requires socialist – indeed, communist – men and women, moved by fellow-feeling and a spirit of cooperation; and not, as is common today in both Communist and capitalist countries, by the motives Hobbes ascribed to individuals in the state of nature – "vainglory," "diffidence," and a ceaseless desire to accumulate. For most socialists, the point of politics is precisely to render the Hobbesian vision false – by *creating* socialist men and women.

Thus socialist theory joins ranks with that strain of political thought, exemplified best by Rousseau, according to which the fundamental political drama is played out, as it were, upon the will of each citizen. For Rousseau, the central problem of political life is to construct institutions that shape individuals so that they may be moved by the right sort of will, the general will – that aims at the advantage of the whole community – and not the private will that aims at each individual's private interest, the interests of vainglorious, diffident accumulators. Informed by this view of politics, opponents of exploitation should seek to transform motivational structures in order to render exploitation in all its forms socially unnecessary. In doing so, material equality and therefore also equality of opportunity are served. The egalitarian project is advanced. And, for that reason, as we shall go on to see, *our* world becomes more just. We will return to these specifically political dimensions of socialist theory in Chapter 4 and then again in Chapter 6, where Rousseauean motifs in Marxism and related strains of socialist theory will be examined more fully.[25]

Rawlsian justice

Exploitation, conceived the way Roemer suggests, bears a plain conceptual affinity with Rawlsian justice. This affinity is worth exploring, not least for its implications for the comparative assessment of socialism and capitalism.

We have already noted the link between equality in its various senses and justice. And we have noted too that exploitation is generally held to be a form of *injustice*; or, more precisely, a way of generating unjust inequalities. The connection between exploitation and injustice is sometimes overlooked by writers in the dominant tradition who accord exploitation scant attention. In this regard, Rawls is no exception. The connection between exploitation and injustice is also clouded – and sometimes even denied – by some who have contributed importantly to the analysis of exploitation.[26] However, I think it is well to acknowledge the connection between exploitation and injustice, if only to recognize the full implications of the emerging consensus on equality that underlies contemporary views of justice – a consensus Rawlsian justice plainly expresses.

Rawls's account of justice is hardly uncontroversial. It expressly opposes important theories of justice offered up by thinkers within the dominant tradition – specifically, utilitarian accounts and also views according to which distributive justice is reducible to respect for individuals' "rights." Still, for reasons that will emerge in due course, I think it fair to regard Rawlsian justice as the best expression of the dominant view of justice as fairness.

Rawlsian justice is summarized in the following two principles:

First, each person is to have an equal right to the most extensive basic liberty compatible with a similar liberty for others; and

Second, social and economic inequalities are to be arranged so that they are both (a) to the greatest benefit of the least advantaged; and (b) attached to offices and positions open to all under conditions of fair equality of opportunity.[27]

77

The first principle articulates the notion of formal equality that, we have seen, came into prominence with the emergence of capitalism and the decline of the hierarchically structured societies of European feudalism. Where this principle is applied strictly, juridical relations of subordination and domination will always and everywhere count as unjust. Clause (b) of the second principle articulates the emerging consensus on equality of opportunity within the dominant tradition. We have seen how, in contemporary political discourse, equality of opportunity is a value all sides affirm, even as they disagree over what its implementation requires. Rawls himself argues for an interpretation of equality of opportunity that tends towards what I have called the left-wing understanding. But however equality of opportunity is finally construed, it figures essentially, in Rawls's view, in our sense of justice. For Rawls, then, justice is a profoundly egalitarian notion: involving, at the very least, a commitment both to formal equality and to equality of opportunity.

The celebrated *difference principle*, clause (a) of the second of the principles of justice, is also egalitarian, even if it does not strictly enjoin equal distributions under most circumstances. Rather, it stipulates a *presumption* for egalitarian distributions, a presumption for material equality. That presumption can, however, be contravened. Deviations from strict egalitarianism are justified, by this principle, whenever they work to the advantage of those who are least well-off or, as Rawls goes on to explain, to a representative member of that group or "class" (understood strictly as a distributional category) that does least well under the distribution in contention.

It is against this egalitarian sense of justice that socialism and capitalism should be compared. This is not at all to endorse uncritically a Rawlsian account of justice. Indeed, quite the contrary, as we shall go on to see. But it is to take as our standard for comparison the egalitarian intuitions that have come to underlie our sense of fairness, intuitions to which Rawls has given decisive theoretical expression.

Rawlsian justice is a standard that can be more or less well realized under different political economic arrangements. Indeed, in Rawls's view, both socialism and capitalism can each in theory satisfy the principles of justice.[28] I will dispute this claim. To this end, it is useful to reflect, again, on exploitation.

In well-off societies, where there is nothing to be gained in satisfying basic needs by distributing liberties unequally, Rawls argues for a "lexical ordering" of the principles of justice, such that the first principle must be satisfied before the second principle, the difference principle and the stipulation that there be equality of opportunity, applies. This is Rawls's *special theory of justice*: the theory appropriate for developed capitalism and also for socialism. The special theory, according to Rawls, follows from a more general conception of justice, according to which all social goods are to be distributed in the way the difference principle stipulates:

> All social values – liberty and opportunity, income and wealth, and the bases of self-respect – are to be distributed equally unless an unequal distribution of any, or all of these values is to everyone's advantage.[29]

The requirement that the inequalities work to everyone's advantage (as measured by their share of the "primary goods" mentioned in the principle – liberty and opportunity, income and wealth, and the bases of self-respect) is a version of the familiar welfare criterion of Pareto optimality (see Chapter 3). In *A Theory of Justice*, that criterion is used in some formulations of the principles of justice. Its transformation into the maximin criterion, where the objective is to maximize the minimal payoff or, in other words, the welfare of the least well-off group, is an important part of Rawls's argument. This is not the place to recount Rawls's arguments. The point to note here is just that the difference principle, in its final formulations, following from "the general conception of justice," reconstructs in different form the same intuition upon which Roemer's account of exploitation rests.

For both Roemerian exploitation and Rawlsian justice, there is a presumption for egalitarian distribution. In each case too, inequalities are "justified" if they work to the advantage of those who get the lesser distributive share. Indeed, in general there will be a substantial overlap between the exploited coalition as conceived in Roemer's general theory and the least well-off group in the sense of Rawls's difference principle. The designations are not identical because for some particular relation of exploitation, some individuals in society (whose distributive shares Rawls would take into account) may not be involved. They may not be players in the "game." Therefore there might be individuals not in the game even worse off than those in the exploited coalition. But this is a difference in the scope of the respective principles, not in the structure of the argument or in the underlying intuition – the sense of fairness – these principles articulate.

However, there is an important respect in which Rawls's difference principle and the generalized account of exploitation Roemer develops part ways. The difference principle would count as just some (unequal) distributions that arise from exploitative relations. Thus socially necessary exploitation in the static sense would count as just; for if the resulting inequalities were removed, the position of the least well-off group would, by hypothesis, deteriorate – thanks to incentive problems throughout the population. But exploitation *is* a form of injustice; and a proper theory of justice ought to accommodate this understanding and to ground opposition to exploitation, where it exists, in a commitment to justice. Rawls, however, would have us deny the injustice of exploitative relations whenever their elimination would worsen the condition of the least well-off group. I will go on to suggest that a less abstract interpretation of Rawlsian justice than the interpretation Rawls himself proffers would force us to recognize the injustice of exploitative relations, even when that injustice is socially necessary and, for that reason, justifiable.

That Rawls's theory of justice, as it stands, does not acknowledge the injustice of socially necessary exploitation is a consequence of the same damaging abstractness that afflicted characteristic accounts of freedom and equality of opportunity within the dominant tradition. Rawls's casuistry, but not his theory, is objectionably abstract. Specifically, he fails to put in question what must be put in question in making and sustaining charges of injustices: the real property relations that Roemer has shown to be crucial for understanding exploitation.

Within the dominant tradition, a tradition Rawls's theory of justice advances incisively, there is, we have seen, a tendency to see the world through excessively abstract spectacles; and to ignore, inadmissibly and to its detriment, the real world about which, in the end, all moral and political philosophy speaks. This excessive abstractness is, I think, largely eliminable. It is characteristic of dominant tradition thinking, but not implicit in the core conceptual and valuational framework of that tradition. What is tendentially pro-capitalist in the dominant tradition can, I think, be ascribed to this unnecessary and unwarranted abstractness.[30]

The charge of abstractness pertains as much to what is taken for granted as to what is not put in question. Rawls holds that both socialist and capitalist economic arrangements may be just in the sense that under both socialism and capitalism, the special theory of justice (that assigns lexical priority to the first over the second principle of justice) can be realized. But in assessing the situation of the least well-off and determining whether that group (or a representative member of it) could be made better-off, Rawls would have us look only at payoffs under different distributions and not put the rules of the "game" in question. But it is one thing to ask, say, of workers under capitalism whether they would be better off under some redistribution of societal benefits, and quite another to ask whether workers would be better off under socialism. These questions are not equivalent even if in principle socialism and capitalism can distribute benefits equally in accord with the difference principle. Rawls would have us inquire whether a system of progressive taxation and income redistribution towards greater equality would diminish aggregate output in ways that would lessen the distributive share of the least well-off. If not, then a move in this egalitarian direction is warranted. If so, the difference principle requires that we avoid this move. But if this is the question posed, the question of workers' payoffs under socialism is not posed. In practice, then, Rawlsian assessments take prevailing property relations for granted or, what comes to the same thing, fail to put in question the historical specificity of the social relations under which the difference principle is applied.

However, Rawlsian justice, so far as its core idea is to maximize the minimal payoff, need not be abstract in this way. There is nothing in the principles of justice themselves that precludes taking historically specific property relations into account in just the way Roemer does in analyzing exploitation. We need only look beyond the surface of putative distributions to the institutional context. We need only be less (needlessly) abstract.

Recall Rawls's argument for the principles of justice. His strategy is expressly "contractarian" in the sense that the principles of justice, in his view, are those that would be chosen by suitably characterized individuals in a properly described "original

position" (state of nature) where principles for regulating cooperation and conflict fairly (justly) are, so to speak, abstracted out,
though recognized as necessary. Rawls places individuals under a
"veil of ignorance" that removes all knowledge of individuals'
particular circumstances, while leaving general knowledge of
society intact. Here is Rawls's account:

> Somehow we must nullify the effects of specific contingencies
> which put men at odds and tempt them to exploit social and
> natural circumstances to their advantage. Now in order to do
> this I assume that the parties are situated behind a veil of
> ignorance. They do not know how the various alternatives will
> affect their own particular case and are obliged to evaluate
> principles solely on the basis of general considerations . . . . It is
> assumed, then, that the parties do not know certain kinds of
> particular facts. First of all, no one knows his place in society,
> his class position or social status; nor does he know his fortune
> in the distribution of natural assets and abilities, his intelligence
> and strength and the like. Nor again does anyone know his
> conception of the good, the particulars of his rational plan of
> life, or even the special features of his psychology, such as
> aversion to risk or liability to optimism or pessimism.

Moreover, individuals are deprived of knowledge of the
particular circumstances of their own society – its political
arrangements, its level of social and economic development and
even where it stands in the course of historical time. The only
particular facts which parties in the original position are allowed to
know is that their social arrangements, whatever they might be,
are such that principles of justice for regulating cooperation and
conflict are possible and desirable. On the other hand, individuals

> know the general facts about human society . . . . They
> understand political affairs and the principles of economic
> theory; they know the basis of social organization and the laws
> of human psychology. Indeed, the parties are presumed to know
> whatever general facts affect the choice of principles of justice.[31]

Needless to say, in Rawls's view, these general facts about
human society do not include theories of history – like Marx's –
that put fundamental property relations in question. The parties in

the original position are "bourgeois social scientists" under a veil of ignorance.

But if our best account of "political affairs and the principles of economic theory . . . the basis of social organization and the laws of human psychology" requires, as Marxists insist, that we do put fundamental property relations in question, then the theoretical culture Rawls imputes to parties in the original position is tendentiously mistaken. In these terms, what obscures the pro-socialist implications of Rawlsian justice is Rawls's account of the "general facts...[that] affect the choice of principles of justice." Whether Rawlsian justice inclines support for socialism or capitalism depends, in the end, on how the world is; and how it is best accounted for. This is not a question that can be settled definitively in a comparative assessment of socialism and capitalism *in theory*. But it is fair to suggest that Marxism, by putting in question what mainstream social science characteristically abstracts from, has the more plausible case – if only for directly confronting what so many rival traditions ignore, and what, presumably, ought to be explained. If this suggestion is right, it follows that good social science forces consideration of what Rawls – and the dominant tradition generally – ignore. By "correcting" Rawls's view of what is known under the veil of ignorance, we render property relations problematic. Doing so, I suspect, has far-reaching implications for how we assess the justice of social practices and institutions. But it would not impugn Rawls's derivation of the principles of justice. If Rawls is wrong in the theoretical culture he imputes to individuals in the original position, the principles of justice are not themselves impugned.

The abstractness of Rawlsian justice follows from the ahistoricity of the political science, economics, sociology and psychology Rawls tacitly accepts. But the content of the general information individuals have at their disposal in the original position is incidental to the core argument and may be modified or enriched without fundamentally altering the case for the difference principle or for the other tenets of Rawlsian justice – the priority of liberty and fair equality of opportunity. An inordinate abstractness – and nothing else – suggests neutral or pro-capitalist positions. But this abstractness can be overcome without undoing Rawls's major insights.

Overcoming the plainly eliminable abstractness of the more

casuistical aspects of Rawls's theory of justice forces attention upon the injustice of exploitative relations, even when they are socially necessary, and clear recognition of the injustices arising out of what the dominant tradition characteristically, but unnecessarily, removes from critical scrutiny: the character and distribution of property. With its abstract spectacles removed, who can tell what might become visible, even from within the horizons of the dominant tradition!

The point, again, is to put fundamental property relations in question in applications of the difference principle. Of course, at this level of abstraction nothing definitive can be concluded. But I would speculate, with some assurance, that a Rawlsian theory thus repaired would support socialism over capitalism. Equal provision of the greatest feasible liberty and full equality of opportunity are, we have seen, at least as likely under socialism – though not necessarily under state bureaucratic socialism – as under capitalism. And a difference principle read so as to acknowledge exploitation, is likely to lead to the conclusion, under present historical circumstances, where so much if not all of capitalist exploitation is either already socially unnecessary or could be made so easily, that we can maximize the share of primary goods allotted to the least well-off group (or to its representative member) only if we eliminate differential returns to alienable assets. Put differently: in eliminating capitalist exploitation, socialism, other things being equal, is more just.

The situation with state bureaucratic socialism is, again, less clear. In eliminating capitalist exploitation, all socialisms (post-capitalisms) enjoy an advantage over capitalism with respect to justice. But the possible advantages of capitalism over state bureaucratic socialism with respect to freedom may override this advantage. If state bureaucratic socialism does jeopardize the equal distribution of the maximum feasible liberty, state bureaucratic socialism runs afoul of the first principle of justice. We know, of course, that Rawls's first principle *can* be violated in both socialist and capitalist societies. And it is unwise to draw conclusions directly from the historical record. Still, as we have seen, there is a greater systemic threat to freedom under state bureaucratic socialism than under capitalism. Certainly, the principal threat to freedom, even where state bureaucratic domination supplants the rule of capital, is political, not political economic. But the political economic obstacle cannot be over-looked. What is clear in theory, and probably also even in light of the historical evidence, is the advantage socialism, including state bureaucratic socialism, enjoys with respect to the second principle – an advantage consequent upon the elimination of capitalist exploitation, capitalism's distinctive mechanism for generating (unjust) inequalities.

In any case, a definitive comparison is not possible. There is no compelling reason to deny the *prima facie* case enjoyed by state bureaucratic socialism over capitalism as a political economic model. Nor is there good reason to regard that case as definitive. State bureaucratic socialism's problems with freedom may infect its tenability with respect to justice too. I have suggested (in Chapter 1) that these problems can in principle be overcome politically; that the principal threat to freedom, under *any* political economic arrangement, is political, not political economic. Even state bureaucratic socialist societies, with the requisite political will, *can* realize the *prima facie* advantage socialism in general enjoys over capitalism. In Part Two we will see that democratic socialism can realize this advantage less problematically.

There is, therefore, a case to be made for socialism over capitalism with respect to Rawlsian justice and, more generally, the egalitarian sense of fairness Rawlsian justice articulates – despite the indeterminacy that plagues comparative assessments of political economic systems at this level of abstraction, and despite reservations about state bureaucratic socialism. We can thus conclude with some confidence that in theory socialism fares better than capitalism with respect to prevailing distributional values.

Appendix: Non-comparative distributional values

In this chapter and throughout Part One, socialism and capitalism are assessed comparatively, with respect to values constitutive of the dominant theoretical tradition of our political culture. There are, however, a number of non-comparative claims, primarily appeals to justice, that are invoked in support of capitalism or, more rarely, socialism. What characterizes these claims is a view that justice is satisfied only by particular (typically, capitalist) social relations. We can sort these claims into two categories: those that would justify capitalism (or, more rarely, socialism) by appeal to a notion of justice as desert; and those that make essential use of normative theories of property rights.

There exists a substantial pro-capitalist, and a relatively meager pro-socialist, literature falling under these descriptions. Were the objective here to report on debates actually going on, tacitly or explicitly, between pro-socialists and pro-capitalists, it would be necessary to examine this literature carefully and to comment upon it extensively. My view, however, is that non-comparative pro-capitalist and pro-socialist positions are defective in ways that can be easily enough indicated; and that such claims are generally unilluminating for the task at hand – the comparative assessment of socialism and capitalism within the conceptual and valuational framework of the dominant tradition. To address non-comparative claims for capitalism or socialism exhaustively would be tedious and, for the most part, irrelevant. I address the underpinnings of at least some of these positions in the course of the main business of this study. Difficulties in the way of motivating clear implementations of substantive principles of justice of a sort that would, in turn, motivate claims for just deserts, have already been discussed. The problematic character of the notion of rights – and *a fortiori* property rights – will be a theme of Chapter 4. It must suffice here to call attention, very briefly, to some particular non-comparative claims on behalf of capitalism and socialism. These arguments are pertinent less for their philosophical perspicuity than for their importance, often implicit, in contemporary discussions. The very brief and incomplete survey to follow will accept the schematic distinction, indicated above, between desert and property rights claims. There is, of course, a sense in which those who claim X because they deserve it, claim a right to X. This, however, is a broader use of the concept of right than is intended here (or in Chapter 4, where socialism and capitalism are compared with respect to how well they afford respect for rights). Desert claims can be proffered even by those who would deny the viability of appeals to rights, in the sense of Chapter 4. Roughly, desert claims are entitlements generated by applications of substantive principles of justice. Rights claims are generated independently of such considerations.

Among desert claims are those that rely, in a way that purports to be non-controversial, upon the substantive principle "to each according to productive contribution." This principle is plausible only if there is some theoretically well-motivated and unambiguous way to implement it. To this end, some pro-capitalist writers have appealed to the conceptual apparatus of neo-classical economic theory.[32] It can indeed be shown that idealized capitalist markets return to each individual a share directly proportional to the marginal product of each particular technical input he or she provides (where the marginal product of an input is defined as the extra output resulting from the addition of an extra unit of that input, holding all other inputs constant). From this result, it is natural to conclude that capitalist markets or, more strictly, idealized capitalist markets (that satisfy conditions only approximated in actually existing market arrangements), allocate benefits justly; that is, in proportion to productive contribution. The returns accruing to capitalists in the form of profits are returns on capital inputs. Wages paid to workers are returns on labor expended. However, this result, or at least its ethical interpretation, is plainly an artifact of the analytical tools employed. Suppliers of capital are held to deserve a return because capital is defined as a productive input. But what, if anything, is the ethical significance of this definition? What warrants the transition from an analytical description, according to which capital is a technical input to the production process, to an ethical judgment in which, in accordance with the principle "to each according to productive contribution," supplying capital is, under idealized conditions, grounds for precisely that share of wealth capitalists gain in the form of profits?

Pro-capitalist economists and others, sensitive to these questions, have suggested that suppliers of capital do indeed serve a tangible productive function *of ethical significance*: they innovate. This, however, is a weak retort; for capitalists hardly innovate in proportion to the returns accruing to invested capital. Some capitalists have, indeed, innovated; and we might concede, for the sake of argument, what is almost certainly false, that most capitalists became capitalists by dint of savings from wages and successful innovation, or through the free gift of someone else, an ancestor presumably, who gained ownership of capital by this ethically pertinent route in the past. Even so, we might wonder what warrants returns on capital inputs. For even if all capitalists or their benefactors were in fact, at one time, innovators, capitalists do not continuously innovate in the way direct producers continuously supply labor inputs. Yet the return on capital invested is continuous, continuing sometimes for generations. It is as though a single innovation counts as a perpetual contribution, while the direct producers' contributions expire with the duration of the labor expended. Then, even if we grant that innovation is an ethically significant productive contribution and that capitalists innovate, there is still no warrant for returns to capital of the sort capitalism provides (unless, of course, we stipulate – arbitrarily and implausibly – that the production cycle for which an innovation is to count as a productive contribution shall include all the time for which, on a given investment, a capitalist enjoys returns).

Moreover, there is no reason even to grant what has, for the sake of argument, been conceded: that capitalists innovate. Of course, like anyone else (including direct producers), capitalists *may* innovate. Arguably, as a matter of historical fact, innovation may once have been an activity characteristically performed by individuals who were owners of capital. Nowadays, however, particularly with the growth of large and complex enterprises, capitalists are likely to hire others to perform those tasks, like innovation, that pro-capitalist doctrine typically ascribes to capitalists themselves: managers, researchers, accountants, lawyers, and so on. That this hiring out of the capitalists' putative tasks is possible underscores what should be an obvious point, even if it is frequently overlooked: that when capitalists perform tasks, like innovation, that are, plausibly, of some distributional relevance, they do not do so *qua* capitalists. Capitalists *qua* capitalists take returns on privately owned assets (in minimal capitalism) and exercise ultimate control over the disposition of these assets (in full-fledged capitalism). Whatever else they may do, including the ethically significant productive functions they allegedly perform, is extraneous to that social role and logically (if not always historically) independent of it. What neo-classical economic theory asserts is *only* that capitalists provide a technical input to the production process; they provide capital. Whatever else individuals who are capitalists may do, they do not do as capitalists. These productive contributions might justify returns to the particular individuals who perform them, individuals who are also capitalists. It might justify a *wage*; a return for productive labor expended. But these contributions would not justify capitalists' *profits*, returns based solely on *ownership* of productive assets. That distinctive, technical "contribution" of the capitalist is apparently not, in any ethically significant sense, a productive contribution of the sort that the substantive principle of justice, "to each according to productive contribution," can include as a basis for just distributions.

What is probably the only historically important, non-comparative pro-socialist argument also slides from descriptive, economic categories to moral considerations. Orthodox Marxists advance a labor theory of value, according to which the value of a commodity (and ultimately, therefore, its price) is directly proportional to socially necessary embodied labor times. On this basis, it is natural to conclude that labor is the sole *source* of value; or, in more contemporary terms, the unique value-producing factor of production. Then, if we identify productive contribution with value-producing activity in the sense understood by the labor theory of value, it would seem to follow that direct producers, the sole suppliers of labor inputs, deserve the whole product (or its equivalent when traded on the market). Wages ought, therefore, to equal 100 per cent of value produced. Capitalists' profits, then, are unjustified deductions from wages. And if capitalist profits are unjustifiable, capitalism must be unjustified – as would be any political economic system that affords returns to individuals who are not suppliers of labor inputs. From this conclusion, pro-socialist inferences are customarily drawn.

However, upon reflection, this argument seems more a *reductio ad absurdum* – directed against the claim that labor is the sole productive contribution relevant for regulating distributions – than a plausible argument for socialism. The final inference, that everything produced (or its equivalent) should go to the workers, is plainly incompatible with most socialists' vision of socialism, according to which non-producers (though, of course, not capitalists) share substantially in social wealth, where perhaps even income and other social benefits are distributed strictly equally. Occasional sloganeering apart, socialists can hardly maintain literally that those who do not work (productively, in the sense of the labor theory of value) should not eat. In addition, the argument just sketched implies that, under capitalism, all non-producers, not just capitalists, are exploiters of direct producers; for the shares going to non-producers (that is, to all but the workers in the very narrowest sense) are, like capitalists' profits, deductions from the total social product which, in this view, ought to be paid out as wages. This conclusion plainly contradicts the view commonly accepted among socialists, including Marxists.

The plausibility of this pro-socialist argument, like the plausibility of the pro-capitalist argument it mimics, is an artifact of the particular theory of value employed; in this case made more plausible, I suspect, by a widespread, but insufficiently thought-out intuition that wages under capitalism are unfairly low. However that may be, both arguments assume what is highly questionable: that there is warrant for identifying productive activity, in some technical economic sense, with the sort of productive activity proponents of the substantive principle of justice – "to each according to productive activity" – might deem appropriate.

It goes without saying that neither neo-classical production functions nor the labor theory of value in its orthodox formulations are widely regarded as sound tools of economic analysis. But the shortcomings of the economics underlying these defenses and attacks upon capitalist profit are not the issue. What is the issue is the absence of a direct connection between economic theories of value and theories of just distribution. In general, there is no reason for adherents of distribution according to productive contribution to suppose that the only ethically significant productive contributors are those who supply what a particular economic theory deems an input to the production process, nor even to connect these quite distinct senses of "productive contribution" at all.

Appeals to the absolute justice of one or the other political economic system come overwhelmingly from the pro-capitalist side and generally take the form of justifications for capitalists' profits. The problem is, as we have seen, to identify some activity or group of activities that might count unequivocally as the capitalist's contribution *qua* capitalist. Since the various productive activities capitalists actually perform – from supplying labor inputs to managing the production process to introducing technical or organizational innovations – can all be performed by others, and are never performed by capitalists *qua* capitalists, it would appear that no particular contribution or set of contributions can be identified as distinctively the capitalist's. For this reason, some pro-capitalists, following a suggestion of Alfred Marshall's, have proposed an alternative neo-classical justification for capitalists' profits and therefore for capitalism: that profit is a reward for waiting; a return, as it were, on the capitalist's sacrifice.[33]

For waiting or sacrifice to bear ethical significance, it must be thought to serve some productive function. That function is investment. By deferring consumption, the capitalist provides resources for investment in future growth. Now, for critics of capitalism, justifying capitalists' profits by appeal to the sacrifice of capitalists will, at first, appear preposterous. The deferred consumption of rich owners of property seems small sacrifice indeed in comparison with the deprivations endured by direct producers. But this objection misses the point; for "sacrifice" is not intended here as a synonym for "deprivation." Rather, the sense of Marshall's contention is that, no matter how well capitalists may live or what deprivations workers might face, capitalists' savings, in so far as they take the form of investments, serve an indispensable productive function.

This claim is not at all an artifact of any particular economic theory or mode of analysis. Investment is indeed indispensable. But is it, strictly, a productive contribution?[34] I think not. The level and type of investment would seem to be, instead, a paradigm of public choice (in the sense to be discussed in Chapter 4), an issue bearing on the whole community that must be addressed somehow or other. Under capitalism, investment decisions are characteristically privatized and decentralized. They are generally not subject to public deliberation and collective choice. The merits and demerits of this characteristic of capitalism, already an issue in Chapter 1, will be considered in the following chapters. It will become clear that the privatization of investment choices under capitalism is not, unequivocally, a mark in capitalism's favor. But however that may be, it seems that investment, properly understood, is not a productive contribution at all – that is, a contribution to the *process* of production – but a public choice (albeit one that, under capitalism, is usually made privately). This recognition deflates the ethical significance of Marshall's suggestion. To note that, under capitalism, capitalists do not consume all that is not paid out in wages and rent, but instead invest a portion of the returns they receive, is hardly to justify capitalist profit and therefore capitalism. It is, rather, to call attention to how investment decisions under capitalism are typically made.

Sacrifice appears to be a productive contribution only, as it were, within a capitalist frame of reference. From a more general vantage point that puts capitalism itself in question, Marshall's suggestion looks much less plausible. To defend capitalism by appeal to the sacrifice of capitalists is not to defend capitalism so much as to describe it.

Similar considerations apply to attempts to justify capitalists' profits as rewards for the risks capitalists take in investing. Under capitalism, capitalists undertake risks. They can lose the capital they invest. Should an enterprise fail, its workers may suffer. But workers, the argument goes, can always go elsewhere. Their productive asset, the capacity to labor, is not undone by the failure of the enterprise. It is transferable. Capitalists, on the other hand, cannot simply transfer capital out of a failed enterprise. When the enterprise fails, the investment is gone. This difference is sometimes advanced in justification of capitalist profit and therefore in justification of capitalism. But will it do?

The plain answer is that it will *not* do for roughly the reason that the appeal to sacrifice will not do: one does not justify a political economic system by describing its particular manner of addressing trans-structural economic exigencies. Risk is a fact of life that all economic enterprises – indeed, all human enterprises – must in one way or another confront. If, under capitalism, risk is distributed in such a way that capitalists shoulder the greatest burden of it, that is not by itself a justification for anything; it is only a description of how capitalism characteristically distributes risks.

Were capitalism taken as given, the distribution of risks under it might well be thought to justify returns to capitalists. (It would still need to be shown, though, that capitalists' profits are somehow commensurate with the risks they have undertaken; that there is some proportionality between risk-taking and profit.) But we are not asking whether, given capitalism, we can justify returns to capitalists; but whether capitalism can be justified, by appeal to some productive contribution of capitalists. The answer, again, is no.

Two further considerations mitigate the force of appealing to risk to justify returns to capitalists. First, we should realize that the risks capitalist enterprises face are themselves, to some very substantial extent, intra-systemic. All human activity is undertaken in uncertainty; and risk is therefore inexorable. But capitalist economic activity is particularly, and unnecessarily, risky – just because capitalist markets are merciless towards uncompetitive enterprises. Capitalist firms face intra-systemic obstacles in the way of survival that exacerbate considerably the risk faced by all human endeavors. It is disingenuous to purport to justify returns to capitalists by appeal to risk-taking, when the risks capitalists confront are, to a very large degree, system induced. It will not do to use risk to justify returns to capitalists, when many of the risks capitalists take are socially unnecessary consequences not of "how things are," but of how capitalism is. Second, in actually existing capitalism it is seldom the case, particularly with large-scale enterprises, that capitalists in fact take the risks ascribed to them in theory. Risk is diffused through state interventions of one sort or another – from the provision of investment guarantees through the manipulation of tax policy. In fact, major capitalist enterprises nowadays risk very little. That this should be so shows that risk-taking, however widely ascribed to capitalists in theory, is not a "productive contribution" necessarily assigned to capitalists, even within capitalism. Capitalists shoulder the burden of risk in theory, only if the theory abstracts from the role of the state. But there is nothing in our account of capitalism that precludes state intervention to the point where risk-taking is no longer the exclusive or even principal province of capitalists. If capitalists are thought to shoulder the overwhelming burden of risk, or if they have ever in fact done so historically, it is, in the end, for historically contingent reasons – because the state or comparable institutions are thought to play or in fact do play little role in economic affairs. It is not, strictly, in virtue of capitalism itself.

These brief remarks on sacrifice and risk aim to impugn the suggestion that capitalist profit can be justified absolutely, by appeal to some productive contribution of capitalists. However, it is not at all my purpose to deny that distribution according to productive contribution *can* have moral force. It seems clear, for example, that differential expenditures of *effort* – different work/leisure trade-offs – should be rewarded differentially; and these differences are, very directly, differences in productive contribution. The plausibility of distribution according to productive contribution raises important problems for socialist ethics. It is important to determine, for example, what deviations, if any, from strictly egalitarian distributions socialists should advocate for moral, as opposed to strictly instrumental, reasons. It does seem fair, after all, that workers who work harder than their fellow-workers should get more; while it seems unfair, though perhaps "socially necessary" for the foreseeable future, that workers with greater skills than their fellow-workers or workers who work with more advanced technology (and, for that reason, produce more) should get larger distributive shares. The elaboration of these intuitions would be out of place here. However, to allay misunderstanding, it is important to stress that while appeals to desert to justify capitalism – or socialism – fail, it does not follow that all appeals to desert are conceptually defective and without moral force.

The other category of non-comparative appeals to distributional values employs a notion of property rights, independent of claims for deserts. John Locke's defense of private property and its unlimited acquisition is the prototype of this sort of argument.[35] Neo-Lockean defenses of capitalism are commonly advanced in pro-capitalist libertarian literature, of which Robert Nozick's *Anarchy, State, and Utopia* is exemplary.[36] I will suggest in Chapter 4 that rights ascriptions of a kind needed to defend capitalism are without theoretical warrant and that rights theory is conceptually defective, though very likely "socially necessary." Here I will indicate some reasons for thinking neo-Lockean positions of the sort Nozick advances unlikely defenses of capitalism, whatever we ultimately make of their conceptual bases.

For Rawls but also for utilitarians and strict egalitarians, justice is a matter of achieving a certain structure or "pattern" of distributions. Then, since there is no reason to expect capitalist markets to allocate benefits in accord with these patterns, justice will require state organized (coercively implemented) *redistributions* – to "correct" market allocations. But if there are inviolable rights to private property – as Nozick, following Locke, supposes – these redistributive measures would violate rights. There would, then, be a conflict between rights claims and the requirements of justice. However, this outcome reveals an incoherence. Justice and rights claims cannot conflict, since respect for rights, in this view, is what justice means. Either our view of rights or our view of justice must therefore give way.

Neo-Lockeans would retain rights and revise justice. Justice cannot be a matter of conformity to patterns, as it is for Rawls. Justice is, instead, an account of *entitlements*, their generation and transfer. Patterned principles of justice thus give way to "entitlement theories."

Following Nozick, we may note an analogy between the structure of entitlement theories of justice that appeal to Lockean rights and deductive arguments. Deductive arguments are sequences of sentences in which each sentence is either a premise of the argument, taken as given, or else follows from preceding sentences by truth-preserving rules of inference. Then, if the premises are true and the argument is correctly developed according to the specified rules, the conclusion must be true too; for the conclusion of a deductive argument is just the last sentence in the sequence. Its truth carries over, as it were, from the truth of the premises, by the operation of the truth-preserving rules that warrant the move from one sentence to another. Entitlement theories of justice have two analogous components.[37] Corresponding to the premises of a deductive argument is an account of the justice of the initial distribution of assets, the "baseline" that will serve as the starting-point for the assessment of what is to come. Corresponding to truth-preserving rules of inference are justice-preserving rules of transfer. Then whatever results from a just baseline through justice-preserving rules is just, in precisely the way that whatever follows from true premises by truth-preserving rules of inference is true.

For Nozick, following Locke, patterned conceptions of justice err in being insufficiently historical. What is relevant is the history of a distribution, not its structure. It is therefore of no importance what a distribution is at a given moment. What matters is how that distribution came about. If we suppose, as neo-Lockeans do, that markets, including capitalist markets, are justice-preserving – in the way that logical rules of inference are truth-preserving – it would follow that justice proscribes redistributive state interventionist policies that seek to implement patterns. Contrary to what

Rawlsians and other mainstream social philosophers think, justice requires, in Nozick's view, a policy of strict adherence to *laissez-faire* capitalism, regardless of the pattern that may result.

At first glance, this position appears forthrightly pro-capitalist and plainly anti-socialist. But does it in fact support capitalism? I think not, even if – for the sake of argument – we concede its use of Lockean property rights. The principal problem is, to resume the analogy with deductive arguments, to get satisfactory premises. What must be shown is that the initial distribution of assets is rightful; that the "baseline" arose in a way that violated no one's rights. For if capitalist markets are, ideally, justice-preserving, as entitlement theorists maintain, capitalist market allocations will be just only if assets were first acquired in a rightful way. We know, of course, that by this standard, existing distributions in capitalist societies must be manifestly unjust; for actual capitalism arose, in large part, in consequence of plunder and expropriation – against a background of feudal exploitation (in Europe) and the displacement and massacre of indigenous populations (in the Americas and other outposts of European civilization). By no account of rightful acquisition, emphatically including Nozick's with his insistence on respect for persons and their "rights," could the initial distribution of assets preceding actually existing capitalism be thought rightful. But, again, we are not assessing actual societies, but their models. Could not capitalism arise from a just initial distribution, even if in fact it did not?

It is clear that capitalism could not arise from an acceptable baseline; though, to defend this assertion decisively, we need a substantive *theory* of capitalism's pre-history (see Chapter 5). There is, of course, no logical impossibility in fulfilling the requirements of justice in acquisition; but neither is there any logical impossibility in capitalist markets allocating resources in accordance with some pattern, Rawlsian or otherwise. The latter eventuality is, however, extremely unlikely. There is no reason why capitalist market allocations should conform to any particular pattern whatever, let alone to patterns deemed just. Should market allocations actually conform to some pattern, it can only be by chance. (This is why, in Rawls's view, justice demands substantial state-organized redistribution of assets.) There is, I think, an even stronger reason why the initial distribution of assets preceding capitalism could not be just in the sense required by entitlement theories. For capitalism's pre-history with respect to distributional matters is not open in the way market allocations are, but relatively determinate.

Capitalism, we know, even without a general theory of history, but from what we know *about* history, is the successor of political economic forms based on property in persons and the division of society into dominant and subordinate social strata. These forms effectively deny the formal equality of persons, and blatantly violate what rights theorists deem inviolable. It could hardly be otherwise. The very notions of formal equality and individuals' rights are, we know, contemporaneous, roughly, with the emergence of capitalism. It is virtually inconceivable, though logically possible, to imagine these values satisfied before they are even conceived.

There is a problem with the other principal component of entitlement theories too – the supposed analogy between market transactions and truth-preserving rules of inference. Pro-capitalist entitlement theorists think market transactions justice-preserving for roughly the following reason: that if two parties seek voluntarily to engage in trade, it would be unfair (unjust) to prevent the transaction. Then whatever is voluntarily entered into is just (provided, of course, that the prior distribution of assets traded is just); and so the outcome of the trade must be just. The underlying intuition parallels the intuition connecting market transactions with freedom: that if two parties seek, voluntarily, to engage in trade, it would be an inadmissible restriction of their freedom to prevent the transaction. In each case, however, this intuition warrants a *prima facie* case; but no more. For there are at least two sorts of considerations that override the *prima facie* case. First, as we have seen for freedom (in Chapter 1), the argument based on this intuition is defectively abstract. It ignores the institutional context within which market transactions occur; and that context, particularly where there are gross inequalities of wealth, may radically diminish our sense of the freedom – or justice – of the transaction warranted by our initial intuition. Second, the rationale just given ignores effects upon third parties, not directly involved in the transactions in question, but affected by them. The question of "external effects," effects upon third parties, and other market "incompetences" and shortcomings will be resumed in Chapter 3. What can be concluded here is that the

justice-preserving character of market transactions is itself doubtful, particularly if we add the institutional specification that the
markets in question are capitalist markets, operating in capitalist
societies, against a background of unequally distributed power and
wealth.

Therefore, even if we grant the very doubtful conceptual
structure of entitlement theories of justice, it still would not follow
necessarily that these theories support actual or even historically
possible capitalisms, as many of their proponents suppose. What is
defended, at best, is an idealized, sanitized and thoroughly
unfeasible capitalism – where initial assets are somehow distributed rightfully and where idealized market relations, with only
negligible external effects, are justice-preserving.

3
Aggregative values

Socialism and capitalism may also be compared with respect to aggregative standards. Where aggregative standards are in contention, the concern is not, as in the last chapter, with how what there is is distributed, but with *how much* there is. Plainly the distinction is somewhat forced. We have already seen that assessments of distributions can depend, in part, on how much there is to be distributed. We have seen too how different patterns of distribution can affect outputs and therefore, presumably, the degree to which aggregative values are realized. Still, for analytic purposes, these sorts of evaluative standards may be distinguished.

The issue is not physical output *per se*, but the impact of physical output – and other effects of political economic arrangements – upon human well-being. The fundamental aggregative value, then, is what is commonly designated *social welfare*. A particular view of this standard is characteristic of dominant tradition thinking. Social welfare is conceived as a combination of individuals' welfares, where individuals' welfares are reducible, ultimately, to the satisfaction of their wants.[1] When welfare is construed in this way, there are hardly any determinate conclusions to be drawn, with even moderate plausibility, in comparisons of socialism and capitalism. However, when the standard understanding is expanded in a way that seems justifiable and also faithful to the spirit of the dominant view, the area of indeterminacy diminishes considerably, and the evaluation turns in socialism's favor.

Welfare is connected historically to the economic concept of *efficiency*. Very often, debates over the relative merits of socialism and capitalism turn on the supposed efficiency advantages and shortcomings of these rival systems. It is therefore appropriate to consider some of these claims here. In this regard, it is important to recall that despite historical connections and even conceptual affinities between capitalism and markets and socialism and central planning, capitalism should not be identified with market arrangements, nor should socialism be identified with planning. Whatever can be said in behalf of markets and plans or against them, does not automatically translate to points for or against capitalism or socialism. Many pro-capitalist writers effectively confound a plausible, but inconclusive, case for the superior efficiency of markets over plans with a case for capitalism over socialism. It is unwarranted to make this connection, though there are indeed pro-capitalist conclusions that follow from some pro-market considerations. Altogether, capitalism probably does fare better than socialism with respect to efficiency, for a number of reasons; but, as we shall see, this advantage is not unequivocally a mark in capitalism's favor.

Welfare is most naturally expressed in utilitarian formulations. This is as we should expect, for utilitarianism holds that in assessing social, political, and economic arrangements, our concern should be to maximize the satisfaction of individuals' interests, and thereby to advance their well-being or welfare.[2] However, it should not be thought that the dominant tradition need be committed to utilitarianism, in so far as it advances aggregative concerns. Within the broad parameters of that tradition, interests can be handled in a variety of non-utilitarian ways. It would violate the spirit and letter of the dominant tradition to deny that individuals' interests are of ultimate importance in assessing social and political arrangements. However, we are not required to treat interests as utilitarians and their successors do. Still, utilitarianism is a convenient point of departure for discussions of the dominant tradition's aggregative standards.

Welfare

If, in utilitarian fashion, we construe individual well-being as the satisfaction of individuals' interests, then social well-being or *welfare*, the logical sum of individual well-beings, is the sum of individuals' interest satisfactions. Welfare, then, is aggregate interest satisfaction.

Interests are reducible to wants. Characteristically, within the dominant tradition, wants and interests are identified. This identification is particularly evident – and damaging – in accounts of efficiency. In what follows I will suggest that interests may deviate from express wants or even oppose them. But even where wants and interests are in conflict, interests are reducible ultimately to desires. The dominant tradition cannot allow ideal standards that can be specified independently of desires, although ideal-regarding uses of "interest" may sometimes figure in mainstream political discourse.[3] Our interests may be *discoverable* by others. There may even be circumstances when others are better able than we are ourselves to ascertain what our interests are. But interests cannot be *imputed* to us by others who claim to know what is good for us in virtue of standards logically independent of our wants.

Classical utilitarianism provides a particularly salient reconstruction of the notion of social welfare. If W_1, W_2, ..., W_n represent the welfares of individuals 1, 2, ..., n, respectively, then W_s, social welfare, is the logical sum of W_1, W_2, ..., W_n. In so far as the point is to achieve the greatest possible aggregate welfare, the point is to maximize the value W_s. If a loss for some individuals is offset by corresponding gains for others, there is no difference in the value of W_s – aggregate welfare remains unchanged. If a loss is more than offset by gains for others, no matter how upsetting for distributional patterns or even for the well-being of particular individuals, to the degree a concern for aggregate welfare dominates the upset distributional standard or concern for *particular individuals*' well-being, the change is warranted. Changes that are motivated by distributional values, but that would lower aggregate welfare, are proscribed by this standard.

To conceive social welfare as classical utilitarianism supposes, individual welfares must be representable as additive magnitudes. This magnitude is designated "utility." In utilitarian analyses of welfare, "utility" is a measure of satisfaction (or, as was more commonly maintained throughout most of utilitarianism's history, of pleasure or happiness). Traditional utilitarians believed, therefore, that, at least in principle, we should be able to construct a function for mapping individuals' satisfactions (or pleasures or happiness) onto magnitudes that can be added and subtracted. Such a function is commonly designated a *cardinal utility function* because the aim is to represent satisfactions (or pleasures or happiness) by cardinal numbers. A cardinal utility function would represent information about individuals' degrees of satisfaction (or pleasure). That is, it would make *intra-personal* comparisons of utility. In doing so, it would represent how individuals rank the alternatives in contention and also how much they value these alternatives. It would record both preference *orderings* and *intensities.*

Beyond these requirements, if social welfare is to be understood as the sum of individuals' welfares, the intra-personal utility scales of different individuals, as specified by their cardinal utility functions, must somehow be rendered comparable. In addition to constructing cardinal utility functions for all individuals whose welfare is to be combined, we must also be able to make *inter-personal* comparisons of utilities. The former task may well be intractable as a practical matter; the latter task runs up against what appear to be insurmountable epistemological difficulties. Intuitively, as do all theorists who fall within the parameters of the dominant tradition, utilitarians want individuals to count equally in the determination of aggregative consequences, whatever they be. Thus in ordinary voting, liberal democrats insist – in theory, though not always in practice – that each individual count equally in the determination of social choices.[4] Likewise, in determining aggregative welfare, individuals ought to count equally. But how, in measuring intensities of preference, are we to equilibrate individuals' capacities for satisfaction (or, alternatively, for pleasure or happiness)? There seems to be no theoretically well-motivated way to do so, even in principle; particularly if we take seriously the post-Cartesian problem of "other minds," and suppose that we cannot have access epistemologically to any mental life but our own. If knowledge of other minds is problematic, the very *meaningfulness* of inter-personal comparisons of utility is problematic too. And even if this epistemological problem is bracketed, or considered benign, how are we actually to go about rendering individuals' utility scales inter-personally comparable?

For the relatively limited purposes of economic analysis, utilitarian welfare economists have registered some conceptual advances in the face of these practical and epistemological difficulties. But even so, since the 1930s, largely thanks to sensitivity to the problem of other minds and thanks also to the growing influence of behaviorism (and a consequent distrust of "mentalistic" concepts), traditional utilitarian analyses of welfare, even in that relatively limited sphere that can be "brought under the measuring rod of money," have given way to what came to be called the New Welfare Economics.

The New Welfare Economics is ordinalist, not utilitarian. Inasmuch as behavior alone was to count, preference intensity – which is not perspicuously registered in behavior – effectively drops out of welfare assessments. It no longer seemed necessary, therefore, to face the apparently intractable problem of constructing cardinal utility functions for intra-personal comparisons of utility, nor the apparently impossible task of making inter-personal comparisons. It was enough, it seemed, to record information about individuals' rankings of alternative options in contention, and to aggregate these rankings. Ordinal representations of actual or hypothetical choices suffice to represent this information. Utility, then, as an additive magnitude, ceased to figure in welfare assessments. The point is just to combine orderings of alternative options in contention – to produce a social ordering of these same options.

Voting is a familiar example of ordinalist aggregation. We can suppose that voters have rankings of the alternatives in contention and therefore that in actual voting, they are not merely choosing arbitrarily, but in accordance with their ordering. Majority rule voting and its close approximations may then be construed as a procedure for aggregating these choices. Voting will therefore produce a societal ordering of these options. If O_1, O_2, ..., O_n represent the orderings of individuals 1, 2, ..., n, respectively, of the alternatives in contention, and O_s represents the social ordering, then majority rule voting may be viewed as a "device" for combining O_1, O_2, ..., O_n to generate O_s.[5] This can be illustrated diagrammatically:

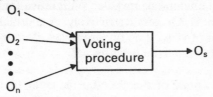

The voting procedure is a "social welfare function," a function for mapping individuals' choices, represented ordinally, as orderings of the alternatives in contention, into a social ordering of these alternatives. Social welfare too is conceivable this way. An appropriately specified social welfare function combines individual orderings to produce a social ordering; and that social ordering effectively maximizes welfare in the sense that each individual does as well as possible – in realizing preferences (represented by orderings) – given the constraint that, in combining individuals' orderings, all individuals, each seeking to do as well for themselves as they are able, figure equally in the determination of the outcome.

In shifting to ordinal analyses of welfare, the idea of the aggregative maximum, as traditional utilitarians conceive it, becomes problematic. The greatest possible social welfare can no longer be conceived as the largest sum of individual utilities. But it is precisely a notion of the aggregative maximum, of the sort traditional utilitarianism provided, that we need, if we are to make comparative welfare assessments. Following the lead of Vilfredo Pareto, welfare economists have responded to this exigency by developing what is, in effect, a non-utilitarian concept of the aggregative maximum. What Pareto realized was that, at least in some circumstances, it *is* possible to make unexceptionable welfare comparisons without relying upon inter-personal comparisons of utility, and even without representing individuals' interest satisfactions as utility. Thus, if one option is judged superior to another by all individuals whose welfare is to be taken into account – if it is unanimously preferred to its alternatives – then surely the unanimously preferred alternative is superior from a welfare point of view. Unanimous preference, in other words, is an unambiguous sign of welfare superiority – even without inter-personal welfare comparisons, and with only individuals' rankings taken into account. If everyone is better off under A than under B, as evidenced by a unanimous revealed preference for A over B, then A is better than B. Or, less restrictively, A is preferable to B from a welfare point of view, if no one is worse off under A than under B, and at least one person is better off.

The chief drawback of the Paretian account of the aggregative maximum is that it can seldom be applied. Whenever unanimity of preference is lacking, as it generally is, there is no Paretian choice. However, the Paretian criterion can be extended. The conceptual strategy employed to this end utilizes the notion of "compensation." Let us suppose that all welfare considerations can be represented in amounts of money, so that compensation can always be depicted as monetary compensation. To simplify further, suppose that society consists of just two individuals, X and Y, and that we want to make a comparative welfare assessment of two mutually exclusive "social states," A and B. If both X and Y were to prefer A to B, then clearly A would be socially preferred and would be the welfare choice. But what if X prefers A to B; and Y prefers B to A? Were we able to construct inter-personally meaningful cardinal utility scales for X and Y, we could discover the aggregative maximum directly, by adding up the utility for X and Y under A and B, respectively. The higher sum would be the aggregative maximum. But if we abandon the analysis of welfare as utility and consider just preference rankings as revealed by actual or hypothetical choices, we cannot add utilities. Still, it would seem that if, for example, X vastly prefers A to B, while Y only slightly prefers B to A (where "vastly" and "slightly" are understood qualitatively), then A is superior to B from a welfare point of view. In such cases, X should be prepared to offer Y (monetary) compensation for his or her loss, sufficient to bring Y back up to his or her welfare level under B. Then X would still be better off, and Y would be no worse off. Unanimity would be achieved; the Paretian aggregative maximum would be realized.

However, this result is reached only if compensation actually is paid. Welfare economists also attempt welfare comparisons on the basis of possible compensation payments. Then social state A would be preferred to B, on welfare grounds, if those who are better off under A than under B *could* compensate those who are worse off sufficiently to bring them back up to the welfare level they would enjoy under B. In these circumstances, since compensation is not actually paid, there will be losers as well as winners. All that is required is the ability to render full compensation. But how can we know when this ability exists? How can we know compensation could be paid in a way that would restore losers' welfare positions, without having some independent measure of the welfare positions of the affected parties – that is, without inter-personal comparisons of utility? We can tell what the possibilities for monetary compensation are, and can therefore specify conventions which, when satisfied, can count as fulfilling the criterion of hypothetical compensation. But we cannot tell when welfare compensation is possible (even assuming all welfare levels have monetary equivalents), unless we are able to compare individuals' utilities in a theoretically meaningful way. But it was just such intractable difficulties in the way of making inter-personal comparisons of utility that motivated this alternative way of construing the aggregative maximum.

Whatever their use in economic analyses, then, hypothetical compensation principles do not retrieve the information classical utilitarian analyses of welfare purport to convey. The Pareto criterion, and its extension through *actual* compensation payments, *will* retrieve the core intuition of the utilitarian position; but its range of applicability, as noted, is limited. That range can be extended through possible compensation principles – but only at the cost of severing the connection with welfare as traditionally conceived. Despite what is often assumed, the possibility of compensation need not indicate a welfare advantage. Thus contemporary welfarism strays from the intuition classical utilitarianism sought to express.

A *Pareto optimum* is a position from which it is impossible to improve anyone's welfare, in the sense of moving that person to a preferred position, without impairing someone else's welfare – that is, without moving someone else to a less preferred position. Pareto optima therefore differ radically from classical utilitarian notions of optimal welfare positions. For there are many – indeed, in principle, infinitely many – Pareto optimal positions, embodying, we may suppose, widely disparate levels of what classical utilitarianism would recognize as aggregate welfare. Classical utilitarianism recognized a unique social optimum: the aggregative maximum. For ordinalists, the socially optimal level of welfare need not be identical with the aggregative maximum (however conceived); nor is it unique.

In consequence, where Pareto optimality is taken as the welfare standard, support for the status quo, whatever it happens to be, is built into welfare assessments. For the status quo, the prevailing welfare allotment becomes our baseline for welfare comparisons. We have no warrant for altering the status quo, unless the proposed change is superior according to Pareto's criterion, a standard that will be difficult in most circumstances to realize. Thus an economy can be optimal in the Paretian sense, even when a few people are extremely well-off and others very poorly-off, so long as the poor cannot be made better-off without lowering the welfare levels of the well-off. In this way, the status quo is privileged; a conservative bias is introduced into welfare assessments. No comparable bias is suggested by classical utilitarianism.

Efficiency and the rationality of outcomes

Intuitively, an "efficient" use of resources is a use that accords well with individuals' interests. An allocation of resources is more or less efficient, according to how instrumental it is in realizing these interests. In technical economic discussions efficiency is identified with Pareto optimality. In this way, efficiency considerations are apparently joined to welfare considerations.

However, we have seen that the putative connection is severed when the Pareto criterion is extended through the device of possible compensation principles. Economic discussions of efficiency, therefore, bear little direct connection to welfare. Even at an intuitive level, the link between welfare and efficiency is problematic, as we shall see; and what can be said in behalf of socialism or capitalism with respect to efficiency is of only doubtful relevance for assessing how well these rival systems stand in light of the aggregative values of the dominant tradition.

At the level of abstraction and qualitative evaluation appropriate for comparing socialism and capitalism, finely honed concepts of efficiency of the sort useful in economic analyses have no precise application. In speculating on the consequences for efficiency of alternative political economic arrangements, we can hardly expect to show that everyone is – or could be made – better off under one allocation or another. We can still speak of efficiency, of course; but informally, according to its intuitive sense. In comparing markets and plans – and finally socialism and capitalism – it will be our informal understanding that will be appealed to. The question is: how well are individuals' interests likely to be served by socialism and capitalism, respectively?

Plainly, efficiency should not be identified with maximum

productivity. It is not even clear what maximum productivity is – since in principle we could always increase production, at least in the short run, by depleting productive resources, including labor. When is a plant functioning at full capacity? The answer depends, in part, on what we take to be the normal intensity of labor and also on what we regard as the proper rate of savings and provision for future production. These are historically relative norms. In general, full employment of productive capacities, however understood, is seldom the optimal use of economic resources. In general, producing as much as possible is irrational, both at the micro level (for capitalist firms, intent on maximizing profits) and at the macro level (where crises of over-production would threaten both socialist and capitalist economies). Efficiency is not a matter of using resources to produce as much as possible, but of using resources to maximize human satisfaction.

If human satisfaction is, in turn, measured by aggregate willingness to pay for goods and services, as it typically is, and if the distribution of wealth and income are not put in question for welfare assessments, as they generally are not, then those with more assets will have more say than those with less in determinations of efficient resource allocations. If there is more effective demand for luxury items than for necessities, economic resources, if they are to be used efficiently, *ought* to be used to satisfy this demand. Resources ought to be put to this use, no matter how urgent rival demands might be, provided those who put these rival demands forward lack the assets to make them effective.

It might therefore be concluded that an efficient economy is potentially an irrational economy; an economy radically out of line with recognized and urgent human needs. I think this reproach is plausible. However, it is not easily integrated into the dominant tradition's way of conceiving aggregative values. The point is not just that behavior that is rational on the micro level might result in socially sub-optimal outcomes. That possibility will be addressed presently, in connection with the relative merits of markets and planning mechanisms, respectively. The problem is that so long as welfare and efficiency are understood as they are within the dominant tradition, it is not clear how to conceive the rationality or irrationality of outcomes.

If, for the sake of argument, we concede the intended, but dubious, connection between efficiency and welfare, and construe welfare, again, according to the particularly perspicuous utilitarian formulation, the difficulty is plainly evident. Individual welfare is a measure of individual interest satisfaction and social welfare is the sum of individual welfares. But interests are reducible to wants; that is, to non- or extra-rational desires. Therefore interests cannot be faulted as irrational. Our interests – the ends of our actions – are neither rational nor irrational; for reason does not rule on the content of our ends. It is instrumental, not substantive; it concerns the adaptation of means to ends, not the ends themselves.[6]

People may pursue ends irrationally; and inefficiencies, in the welfare economic sense, may result. Thus, allocations of goods and services may be irrationally achieved, but they can never in themselves be either rational or irrational. If the rich get luxuries while the poor fail to get the necessities they require, the situation is neither more nor less than a reflection of people's desires, as registered by their willingness to pay for goods and services, taking the distribution of assets among them – and therefore their means for realizing their interests – as given. There may be good reasons for faulting the outcome, but not apparently on grounds of irrationality.

This conclusion is warranted, I think, according to the standard understanding of social welfare. But the dominant tradition's conceptual horizons can be expanded to accommodate at least part of what is intended when allocations are faulted for their irrationality. What is required is a way to assess ends substantively, while still supposing that reason does not rule on the content of our ends.

A candidate for this task would be a theory of human needs. Had we such a theory, we could assess social arrangements according to how well needs – conceived independently of wants – are satisfied. We would then have an aggregative standard distinct from welfare. I can see no reason in general why the dominant tradition could not accommodate a theory of needs. However, within the dominant tradition, characteristically, needs are seldom appealed to except at a pre-theoretical level; and there nowhere exists, in any case, an elaborated theory of needs of sufficient specificity to be useful for assessing political economic systems. To praise or blame socialism or capitalism for fulfilling or failing to fulfill human needs is not – yet, at least – a claim that can be elaborated theoretically.

Another strategy, closer to both the spirit and letter of the standard view, would be to ascertain wants apart from revealed market preferences. Revealed market preferences are doubtful, we have seen, because they depend upon a prior distribution of assets that accords undue weight to the choices of those with the resources to make their demands effective. Were there a way to discern wants independently – say, by questionnaires or other polling techniques – we could, in principle, arrive at a standard against which existing allocations could be compared. The difficulties here are practical, not theoretical. Assuming these difficulties were overcome, however, we would have only provided ourselves grounds for faulting market allocations for their incompetence in accommodating actual wants. This reproach is still at some remove from what is usually intended by charges of irrationality.

We can retrieve some of what is intended by that charge if we distinguish what we might call "true wants" from express wants, whether revealed in market choices or in some other way. True wants may be defined counterfactually. Our true wants would be our ends, supposing we had adequately reflected on our choices in light of full knowledge of the consequences and alternatives (or some reasonable approximation thereto). Our true wants, then, are our wants in so far as we are *prudent*. Plainly, true wants can deviate from express wants. But true wants are still reducible, ultimately, to desires. In speaking of true wants, then, we have not passed over into ideal-regarding standards. We are not supposing that reason rules substantively on the content of our ends. The concept of true wants deviates from the standard view, but is compatible with its underlying assumptions. In the concluding section of this chapter, this notion will play a role in an argument for the welfare advantages of socialism. First, however, it will be well to investigate the received view further, and particularly to explore some supposed efficiency advantages and shortcomings of markets and plans, and finally of socialism and capitalism.

Markets and efficiency

We know that capitalism cannot dispense entirely with markets and that socialism cannot rely entirely upon markets. Still, we should not automatically conclude that what can be said in defense of market arrangements redounds to capitalism's advantage; and that what can be said in behalf of central planning is tantamount to a defense of socialism. Capitalism can rely substantially on planning mechanisms; and socialism is compatible with very substantial reliance on markets. Even so, if only in deference to their very close historical connection, points made for or against markets or for or against central planning may be considered at least tendentially pro- or anti-capitalist or pro- or anti-socialist, respectively. In considering the efficiency of markets, we should be sensitive to these connections, but also wary of drawing hasty conclusions on their basis.

Intuitively, the case for markets with respect to welfare goes as follows: market transactions are, by definition, voluntary, bilateral agreements, undertaken, by hypothesis, in the interests of each of the transacting parties. Market transactions, then, have the consequence of moving the transacting parties to preferred positions. In doing so, by any welfare standard, social welfare is advanced. Each of the transacting parties' welfare positions is improved; and social welfare, a combination of individuals' welfares, rises accordingly.

There is therefore a *prima facie* case favoring markets over alternative allocation mechanisms (though not necessarily a case for capitalist markets). This case would be compelling so long as contravening considerations do not overwhelm the *prima facie* advantages markets enjoy. There are, however, considerations that impugn the efficiency of market allocations; and therefore, to the extent efficiency (understood informally) and welfare are joined, their supposed welfare advantages. I will list and comment upon some apparent failings of markets. Then, in the next section, in anticipation of drawing up a balanced assessment, I will list and consider some failings of central planning.

The relative importance of the items in the list that follows will vary with particular circumstances. Therefore nothing hinges on the order in which market incapacities are listed. The important categorial distinction is between shortcomings of the market model itself, and failings that are likely to arise in actual market arrangements, but not in the idealized model.[7]

111

Among the former are those situations in which, by voluntary bilateral agreements, groups or individuals who are not parties to particular transactions, find their interests affected in ways that the market cannot count. These "external effects" fall into two principal categories:

1 *External diseconomies.* There may be "real" costs of production that are not registered through the market mechanism. For example, when a factory produces a product but, in doing so, pollutes the air, the factory is depleting a resource – air – that the market mechanism does not count in its production costs. Therefore the price of the factory's product, as set by the market, does not represent the "real" economic cost of the product. The market price is therefore not the price at which the product would sell were all costs counted, as they would be, by definition, in a perfectly efficient economy. External diseconomies are an endogenous source of inefficiency. So long as market transactions affect third parties adversely, there will be costs that the market price does not represent.

2 *External economies.* Similarly, there may be uncounted benefits that the market does not register. Enterprises may benefit from, say, transportation or communications systems paid for, in part, by individuals or firms who do not utilize them. Or a factory's training program may benefit other factories, by training workers who then drift to other firms that have not paid training costs. These uncounted benefits, like uncounted costs, detract from the efficiency of market allocations, for they are not correctly registered in the market pricing system.

More generally, whenever there are costs that the market cannot count, there is a falling away from efficiency. In principle, government intervention can always rectify these shortcomings by requiring that "efficiency prices" be paid. But the market by itself cannot always achieve this end. Under central planning, on the other hand, the government always intervenes in the determination of prices. In theory, then, central planners can do what the market mechanism by itself cannot: they can impute efficiency prices even in the face of what, in a market system, would be an external effect.

In addition, there are certain sorts of goods, *public goods*, that are of such a nature that their effects spill over to everyone, in a way that undercuts the incentive of any particular individual or group to expend resources for their support. It is in everyone's interest that there be public goods, but in no one's interest to pay for them. Everyone wants to be a "free rider." A standard example is national defense. In the nature of the case, an army cannot selectively protect or fight for some individuals within a given population, and not others. It cannot defend just those who voluntarily contribute resources to support a system of national defense, and let others fend for themselves. Arguably, everyone has an interest in national defense; but there are no market incentives for bringing it about. For goods of this sort, it seems authority is required to impose the requisite charges on users. If there are to be public goods at all, authority is needed to countervail each individual's interest in remaining a free rider. Coordinating individuals' behaviors to support and maintain public goods therefore requires non-market mechanisms; for markets even in principle cannot motivate the required level of social coordination. With central planning, an apparatus for charging for public goods is already in place. In theory, central planners can do what markets cannot.

Likewise, if there are social tasks of a sort that impose severe costs on sections of the population, such that the adversely affected parties would never voluntarily incur these costs, the market mechanism will be incapable of accomplishing these tasks. Markets can organize only voluntary, mutually advantageous feats of social coordination. Systems of public works, particularly those of an ambitious and far-reaching kind, generally work to the detriment of significant sections of the population, and would therefore be unachievable without non-market, authoritative coordination. So too does a good deal of social policy that aims at social and economic "development." Development, in most circumstances, requires substantial redistribution of land and movements of population – and perhaps also a marked decline in standards of living, particularly in the countryside, that may continue for generations. Be that as it may, much of the world's population and nearly all of its leaders regard development and all that goes along with it as "dynamically necessary." But markets, by themselves, cannot achieve this goal. Strictly speaking, this is not quite a market inefficiency so much as a failure of markets as such, even were they perfectly efficient. Markets can only coordinate behavior through voluntary consent. What cannot be accomplished this way cannot be accomplished by markets. Again, as in strict cases of market inefficiencies, economic systems that rely on central planning already have the appropriate coordinating mechanisms in place.

Among reasons why actual markets are likely to be inefficient, even when the market model is in principle adequate for the task at hand, three considerations seem particularly salient. First of all, the idealized model supposes there are no monopolistic distortions of the price system. Where monopolies exist, efficiency prices are not realized through the market pricing system. But where markets operate unimpeded by external controls on accumulation, as they generally do under capitalism, there is a tendency for wealth to concentrate and for monopolistic price distortions to result. In this way, real world markets exhibit a tendency – a tendency that is widely realized – to deviate from the model. Second, the model supposes that consumers are in fact "competent"; that they are capable of choosing in accord with their interests. But consumer competence is generally an unrealistic expectation in a complex economy. It requires knowledge and reflection that can hardly be attained by everyone all the time. In practice, it requires much effort to become, say, a competent consumer of medical services; but will that consumer also have the time and be willing to expend the effort to develop expertise in buying insurance or automobiles or computers? Here, again, central planning enjoys an advantage. For central planning institutions will have the resources to acquire information better than could individuals acting by themselves, without special resources. In principle, of course, a similar result could be organized through voluntary associations, such as consumer groups. But even if such groups were organized extra-governmentally, through voluntary subscriptions, there are bound to be free-rider effects that detract from their efficiency. Finally, in real world markets, there are costs in realizing market transactions – in record keeping, legal fees, transportation, and so on. All of these costs detract from efficiency. In actually existing capitalist societies, transaction costs are often considerable; but it is moot whether in this regard central planning systems enjoy an advantage. For there are costs too in maintaining bureaucratic authority structures and implementing planning decisions.

There is, in any case, a *prima facie* case favoring plans over markets with respect to each of the other market incapacities listed. As we will see, however, it is far from sure that this *prima facie* case can, in the end, be sustained. However that may be, it is incontrovertible that markets are not always adequate for coordinating economic behavior efficiently, even in principle; and that actual markets are bound to fall short, so far as efficiency is a value, from what the market model purports to provide.

Plans and efficiency

Markets can coordinate behavior only to the extent coordination can be achieved through voluntary transactions. In cases where coordination cannot be achieved this way – whether for the very general reasons just cited or for more immediate political reasons – central planning enjoys a clear advantage. But there are shortcomings to the planning model also; "incapacities" that detract from overall efficiency. In principle, of course, planned economies *can* price goods and services at efficiency prices, and therefore *can* allocate economic resources efficiently. The incapacities of central planning are of a more practical nature. They result from the enormous complexity of socio-economic organization. The efficiency advantages of markets, and disadvantages of planned economies, center around the difficulty of making global choices – choices for entire, complex societies. In markets, decision-making is radically decentralized. It is therefore more tractable. Pro-capitalists and even some socialists are quick to proclaim the efficiency advantages of markets over plans. These supposed advantages are largely a consequence of the fact that markets simplify – and plans complicate – economic choices.

All modern social institutions that coordinate individual behaviors, whether they be governments and central planning offices, or the managements of large capitalist corporations, rely to some extent on hierarchically organized, bureaucratic structures. Administration could not function otherwise. Actual bureaucracies sometimes function smoothly; sometimes they are inept. It is not inconceivable that some bureaucratic inefficiencies are consequences, as it were, of insufficient bureaucratization. A better-oiled machine could do the job better. However, there do seem to be some unavoidable shortcomings of bureaucratic administration, particularly at the level of central planning agencies, whose task is to coordinate entire economies. Defenders of markets (who are also, for the most part, defenders of capitalism) have been industrious in describing bureaucratic inefficiencies. The items in the list that follows are therefore widely familiar, and can be noted without much comment.[8]

1 There is an incentive, within bureaucracies, to under-represent capacities, for fear that one's superiors may expect too much. In other words, the incentive structure within bureaucracies, far from encouraging productivity, actually discourages it. A consequence may be that accurate information will not be conveyed up the administrative hierarchy. Then planners will not always have correct information upon which to base their calculations and construct their plans.

2 Moreover, the information planners have, even were it accurate, will often be too abundant to process, even with sophisticated techniques of economic analysis and computer technology. Even the largest and best equipped bureaucracies may be overwhelmed by the tasks set before them.

3 There can be problems too with the control of subordinate agencies. There is a tendency, for any number of well-known reasons, for subordinate agencies to pursue their own, relatively independent interests; escaping the authority of their superiors and even engaging in internecine battles with other agencies. In many capitalist countries, these failures of *internal organization* are rife, particularly in the military and in some large corporations. They are endemic in the countries of actually existing socialism. The more market arrangements give way to bureaucratic control, the more debilitating this problem is likely to be.

4 Finally, as the experience of existing socialism attests, there is a tendency in planned economies for "shadow markets" to form. There will be trading of favors and services within bureaucracies, and collections of "debts." But in shadow markets, there is bound to be lack of clarity about the terms of trade. Efficient markets require a universally acknowledged medium of exchange (money) and clearly posted prices. Shadow

markets, lacking these market tools, are clumsy and inefficient. Their inefficiency detracts from the overall efficiency of the system.

These and other shortcomings can render planned economies woefully inefficient, as observers of contemporary Communism are eager to note. In theory, of course, planners can always allocate resources efficiently, something impersonal markets cannot always do. But the instruments planners have at hand to achieve efficient allocations can, in their actual implementation, effectively undo any (theoretical) efficiency advantages there may be to plans over markets. The Communist countries *do* provide ample evidence bearing out these speculations, as do many inefficiently run institutions in capitalist societies. That evidence is not at all encouraging for those who favor plans over markets.

Markets versus plans

Just as a list of market incapacities suggests the superiority of central planning, even a brief look at some inefficiencies of planned economies suggests the wisdom of relying on markets to allocate goods and services. To repeat: the main advantage of markets lies precisely in their alternative way of addressing what makes real-world planning systems inefficient: the complexity of socio-economic organization. Market systems transform complex decision problems into drastically simplified ones, by radically decentralizing them. Under central planning, someone must decide how goods and services are to be allocated, what is to be produced, how much is to be set aside for savings, how much is to be invested, and so on. In markets, no one confronts these global choices. The problems remain, of course; but "solutions" emerge when each of many individuals and firms grapples with the far simpler problem of determining what it is in their interest to do, given existing market conditions. Society then takes care of itself.

This wonderfully simplifying character of markets was already clearly understood by Adam Smith in his insistence that in a community of self-interested, rational agents, an Invisible Hand works to insure the public good.[9] Social welfare, Smith argued, is advanced by individuals seeking to promote their own individual welfares, not by individuals setting about to promote social welfare as such. In recent years, this intuition has been given rigorous mathematical formulation. Assuming a number of unrealized – and probably unrealizable – conditions, it can be shown that markets, in equilibrium, provide optimal allocations of economic resources. Moreover, markets achieve this feat of coordination without coordinators! Of course, actual markets may not coordinate quite so efficiently as markets do in theory. But even if actual markets fall short of the ideal (since the conditions for achieving optimal allocations do not generally pertain), they still do coordinate economic activity better, arguably, than can be achieved in any alternative way. For even inefficient markets succeed in simplifying what would otherwise be an enormously complex – and very likely insurmountable – set of decision problems into a host of relatively simple choices we all, individually, are competent to make.

There is, of course, a drawback to solving social choice problems as markets do. Questions of public policy are effectively removed from the public arena. This market feature is particularly evident in capitalist markets, where there must always be some "civil society," extending into questions of *control* over society's principal means of production. How many automobiles a society should produce in a year is a question bearing directly or indirectly on the lives of nearly everyone. Arguably, therefore, it is the sort of question that ought to be addressed in the public arena (see Chapter 4). However, if this question is left for markets to decide, it is never addressed publicly. It is, in fact, never made by anyone, but results instead from the individual choices of managers of firms, responding to market pressures and expectations. Where there is substantial reliance on the market mechanism, many likely public questions are privatized. I have already suggested that this situation is detrimental for autonomy (see Chapter 1). In the next chapter, I will argue that it is also detrimental for democracy. These charges, if they can be sustained, should be taken into consideration in any balanced, comparative assessment of markets and plans. For better or worse, markets do radically depoliticize questions of public policy.

Centralized coordination requires more than just assigning priorities to different economic projects and tasks. That problem can be addressed through the political process or in bureaucratic organizations. Nor can all the blame for planning inefficiencies be ascribed to information overloads or other planning incapacities. At its root, the problem is that the choices planners make have effects throughout the entire economy. Knowing these effects is a precondition for planning effectively. But to know these effects, planners must know the real cost of things; they need to know what, if we are to have X, we must give up. With the (substantial) reservations already noted, this is just what the market mechanism accomplishes. When pricing is removed from the discipline of the market, planners do not have this source of information. They must therefore discover alternative ways to determine the information market prices ideally represent. Theoretically, this problem is not insurmountable; but it is of staggering dimensions in complex, highly interdependent, economies.

Moreover, where market incentives are at work, economic agents are motivated to use productive capacities efficiently. In so far as the payoff for any individual *is* the market allocation, each individual is in a cost-price squeeze that constrains her or his behavior – presumably in the direction of the most efficient use of resources. This claim will require qualification, particularly for capitalist markets. But it is not implausible to hold, pending further consideration, that those who own productive resources under capitalism, the capitalists, have a compelling incentive to see to it that the productive capacities they own are utilized efficiently. For their returns depend on how what they own is used. On the other hand, in planned economies, we know the incentives are, if anything, counter-efficient. Those in commanding positions are too often motivated to use resources inefficiently.

In sum, then, despite their imperfections and plain incapacities, markets do seem to fare better than plans. They radically decentralize and simplify economic decision-making; and they provide incentives for acting efficiently. Whatever their shortcomings, actual markets plainly have accomplished a great deal. Whether they have achieved more than central planning has – or could – cannot be settled by speculation alone. As in so many other cases, particular circumstances – and, above all, historical legacies – must be taken into account in making assessments. In principle, planning is capable of achieving all that markets cannot. Still, it is far from clear that in practice planning is an effective way of setting about economic tasks efficiently, except in special cases.

Where there are particular, clearly defined ends in view, planning does seem apt. Thus even the most steadfast, capitalist market societies have resorted to planning for some sectors in time of war – when specific production objectives had to be realized quickly. Successes in targeted areas, however, are generally achieved only at considerable cost to the rest of the economy. Soviet economic history is full of examples of this phenomenon; and today, an awesome military force in the midst of a poorly functioning economy bears witness to it. The historical evidence to date suggests that where the point is to keep the entire economy functioning well, markets have an advantage over planning mechanisms. However, where the point is to mobilize resources to achieve particular ends, planning is clearly the better choice.

Socialism versus capitalism

Capitalism typically relies on markets – in labor and products of labor and, of course, in capital itself. Strictly speaking, however, capitalism requires only that there be private ownership (and therefore some private control) over society's principal means of production. Therefore capitalism requires markets just in capital goods, and can rely on planning in other sectors. However, in consequence of private ownership of means of production, even with substantially more planning, capitalist societies would remain essentially market societies.

Existing socialist societies have relied overwhelmingly on planning; though periodically – as in the New Economic Program (NEP) of 1921–3 in the Soviet Union and in the economic "liberalizations" undertaken in the 1960s and 1970s throughout the Soviet bloc – they too have utilized markets in some sectors. In theory, socialist societies could rely much more on markets than any so far have. But, of course, no socialist society could permit very much in the way of markets in capital goods. Socialism cannot allow the private ownership (control) of society's principal means of production. We must, therefore, be careful, in conceiving "market socialism," to keep in mind what distinguishes socialism from capitalism. A thoroughgoing market socialism, extending even to markets in means of production, would pass over into capitalism. Advocates of market socialism should be wary, therefore, of policies that would accord to a market mechanism effective control over the determination of economic priorities, levels of investment and other key questions of economic policy. Determining how socialist societies can use markets remains an important and unsettled question for socialist theory.

A more natural affinity for markets is perhaps an advantage for capitalism over socialism, with respect to efficiency, though the extent of that advantage is unclear. A clearer advantage for capitalism, already noted, lies in the incentive there is under capitalism for owners of capital to utilize what they own efficiently. Only profitable enterprises survive; unprofitable enterprises fail in market competition. Therefore capitalists who do not see to it that their property yields profits, seal their doom as capitalists. To the extent the profitability of enterprises depends on the efficient use capitalists make of the property they control, capitalists, who ultimately control productive capacities, face a systemic imperative to use these capacities efficiently. Efficiency is therefore an endogenous requirement of the system. In socialism, even "market socialism," there is no corresponding, systemic incentive to utilize resources efficiently. Thus it might be concluded that, where efficiency is a value, capitalism fares better than socialism.

This argument is not without force, particularly if socialist institutions tend to generate disincentives for efficiency, as, it seems, the planning arrangements in place in the Communist countries do. Efficiency is, at best, problematic under socialism, a situation socialists, concerned with efficiency, must confront. But is the pro-capitalist argument as persuasive as may at first appear? Does capitalism, in fact, provide systemic incentives to utilize resources efficiently?

The case for capitalism trades on identifying the efficient use of resources with the profitability of enterprises. There plainly is a link. Inefficient firms would not normally be profitable, unless of course they enjoyed monopoly advantages or state protection or otherwise avoided market "discipline." But profits can be realized in ways that do not, in any plausible sense, involve the efficient utilization of resources. One would be hard put to defend most forms of speculation, for example, by appeal to efficiency considerations; yet speculation can be a profit-maximizing strategy. Profitability and efficiency should not be confounded.

The case for the systemic efficiency advantages of capitalism over socialism is not without merit, but neither is it unequivocally the final word.

The efficient allocation of resources is surely of considerable importance when, as throughout most of human history, productive capacities are relatively undeveloped. Then inefficiencies are likely to frustrate interests, with significant consequences for individual and collective well-being. However, throughout most of human history, the efficient allocation of resources has been an unachievable objective. In the absence of generalized market relations – or alternative, central planning institutions that aim at the efficient allocation of resources – there were no mechanisms capable of allocating resources efficiently. It is only with the development of capitalism that efficiency became an achievable value. But capitalism has contributed enormously to the development of productive capacities, to the point where efficiency has become increasingly unimportant. Efficiency, it seems, is a value of ever diminishing appeal; a value that, in so far as it is realized, "withers away."

It is from this deflationary perspective that we should evaluate capitalism's plainest efficiency advantage: the systemic incentive it provides to innovate, to introduce new products and techniques. Under capitalism, entrepreneurs can capitalize on successful innovations, and reap significant rewards. Innovations are therefore likely. Socialist societies, intent on promoting innovation, would need to find a functional equivalent for the material incentives capitalism offers. There is no reason in principle why socialist societies could not do so (if nothing else, they could reward innovators materially); but neither is there a systemic imperative favoring innovation, as there is under capitalism. To the extent innovation promotes welfare, capitalism's advantages in this respect do amount to welfare advantages for capitalism.

Capitalism does seem to have welfare advantages, then, albeit of ever diminishing importance. However, welfare advantages under capitalism are not always unmixed blessings. We know it is profitability, not efficiency *per se*, that constrains the use of productive resources under capitalism. We know too that policies that promote the profitability of enterprises can have untoward consequences. In particular historical conditions, such policies may result in, among other things, widespread unemployment, waste production, the degradation of labor, depletion of the environment, and the marginalization of entire regions and sectors of the population. We have considered some difficulties in the way of conceiving these "global irrationalities" within the conceptual and valuational framework of the dominant tradition. Whether or not these difficulties can be overcome, the fact that efficiency under capitalism can have these results raises doubts about the value of efficiency generally, at least in conditions of relative abundance. It may be that efficiency not only becomes increasingly unimportant as it is realized, but that its realization, in determinate historical conditions, can actually *impede* the realization of the dominant tradition's aggregative concerns. It is far from clear, therefore, that there is much advantage for pro-capitalists in the efficiency advantages capitalism might enjoy.

Socialism and welfare

It is surely worth comparing markets and plans and capitalism and socialism with respect to efficiency, if only because so much pro- and anti-capitalist and pro- and anti-socialist debate turns on these questions. Moreover, as we have seen, the question of efficiency is linked, historically and also conceptually (though not so clearly as many suppose) with the dominant tradition's view of social welfare. However, the pertinent question in assessing socialism and capitalism with respect to the aggregative values of the dominant tradition is not whether the one or the other political economic system is likely to be more efficient. Efficiency is too tenuously linked to welfare and also, in most circumstances, too unimportant and even dubious in its own right. The pertinent question, instead, is more directly whether socialism or capitalism can best be expected to advance social welfare. This question, though, is evidently problematic.

Under which system of political economy are we likely to be better off? Which will better address our interests? The focus on efficiency at least gave these questions some specificity. Without that focus, the question retains its sense; but it eludes a determinate response. More precise institutional specifications would help to restore specificity; but at the level of abstraction at

123

which our investigation is posed, it seems there is nothing more definite to conclude.

Nothing, that is, unless we strain the limits of the conceptual framework of the dominant tradition by enriching our understanding of social welfare. We know that the dominant tradition cannot countenance appeals to interests irreducible to wants. Therefore we cannot construe welfare in an ideal-regarding sense without changing the terms of our question entirely. However, there is nothing contrary to the spirit of the dominant view, if we take up the suggestion made earlier, and construe welfare as the satisfaction of "true," as opposed to merely express, interests. By doing so, we remain within the broad conceptual parameters of the dominant tradition, while providing ourselves with a serviceable welfare standard for comparing socialism and capitalism.

Any feasible comparison will of course be tentative and schematic. Without specifying much more about particular institutional arrangements, it is useless to speculate very assuredly about the likely realization or frustration of wants of one sort or another. Still, I think an argument for socialism can be constructed – by focusing on what we have already seen to be a general characteristic of capitalist, but not socialist, economic systems.

Let us say, then, that our "true wants" are what we would want under ideal conditions – that is, with full knowledge and adequate reflection. Or our "true wants" are what we would want were our "nature" allowed free expression. Then actual wants can deviate from true wants in virtue of inadequate knowledge or reflection or, according to our alternative definition, the suppression of our true natures. Let us suppose too, as many within the dominant political culture do, that we truly want "meaningful work" – work that is fulfilling, edifying, creative and "non-alienating." Now a workplace designed to provide work of this sort is widely thought to be, and very likely is, at odds with the exigencies of capitalist markets. For capitalist firms to be run profitably, it is widely believed (particularly by managers of capitalist enterprises) that severe labor discipline and control, of a sort opposed to what we are supposing human beings "truly want," is crucial. Then, it would follow that individuals working in these enterprises would be better off – their welfare would be advanced – if the labor process were reorganized to make work more "meaningful"; and, in consequence, less profitable. If this argument is right, the requirement of profitability, the guiding requirement of capitalist enterprise, is inimical to at least one, important "true want" – our desire for meaningful work. Socialism, on the other hand, is in no way systemically opposed to a reorganization of the labor process with a view to making work more meaningful.

Of course, socialist societies need not organize the labor process with a view to making work more meaningful, as workers in Communist countries would likely attest. And capitalism probably can do better than it characteristically has. In this regard too, what is decisive are historical legacies, particular institutional arrangements and political will. But there *is* a systemic disadvantage to capitalism, and, for that reason, a case against it in comparison with socialism. The reorganization of the labor process with a view to making work more meaningful conflicts with the endogenously generated imperatives of capitalist market arrangements. How important this case is depends on how much we value "meaningful work." In conditions of relative abundance, where it is moot whether there is much of an interest in augmenting production as such, meaningful work is likely a value most people, including many pro-capitalists, would support – even, if need be, at the expense of efficiency. This type of argument can be generalized. Wherever the realization of particular interests, representing "true wants," would work against the profitability of enterprises, there is a welfare advantage, potentially, for socialism. Socialist societies might not seize these advantages; but there is nothing in their political economic organization that impedes their doing so.

In sum, how socialism and capitalism compare with respect to the aggregative values of the dominant tradition depends, in large measure, on precisely what standard we finally employ. If we focus just on economic efficiency, capitalism fares better than socialism. However, if we enrich the dominant view to retrieve some of what ideal-regarding notions of welfare aim to articulate, there is reason to decide in socialism's favor. I have argued that there is no good reason to focus just on economic efficiency. Efficiency is, at best, a value of ever diminishing importance. On the other hand, a view of welfare rich enough to suggest pro-socialist positions is feasible and appealing. Socialism in principle can always do what capitalism cannot: it can accommodate our "true wants."

4
Political values

Capitalism is widely thought to enjoy an advantage over socialism with respect to such specifically political values as democracy and respect for individuals' rights. Pro-capitalist theorists have, of course, argued for this view; but I suspect its widespread acceptance is based more on an impression of the historical record than on reasoned considerations. The arguments that can be offered in capitalism's behalf are not, for the most part, very persuasive. In view of the weakness of the case for capitalism, and the historical record of actually existing socialism, it would be natural to suppose the contest inconclusive; or to conclude that neither socialism nor capitalism enjoys any particular advantages with respect to political values. I will argue that this conclusion likely can be sustained with respect to individuals' rights; but that when that issue is properly understood, there remains, contrary to initial expectations, an important advantage for socialism. With respect to democracy, however, I will maintain that socialism enjoys a distinct – though plainly not an automatic – advantage.

On rights, my claim, more precisely, is that the issue is poorly conceived. There is indeed a sense in which socialism and capitalism can equally support or deny individuals' rights. But I will hold that rights theory, though important in actual political communities, is conceptually defective. Under capitalism, there appears to be no workable alternative to rights, if capitalist society is to succeed in presenting itself as a morally attractive ideal. Under socialism, however, there *is* a possible remedy for the defects of rights theory – though no existing socialist society has done much to rectify the situation, nor is any likely to do so, so long as the state bureaucratic model remains the governing conception of socialism. The alternative to rights, we shall see, emerges from the radical democratization of the social order.

With regard to democracy, my claim is that, in general, socialism fares better than capitalism, though the area of indeterminacy that plagues comparisons of political economic systems at this level of abstraction, is, in this case too, substantial. As already noted (in Chapter 1), capitalism is necessarily non-democratic in crucial respects, while socialism is not. But, as with freedom, capitalism may still fare better than state bureaucratic socialism with respect to democracy. Clearly, democratic socialism fares best. However, the historical possibility of democratic socialism cannot simply be assumed; nor should its desirability be taken for granted. Both require demonstration. This question is the principal topic of Part Two.

Democracy

Etymologically, democracy designates rule by the *demos* – the mob, the unprivileged, the (common) people. Until well into the nineteenth century, the consensus view was that democracy, understood in this original sense, was a bad thing. Even the founders of contemporary democratic theory – Rousseau, for example – insisted that democratic government, as opposed to rule by monarchs or aristocrats, by those possessing civility and educated to rule, was the very worst way to organize the administration of civil affairs.[1]

However, among those who despised government by the *demos*, there were thinkers such as Rousseau and also Locke who advanced notions of popular sovereignty; and who maintained that the popular sovereign should legislate by pooling the views of its constituent individuals – registered by their votes for alternative options in contention. What these thinkers defended, then, are collective choice procedures that map individuals' choices into social choices that represent the will of the people as sovereign. For the social choice genuinely to represent the popular will, it is crucial, as Rousseau and Locke and many others too maintained, that individual voters count equally in its determination; and that the social choice be determined exclusively by the choices of the individuals whose votes are to be combined. It is choice procedures of this sort that the term *democracy* came to

127

designate, increasingly throughout the nineteenth century, and definitively in this century, particular in liberal democratic polities. In non-liberal democratic societies, whether in the Third World or in the Communist bloc, residues of the older sense of the term are still, to some degree, in force.[2] But the new sense dominates even there. To hold that institutions are democratic is to maintain that collective choices are made democratically; that social choices are functions of individuals' choices (counting individuals' choices equally).

The modern sense of the term bears evident affinities to the older sense, provided the franchise is extended sufficiently to include what, in former times, was designated the *demos*; and provided too that the *demos* is large enough to be nearly coextensive with the voting community. Then democracy, conceived as collective control, effectively *includes* democracy, conceived as rule by the *demos*. It is evident too that the original sense of "democracy" suggests, though it does not strictly imply, the modern sense. Thus in antiquity, where the *demos* ruled, or where their rule was contemplated, democratic collective choice – usually in the form of irregular plebiscites – was acknowledged to be the most natural and effective way to ascertain the people's will. However, with the transition from the original to the modern sense of the term, the class character of democracy is effectively lost. Today, democracy, like the other values of the dominant tradition, is conceived in an essentially individualist framework. The voting community is decomposable into individuals, not classes. And social choices are functions, strictly, of individuals' choices.

This individualist understanding of democracy has come increasingly into conflict with the plainly social character of political life.[3] Recent democratic theory has sought, accordingly, to accommodate this fact, by focusing on the role of "partial associations" that mediate between the individual and the state. At a descriptive level, the claim is that social *groups*, functioning sometimes directly in the political process, as organized "interest groups," and sometimes at the peripheries of the political process, as reference points for ethnic, cultural, religious and even ideological identities – stand between the individual and the state. As a descriptive theory, *pluralism* (as this genre of democratic theory may be called) opposes both the radical individualism of classical liberal democratic theory and also social theories like Marxism that maintain there are social divisions – class divisions, specifically – that are of paramount importance for understanding social and political life, even when individuals group themselves into partial associations organized around different criteria than class membership. In the pluralist view, the important social divisions are just the ones individuals in fact recognize. Class divisions matter, then, only if individuals acknowledge them, and organize around them.

Sometimes too, political theorists advance pluralism as a normative ideal; as a vision of proper political arrangements. Then it is held that there is a positive value to the sort of group identification pluralism recommends, and that a good society would be pluralist. Or, less enthusiastically, it is held that pluralism represents the best feasible realization of values implicit in more traditional (individualist) democratic theory. If, as is everywhere the case, existing political communities are too large and complex for individuals to participate in them effectively, or to achieve identity through them, partial associations can, as it were, take the place of the state. They can function as genuine political communities and do at least part of what the state is supposed to do in theory, but cannot do in practice. Individuals do not lose control of the political process. The state remains democratic in the sense that social choices are still functions of individuals' choices. It is just that individuals are organized into pluralistic subcommunities, and are therefore more or less well represented in the political arena, according to their particular group affiliations. Individuals vote as individuals; but they are politically effective as members of groups. Thus groups do what isolated individuals cannot do, given the size and complexity of actual political entities. Pluralism is a second-best solution; but it is the best feasible democratic solution in a complex world of large political communities and diverse social groups.

Thus, even if the extreme individualism implicit in the modern sense of "democracy" is consciously mitigated, as it is in pluralism, the class perspective of "democracy" in its original uses is not restored; and the core idea – that democracy is a matter of ascertaining the popular will by consulting individuals through voting – remains. Pluralism represents an emendation of the traditional view, not a break from it. It is squarely lodged in the dominant tradition. Its aim is to make democratic theory accord better with political reality, and to present a more attractive – or, at least, a more realistic – picture of political arrangements. In doing so, however, the idea of democracy remains unchanged. Democracy, for pluralists as for classical liberal democrats, is essentially a matter of aggregating individuals' choices into social choices.

As we saw in Chapter 3, democratic choice mechanisms are ordinalist aggregating devices. There is, accordingly, a close connection between democracy and welfare. If our choices as voters represent our preferences, and if our preferences, in turn, represent our wants, as liberal democrats suppose, then the democratic choice, the socially preferred alternative, is also the most desired alternative – ignoring, of course, variations in intensity of preference. The democratic choice is, at the same time, the welfarist choice.[4]

However, if we suppose that what democratic choice mechanisms aggregate are *not* representations of wants, then democratic aggregating is of no welfare significance, as welfare is conceived within the dominant tradition. The link between democratic choice and welfare is then severed. This is, in fact, the position of some democrats within the rival, idealist tradition. Thus, for Rousseau, democratic choice mechanisms do not combine *preferences*, since by hypothesis private interests (interests in realizing particular wants, represented by our schedule of preferences) are superseded in the just state. Democratic choice mechanisms, in Rousseau's view, aggregate judgments as to what the general interest (the interest of the political community, logically distinct from the sum of private interests) is. For Rousseau, then, democratic choice mechanisms are not means for augmenting welfare at all, but serve a quite different purpose: the *discovery* of the general will. Voting in the Rousseauean state is therefore a truth discovery procedure, a means for discovering a matter of fact (just as jury voting, where disinterestedness is also assumed, is supposed to ascertain matters of fact).[5] The link with welfare holds, therefore, only if we suppose what is in fact supposed throughout the dominant political culture: that in collective choice procedures individuals seek outcomes that accord with their particular (that is, "private") interests. A commitment to democratic values is therefore irreducible to a commitment to augmenting welfare, though, in the dominant tradition, these conceptually distinct values are effectively joined. Democracy can be a value apart from welfarist commitments, and can be defended on radically non-welfarist grounds.

For practical purposes, a commitment to democracy amounts to an endorsement of voting procedures. For voting is just a way of combining individuals' choices to generate social choices. In the political arena, there are, in fact, no other significant democratic collective choice procedures. However, not all voting procedures are equally democratic. The most democratic voting procedures are, of course, those that are most responsive to individuals' choices, and that are therefore least weighted for or against a particular option in contention. Plainly the ideal is simple majority rule voting. Where larger than simple numerical majorities are required for an enactment, voting is weighted in favor of the status quo; that is, in favor of the no enactment option. Then the socially most preferred alternative can be blocked by a minority of the electorate, in (partial) violation of democratic commitments. The larger the majority required for an enactment, the more these commitments are violated.

There may, of course, be extra-democratic reasons for adopting collective choice procedures of this sort. For example, it might be deemed desirable to weight the collective choice mechanism in favor of the status quo, precisely to make change difficult. Many political communities adopt this policy for matters of great moment, as when changes in fundamental laws or constitutions are proposed. In such matters, a conservative bias arguably *is* warranted. Then conservative considerations would be weighed against democratic ones, and a balance struck.

Representative governments, the norm in liberal democratic polities, characteristically stray from the ideal model of democratic collective choice (*direct*, simple majority rule voting), for a number of reasons to be considered presently. However, ordinary political discourse, particularly in capitalist countries, casually identifies democracy with representative government. To think clearly about democracy, it is important to disabuse ourselves of that identification. Since even the most "democratic" polities rely so little on ideal democratic choice procedures, it will be well to bear the ideal in mind, as we compare capitalism and socialism with respect to democracy.

Capitalism and democracy

Since the seventeenth century, democratic collective choice has come to be valued in capitalist societies or in societies where capitalist social relations were coming into prominence. However, for a number of reasons, capitalist societies cannot go very far in implementing democratic values. Under capitalism, an ideal of democratic collective choice developed which, in the end, capitalism cannot be expected to sustain very well.

Assuming the connection asserted in Chapter 1 (in comparing socialism and capitalism with respect to capacity-freedom) and argued for in Chapter 2 – assuming, that is, that in general capitalism is likely to fare poorly in realizing material equality – a plain shortcoming of capitalist society with respect to democracy is precisely the degree of material inequality capitalist markets are likely to generate. These inequalities can, of course, be corrected through state interference; but, as we know, the requisite interference, though possible in principle, is unlikely, precisely because of what it is designed to correct: the unequal distribution of effective power under capitalist social relations. Inequality of income and wealth is almost certain to promote inequality of political power. Then the better-off are likely to acquire considerable and inordinate power over the less well-off. Rich and poor each have only one vote; assuming, as has generally come to be the case in existing capitalist societies, that there are no property qualifications for the exercise of the franchise. But the well-off have means of controlling the political process that the poor do not. Wealth buys influence. Even if wealth does not directly buy politicians, as it can and sometimes does, it buys access to means of influencing opinion – of swaying opinion around particular issues and, more important, of defining the terms of debate. To the degree the political process is responsive to public opinion – a very large degree in nearly all actually existing political communities, capitalist or socialist – indirect control over the political process is thereby achieved. This outcome would hold, presumably, wherever there are great material inequalities. However, the rule of wealth is even more secure, as we shall see, under specifically capitalist social relations.

To some degree, inequality of power is potentially offset by the formation of interest groups of the sort pluralist democratic theory describes and advocates. In principle, an organization of poor people could serve as a countervailing force to an organization of bankers or industrialists. But, again, the poor, even if numerous and organized, are not likely to have the resources commanded by the well-off, and will therefore likely not exercise comparable influence. Inequalities of income and wealth *need not* lead directly to oligarchy. But the tendency towards oligarchy is ever present, even where, formally, all individuals count equally.[6]

In so far as material inequalities pose problems for democracy, socialism, by faring better than capitalism with respect to equality, can likely do better than capitalism in this regard too. However, we should not conclude automatically for socialism: first, because, in the state bureaucratic model particularly, there are other ways that some individuals can come to exercise inordinate and anti-democratic power over others; and second, because the *possibility* of democratic socialism remains to be shown. The former issue will be considered presently; the latter, of course, in Part Two. For the present, we must be content with another, very provisional mark in socialism's favor.

A second failing of capitalism has already been noted. It is less immediately evident than the first, but more central, for it depends not upon likely consequences of capitalist social relations, but upon the character of these relations themselves. For democrats, other things being equal,[7] matters affecting the public ought to be decided by the public. Public questions constitute, as it were, the domain of collective choice. Now, the sorts of decisions capitalists make – about the use of the productive resources they own and about the allocation of the product derived from the employment of these resources – plainly affect the public and therefore fall within the public domain. However, under capitalism, questions of this sort are privatized, to the extent that they have to do with the utilization capitalists make of the assets they own. Thus, many public questions never come before the public, and therefore can never become, even in principle, objects of democratic collective choice. In this way, capitalism restricts the scope of democratic choice.

In actually existing capitalism, state regulation and interference do very often impinge, at least peripherally, upon the uses capitalists make of the assets they own. But in the final analysis, even where there is substantial state intervention, fundamental economic choices remain in the private domain. Economic decision-making is necessarily privatized, for public choice in this domain is incompatible with private ownership and therefore with capitalism. Thus, even if all individuals really did count equally in the determination of social choices – not just formally, but substantively – capitalist societies would still fall short of the democratic ideal. For capitalism necessarily depoliticizes the economic, casting it off into the non-political realm of "civil society". Under capitalism it is therefore impossible to democratize – or even politicize – what is so central to public life.[8]

Under socialism, there is no comparable impossibility. Even in actually existing socialist countries, economic decision-making, though patently non-democratic, is at least highly politicized. The distinction capitalism tends to engender between the strictly political and the strictly economic is hardly sustainable in any socialist polity. Socialism, even state bureaucratic socialism, for better or worse, eliminates systemic restrictions upon the scope of public choice. Doing so is hardly sufficient for democratizing the economy, as the record of the Communist countries shows. But it is necessary for achieving a full and radical implementation of the democratic ideal.

Representative government

Wherever, as under capitalism, a separation is maintained between *public* political activities, on the one hand, and *private* economic activities, on the other, democratic choice is restricted in scope. It is excluded from the economic sphere. In practice, however, even in the most professedly democratic of liberal democratic states, democratic choice is restricted far beyond necessity. Typically, the public is consulted infrequently in elections. And elections are held, almost without exception, just to elect representatives to legislative or executive (and sometimes judicial) institutions. The people do not directly decide issues or enact laws. Governance therefore becomes a specialized activity;

separate – and remote – from the daily lives of all but professional "politicians." Indeed, politics itself, so far from permeating all spheres of individuals' lives, as the classical tradition in political theory from Aristotle through Rousseau thought proper and desirable, becomes a career among many – in which a few are engaged professionally, while others, the vast majority, take only occasional interest. Capitalism encourages this state of affairs, even if it does not, strictly, require it. It promotes representative government. Thus capitalism tends to marginalize and professionalize politics.

In these conditions, it is hardly likely that an institutional apparatus will develop for effecting democratic choice joined intimately, as it were, to citizens' daily activities and truly responsive to their interests. There will likely be little, if anything, in the way of workplace or neighborhood democracy. Instead, what can be expected are parliamentary institutions, remote from people's ordinary activities and concerns, connected only very tenuously to those concerns through political parties and other mediating institutions. In existing capitalist societies, it is precisely these institutions of representative government that are thought to implement democratic values. However, the connection between democracy and representative government – a connection suggested and supported by capitalism's characteristic restriction of the scope of public choice – is not what it sometimes seems.[9]

If social choices are to be functions of individuals' choices, each individual counting equally, then it is plain that democrats' commitment should be to *direct* democratic control, where all individuals vote directly on measures or laws, and not to indirect or representative government, where individuals vote for representatives who enact measures or laws in their constituents' behalf. It will be recalled that Rousseau was adamant in insisting that representative government is incompatible with popular sovereignty;[10] and it is worth reflecting upon that insistence, especially in view of the pervasive tendency of liberal democrats to find a commitment to both democracy and representative government unproblematic.

Generally, representative government is considered an innocuous way of implementing democratic values, in circumstances where direct democratic control is impracticable. Thus it is maintained that in modern political communities, it is simply unfeasible, even were it desirable, to assemble the people together to vote. What was possible in the Athenian *polis* and what continues to be appropriate (though in very limited domains) in town meetings, is simply inappropriate for coordinating the behaviors of the multitudes that comprise the citizenry of existing states. Representative government, however, is eminently feasible, according to this view, and serves the same purpose – of insuring popular control over the state – at least tolerably well.

Against this claim, it could be countered, following Rousseau, that representative government does not at all serve the same purpose as direct democratic rule; that it does not, even approximately, implement popular control. To see why, consider the role representatives are supposed to play in liberal democratic governments. Were representative institutions just workable approximations of direct democratic institutions, representatives ought to act, so far as possible, simply as delegates, transmitting the choices of their constituents. Constituencies, then, should be consulted frequently and periodically, and representatives should be bound to transmit their constituents' views. They should serve as conduits, mandated to vote this way or that. However, liberal democrats hardly ever insist that representatives respect their constituents' views. Quite the contrary. Legislators are prized for their independence, not for their fidelity in communicating the choices of those who have elected them. Representatives are supposed to vote according to their *own* best judgments. They are supposed to serve as independent legislators, not as delegates.

Of course legislators typically are compelled to acknowledge their constituents' views as they set about their work. But the compulsion is entirely prudential. Should they stray too far from what their constituents want – or, more strictly, from what a majority of their constituents want – their prospects for re-election may suffer. For some representatives, this consideration may serve as a disincentive for acting independently. But, at best, it is a very weak and indirect constraint. Where elections are held infrequently, as is nearly always the case in liberal democracies, there will have been many votes that a legislator's constituents will assess. A failure to represent the majority view, even on a wide range of issues, might therefore be of little consequence in an overall, balanced assessment of the legislator's record. Moreover, with a well-developed party system in place, constituents may have little control over who their representatives are. They may be able to choose between various parties' candidates, but not select the nominees. And, finally, with the generalized political apathy that remote parliamentary systems of government promote, constituents may not even know or care to what extent their elected representatives have, in fact, represented their views, if indeed they have views at all on questions that come before parliamentary assemblies. In short, where there is representative government, there is typically very little actual popular control over the state.

In reply, it might be held that the independence of representatives is itself a consequence of the impracticability of direct democratic control. It would be difficult èven to imagine an institutional structure that would allow representatives to ascertain their constituents' views in a regular and reliable fashion. Therefore, the argument goes, representatives cannot but act with a substantial measure of independence. Admittedly, this reply is reasonable, though it is easy to exaggerate the difficulty of discovering constituents' views, especially in an age of easy transport and ever-developing communications technology. However, no matter how plausible this rejoinder is, it does not quite capture how representative institutions are conceived within the dominant political culture. Liberal democrats in capitalist countries do sometimes insist upon the necessity of representative institutions for realizing democratic values. And they surely do insist upon the impracticability of direct democracy. But they hardly deplore this situation as a necessary evil, as a democrat should. Instead, liberal democrats make a virtue of necessity. They view representative government as a positive good, not as a concession to the unwieldy realities of modern political life. But representative government is plainly not a very likely way to combine individuals' choices into social choices democratically, precisely because the institutions of representative government, to the extent they *separate* individuals' choices from social choices, *guarantee* that the social choice, the parliamentary enactment, will *not*, in fact, be a function strictly of individuals' choices for the alternatives in contention. As Rousseau long ago pointed out, representative governments usurp democracy, even as they claim to implement it. They are always forms of despotism, though typically benevolent despotisms, in so far as representatives are indeed accountable to those who elected them.

137

Why, then, if representative institutions are non-democratic, do liberal *democrats* support them? There are, I think, two principal reasons: the first having to do with the role of extra-democratic values in the dominant tradition; the second, with the character of politics itself as liberal democrats conceive it. Of these reasons, the first is the more familiar and perhaps also the more revealing. The second, however, is of considerable philosophical interest, particularly for the connection it suggests between liberal democracy and capitalism.

Chief among the extra-democratic considerations that motivate distrust of direct democracy, and, at the same time, support for representative institutions, is a concern for order and civil peace. This concern harks back to Hobbes and indeed even to Saint Augustine and early Christian political theory. But the argument that follows from this concern is essentially the familiar anti-democratic argument that, before the ordinary understanding of "democracy" changed, was nearly universally accepted. The people, according to this view, are not very much to be trusted for maintaining order. They are mercurial and capricious, and easily manipulated. The *demos* lack civility and good sense. They are incapable, in general, of legislating wisely, and incapable of maintaining stable institutions. Better, therefore, that legislation be entrusted to those capable of it. Nowadays, to be sure, with democracy generally valued positively, the anti-democratic consequences of this position are seldom recognized, at least in theory. Proponents of this line of argument nowadays would deny that the "solution" lies in authoritarian or dictatorial forms of administration of a sort advocated by, among others, Hobbes and Saint Augustine, the arch-theoreticians of civil order. Instead, they advocate benign, representative "democracy." The point is to have the best of both worlds. Order is assured. And popular control is, nominally, retained. The people rule indirectly, through their representatives. Thus they save themselves from the debilitating consequences of taking their own affairs in hand, while, in theory, retaining control over their own affairs.

A similarly ambivalent stand on democracy follows from yet another, non-democratic reason for advocating direct democracy: a concern for protecting some significant range of individuals' activities from state interference.[11] What is feared is the tyranny of the majority; a tyranny likely to emerge, it is thought, in volatile popular assemblies. Representative governments will be less prone to devolve into tyrannical forms, and more likely, the argument goes, to respect individuals' liberties. Parliaments are less likely than popular assemblies to be volatile and mercurial; and more sensitive to the constitutional requirements of wise governance. It might seem, then, that outright despotisms, so long as they are benevolent and committed to liberal values, would be the best form of governance. Many early liberal writers were indeed inclined to support benevolent despotisms. But the positive evaluation nowadays accorded democratic collective choice – and doubtless too the historical experience of life under actual despotisms – militates against this conclusion. Representative government therefore emerges as the best solution. It is, to repeat, a benevolent despotism in all but name. It is benevolent to the extent representatives are accountable to those they represent. And it is despotic because, appearance to the contrary, the people do *not* rule. Representative government therefore accords with liberal requirements without jarring democratic sensibilities.

Still, however they may be depicted, representative institutions are anti-democratic in effect. They are based upon distrust of the people, the *demos*. But democracy is rule by the *demos* or, in modern "individualist" guise, popular collective choice. Therefore democrats must trust the people. For democrats, if there is to be distrust, it should be directed, following Rousseau, against those who would rule in the people's behalf. Proponents of order should indeed be wary of what might upset stability, and proponents of liberal values are wise to fear the encroachments of governments. But for genuine democrats there is no special reason to fear direct democratic rule more than any other form of civil administration, and particularly no reason to prefer representative government. As in ancient times, so too today, the democrat accords to the *demos* precisely that trust the anti-democrat would deny.

In the final analysis, I doubt that any of the standard justifications for representative government – the unworkability of direct democracy, a commitment to order or liberal values – whatever their discord with democratic values, will suffice to explain the nearly universal appeal of representative institutions in capitalist societies where genuinely democratic values have, after all, developed and found sustenance. To account for that appeal – and for the ambivalence practicing liberal democrats in capitalist societies exhibit – I think it is necessary to reflect, again, on the role of the state in capitalist society, and more generally on the nature of politics under capitalism.

We know that under capitalism there must be some private control over society's principal means of production, and therefore some civil society, some domain apart from the political. In liberal democratic capitalist states, characteristically, civil society is substantial. What is of prime importance to individuals is generally understood to be essentially non-political. It is in civil society, not the state, that individuals normally pursue their ends. The market is the arena where the business of life is conducted, not the assemblies of the people. Of course, in existing capitalisms, the state may penetrate civil society and interfere with individuals' private pursuits – to facilitate or impede their realization. But the pursuits themselves remain essentially non-political. Locke's account of the foundation of the (liberal) state, a founding document of the dominant view,[12] is emphatic on this point. For Locke, property rights – including the right to accumulate private property virtually without limitation – precede the state logically and, if the quasi-historical story Locke tells of the origins of states is taken at its word, also temporally. The state is devised to protect and enforce antecedent property rights. The dominant tradition continues this position in its characteristic tendency to distinguish the social (including the economic) from the political – and its characteristic subordination of the latter to the former.[13] Not the state but civil society is the sphere of human self-realization, the arena where human energies are best and most productively expended. To devote time and concern to specifically political matters is therefore to deflect attention away from where it is best employed. It is to squander on the state – which should function largely, as Locke thought, to protect and promote the acquisition of (private) property – energy that could otherwise be employed directly in the capitalist marketplace.

It is therefore best, under capitalism, to discourage a high degree of political participation, and to encourage the rigorous separation of the economic and social from the political that capitalism tendentially promotes. Better to professionalize politics than to politicize society and have politics permeate the social order. The state is a necessary evil; and those who attend to its affairs engage in an undesirable, though necessary, business. That that business be well managed is, of course, of tremendous importance. Among other things, the well-being of capitalist markets depends on it. It is appropriate, therefore, that politics be given an incentive structure comparable to that provided in the marketplace, to encourage the talented to undertake the tasks of governmental administration. In existing capitalist societies, accordingly, politics is conducted as a career among many; where the rewards – in money and, of course, in power – can be considerable. But it is still only a career, and not, as in classical political philosophy, an expression of our nature as "political beings." Politics thus becomes, strictly, a vocation; a career of public service, undertaken by professionals, with only minimal participation by the people themselves.

Representative government depoliticizes without expressly repudiating democratic values. Where citizens govern directly, the sphere of the political is expanded and civil society contracts correspondingly. Where citizens elect representatives, however, the sphere of the political is diminished. Even if, as in existing capitalist states, the state apparatus expands, enlarging the sphere of bureaucratic control and domination over the economy, the task of administration is still increasingly professionalized and depoliticized. The state apparatus may become ever more important, while the importance of politics, paradoxically, diminishes.

We know, of course, that throughout much of the history of political thought, politics is not at all conceived as a career among many, but as a component – indeed, a central component – of truly human life. Liberal democratic politics is as historically particular as are the key valuational notions that comprise its theory. Moreover, as we have seen, an explanation for this particularity is readily at hand. Liberal democratic politics – a depoliticized politics of minimal participation by the many and professional public service by the few – expresses precisely what capitalism tends to promote: the privatization of public life. It is capitalism, I would hazard, that militates against a "classical" view of politics as a principal expression of essential humanity, and promotes instead the characteristically liberal view of politics as a career among many. Capitalism therefore promotes, even if it does not strictly require, representative institutions. It effectively undermines democratic values, even while the dominant liberal democratic tradition in political theory, a tradition historically linked to capitalism, continues to support these values, at least in name.

On the other hand, socialism introduces no systemic tendency to devalue the political. Neither for this reason, nor for any of the reasons discussed previously, does socialism display any bias against direct democracy. The degree of democratization under socialism is, of course, what distinguishes what I have called the state bureaucratic from the democratic model. If we imagine possible socialisms arrayed along a continuum, with the state bureaucratic model at one pole and the democratic model at the other, actually existing socialisms, viewed as instantiations of the models arrayed along the continuum, fall squarely on the state bureaucratic side. As everyone knows, and as pro-capitalists are eager to note, these societies fare poorly with respect to democratic values. They lack even that semblance of democratic control provided by representative institutions in liberal democratic states. Still, even in socialisms that exemplify the state bureaucratic model, politics is in command. Thus even the most non-democratic, state bureaucratic socialisms are free from a very substantial obstacle to democratization that capitalism, unavoidably, confronts. Under capitalism, underlying property relations militate against the full implementation of democratic values (even as they can accommodate their nominal realization). Under socialism there are no obstacles from this quarter. In Part Two, I will argue that there are no insurmountable obstacles from other quarters either, and that *democratic* socialism is indeed on the historical agenda.

Rights

Respect for rights is another specifically political standard against which socialism and capitalism may be compared. As with democracy, some existing capitalist societies plainly do better in this regard than do any existing socialist societies. And, as with democracy, the connection appears to be rooted historically. Very generally, a concern for rights, outside specifically legal contexts, developed along with other components of the dominant tradition contemporaneously with capitalism – in England, North America and in parts of Western Europe. However, unlike other dominant tradition values, rights theory has not had, from its inception, a continuous history. Utilitarians, particularly, have opposed the concept, for reasons roughly similar to those to be adduced here. I shall argue that this standard is indeed more problematic than any of the other standards against which socialism and capitalism may be compared. But whatever we finally make of rights, rights theory today enjoys some prominence within the dominant political culture.

Even if there were a demonstrable causal connection between the rise of capitalism and concern for individuals' rights, such that capitalism (or, at least, emerging capitalism) could be shown to *require* that rights be respected, 'it still would not follow that respect for rights *requires* capitalism; nor even would it follow that capitalism provides the best basis for furthering a concern for rights. Respect for rights, as a matter of historical fact, does seem to have developed alongside capitalist social relations – during the English revolutionary upheavals of the seventeenth century. Perhaps a case could be made that, in fact, only in connection with capitalism could this concern have taken root and developed. But it would not follow, even then, that this value can be realized only under capitalism. It is entirely consistent with this view that socialism – including state bureaucratic socialism – can respect individuals' rights too. It might even be, as it was with other dominant tradition values, that a concern for rights developed under capitalism that, in the end, capitalist societies cannot fulfill; and that only socialism can complete the task capitalism began. However, in this case I think that line of argument would be misleading. For it is appropriate to question the concept of rights itself.

Before questioning the concept of rights, a word of caution is in order. It is not at all my intent to dismiss concern for rights, particularly in prevailing historical circumstances. Quite the contrary. For there exists at present no theoretically developed alternative way to articulate what the concept of rights – defectively – aims to express; nor is there any effective practical alternative yet at hand to take the place of struggle for the defense of individuals' rights. To be sure, there are intimations of alternatives, coming largely from outside the dominant tradition; alternatives that, we shall see (in Chapter 6) some Marxists have already begun to explore. But for the time being, in the present

143

circumstances, how well rival political economic systems fare with respect to individuals' rights remains a pertinent question, even if it is not, in the end, the right question to ask.[14] What follows therefore opposes taking rights seriously, but with the important qualification that, at present, we may have to make do with rights; that rights theory, for the foreseeable future, may be "socially necessary." I will argue that there is in fact a connection between capitalism and rights, but not of the sort many pro-capitalist writers, who take the viability of rights claims for granted, maintain; nor even of a sort that, in the end, supports capitalism over socialism. Then I will suggest how examination of the connection between capitalism and rights is useful for indicating shortcomings of both capitalism and rights and also of existing socialist theory.

The historical record apart, there appears to be no reason why socialism and capitalism cannot equally well sustain support for individuals' rights. As with democracy, the likelihood that a particular political community will support rights claims seems to turn on political traditions and culture, not on political economic arrangements. Then the poor record of existing socialist countries in protecting individuals' rights, like their poor record on democracy, cannot be ascribed to the public ownership of society's principal means of production, but instead to a long history of despotic disregard for rights – a disregard pre-dating by centuries the attempt at building socialism, and seldom interrupted by sustained and significant popular resistance. But what of the evident successes some capitalist countries have scored in protecting individuals' rights? Is this too just a question of political culture? Plainly political culture is at least part of the story; but I think there is, in addition, a more intrinsic connection to be probed.

Under capitalism, labor supplied by human beings is, like all other factors of production, subordinated to the requirements of capital accumulation. To this extent, there is no difference between persons (suppliers of labor) and things (non-human means of production). Each is only a commodity, a determinant exchange value, to be used instrumentally as the accumulation process requires. In capitalist societies, capital accumulation is the principal business of civil society; and civil society is, in turn, the sphere where our deepest aspirations for self-realization and fulfillment are enacted. Our sense of fundamental human worth is therefore put in jeopardy by the requirements of capital accumulation. For in this very central arena of human life it seems that, as Kant would have it, persons are treated as "means only," and not as "ends-in-themselves."[15]

The importation of the juridical concept of *right* into moral and social philosophy provides a means for countering the tendency of capitalist markets to transform economic agents into "means only." Rights serve, among other things, to articulate a claim for human dignity. For rights – of the sort political economies may be praised or blamed for protecting or failing to protect – limit markets. They set off an area in which market exigencies – including even the requirements of capital accumulation – may not intrude. Of course, not all rights claims function this way. Many specifically legal rights, and others as well, are exchangeable. There can be a market in rights too. Thus, if I have a right to build a structure on my property, I can surely sell that right – say, to a neighbor who wants a guarantee that no building will obstruct his view. The rights against which socialism and capitalism are compared are not these rights, however, but the sort of rights the dominant tradition deems "natural" or, more aptly, "inalienable." Many putative "human rights" fall in this category.

By definition, *inalienable* rights cannot be bought or sold. Nor are they subject to other market criteria. They are distributed equally. And in general their exercise involves no monetary charge. If, as is common among writers in the dominant tradition, we suppose people to be generally self-interested, we can imagine circumstances in which it would be advantageous for individuals to exchange some of their "inalienable"rights. Thus I might seek to sell, say, my right to vote (assuming the right to vote is deemed an inalienable right, as it is in many political communities); for there is surely some monetary payment I (and nearly anyone else) would prefer to voting. However, where rights are inalienable, this is precisely what I cannot legitimately do. I may be self-interested and acquisitive and I may find it in my interest to "alienate" some of my inalienable rights. But much as my nature and circumstance may incline me, I cannot rightfully do so. Thus by claiming that there are inalienable rights, liberal democrats counter the threat posed to human dignity by human nature, as they understand it, in the context of capitalist market arrangements. Rights establish a sphere of inviolability; an area of human life that cannot legitimately be subordinated to instrumental requirements. Taking capitalist social relations as given, rights save us from ourselves and from each other. They function as a corrective to our tendency to subordinate everything, even our essential humanity, to the requirements of capitalist markets.

Rights therefore *are* inextricably linked to capitalism, but not in the sense that the one furthers or nurtures the other. Rights function instead to correct what capitalist market relations tend to bring about. If left unchecked by inalienable rights, capitalist markets threaten human dignity, and therefore impugn the vision pro-capitalist writers in the dominant tradition seek to advance. For how can we propose as an ideal of proper social and political arrangements a system of practices that degrades persons into things? Rights are necessary to provide a "human face" for capitalism. Without rights, capitalist society would consist just of individual instrumentalities, all bearing no overriding concern for their own or for each other's fundamental dignity.

The attribution of inalienable rights to persons otherwise inserted in capitalist market relations is consistent, to be sure, with the letter of the dominant tradition's valuational commitments. But it does not follow from these commitments, as we shall go on to see. This is why I think rights are best viewed as *correctives* to the dominant theory and practice of politics, and not as an integral part of it.[16] Rights are introduced, so to speak, from outside, in order to counter, not to complete, what the dominant theory suggests. Rights are brought in to correct an otherwise dismal and therefore untenable social vision.

What is wrong with rights?

The problem with this move was recognized long ago by utilitarian critics of rights theory: it is irremediably *ad hoc*, for there is no theoretically well-motivated way to ascribe rights to persons. That assignment, ultimately, is arbitrary. In giving capitalism a human face, rights theory is cosmetic. It makes people *look* different from things. But rights, like the emperor's new clothes, are there only for those who dare not see. Willful blindness, however, is not an adequate foundation for a political practice that genuinely does defend what rights claims seek to express and protect. For rights to work as intended, there must be a way to justify their attribution.

Of course it cannot be proven definitively that rights claims *cannot* be provided an adequate foundation. But the burden of proof can be fairly ascribed to those who would advance claims for rights. Certainly, no adequate foundation for rights has yet been established. And apart from plainly inappropriate theological justifications attempted by Locke and some early natural rights theorists, there has been remarkably little effort expended even in the search for foundations. The historical particularity of rights claims is fatal to the viability of the concept. Without the capitalist assault on fundamental human dignity – or its equivalent in post-capitalist (particularly state bureaucratic socialist) societies – rights talk would drop away for want of sufficient reason. It is because rights do not exist that they had to be invented.

There is in fact no properly liberal democratic justification for rights, beyond the need to correct for the effects of liberal democratic institutions. Contrary to what is widely, though unreflectively, believed, there is in fact an opposition between rights and the dominant tradition's core notions of welfare and freedom. That there is an opposition between rights and welfare is easily seen. Rights theorists would have rights function, so to speak, as trumps against welfarist considerations. They would concede, in general, that we ought to do what advances welfare – but not where doing so leads to the violation of rights. Where there is a conflict between respect for rights and welfare, rights take precedence. Rights and welfare are distinct and sometimes even opposed notions. Indeed, rights are introduced precisely to counter welfarist claims.

An opposition between rights and freedom was supposed in our discussion (in Chapter 1) of the sense in which property, of any sort, restricts freedom (F1). Systems of property are, in effect, systems of juridical rights, rights that are specified in and enforced by law. In general, to assert a right is to advance a claim for restricting (normatively) another's freedom to infringe upon *whatever* that right protects. Thus rights specify moral justifications for limiting the freedom of those to whom rights claims are addressed.[17] If I have a right to free speech, for example, others are unfree to interfere with my speech – a freedom they would have in the absence of my right. The structure of rights ascribed to individuals is therefore a structure of (morally justifiable) unfreedom relations.

This claim may seem odd in view of the fact that, very often, rights are claimed precisely to guarantee individuals' freedoms. However, the conceptual framework within which rights function to guarantee freedoms should be borne in mind. In the absence of specifically political institutions – that is, in a "state of nature" – freedom (F1, liberty) is unrestricted and therefore absolute. However, absolute liberty is untenable and even self-defeating, for it is opposed to our interests as free beings (see Chapter 1). To maximize freedom, liberty must be restricted; the state of nature, according to the familiar story, must be replaced by a (political) state that provides a coercive structure of laws and regulations within which we can pursue our interests and exercise that level of freedom that is optimal. Rights ascriptions are one way of conceiving these restrictions. In so far as rights are enforced by law, we have a coercive apparatus for restricting absolute liberty, in order that we may overcome the devastating sub-optimality of the state of nature. In claiming a right to do something, then, we *are* advancing a claim in behalf of our freedom; or, more strictly, in behalf of our interests as free beings.[18] But in articulating claims for freedom through this device, we are, at the same time, normatively restricting the freedom of others. Rights therefore cannot be derived from the dominant tradition's notion of freedom. Rights oppose freedom, even as they figure in strategies for its implementation.

However, the problem remains: where do these rights come from? For strictly legal rights, the answer is straightforward. Legal rights are products of particular juridical frameworks. They are ascribed by whatever procedures the legal system establishes for that purpose. What is problematic are extra-juridical rights, rights that are conceived prior to states and their legal systems. It is precisely according to how well rights of this sort are respected that socialism and capitalism are compared. But unless a foundation for these rights ascriptions can be supplied, it is moot what a comparison of socialism and capitalism along these lines shows.

There is, at present, no adequate account of foundations for rights ascriptions. Nor is there any reason to expect one can be provided. At best, the burden of proof lies with those who claim that rights ascriptions can be justified; that rights claims do, ultimately, have adequate grounding. I would hazard there is no case to be made, and that utilitarian objections to rights theory are basically sound. Rights are indeed like the emperor's new clothes. Their political role is monumental. But in the end there is nothing there.

Beyond rights

There is no reason why rights cannot function under state bureaucratic socialism as they do under capitalism. Rights could be stipulated: to mark off an area in which individuals are free from state and other interferences and also, if need be, to defend human dignity from the tendency of those who govern to treat persons as things. In existing socialism, there plainly is a need to counter that tendency, even in the absence of the systemic features of capitalism that necessitate rights as a corrective. Removing capitalist market relations is plainly not sufficient for undoing what rights are introduced *ad hoc* to address. In state bureaucratic socialism, there is, it appears, a functional equivalent of capitalist market relations: the organizational requirements of hierarchical systems of command and administration. These requirements, we must conclude, can pose as devastating a threat to freedom and, above all, to essential humanity – to respect for persons as ends-in-themselves – as do capitalist markets. The record of actually existing socialism on rights is as dismal as the record of all but the most brutal capitalist dictatorships. Thus it would seem that socialism – at least, existing socialism – needs rights as desperately as capitalism does: to save human dignity from the threat posed to it by the organization of the social order.

In Chapter 6, I will argue that, in democratic socialism, a theory and practice of politics is likely in which rights talk would pass away, so to speak, for want of a sufficient reason. In anticipation of that argument, I shall conclude here by recalling how, contemporaneously with the dominant tradition but outside it, human dignity and the difference between persons and things – the "rational intuitions" rights claims seek to express – have been theorized *without* recourse to rights. The principal proponent of this alternative strategy is, again, Rousseau.[19]

Part One

For Rousseau, human dignity is assured by *transformative institutions*, institutions that educate and form individuals into the rational, autonomous beings they always are potentially. The point of Rousseauean politics is to lead people to do spontaneously what rights theorists would have them do, if at all, through coercively enforced rights claims. The sovereignty of the general will – through which alone, in Rousseau's view, essential human dignity is realizable – is attained by changing human beings – from the rational egoists we find in the state of nature to citizens who value the general interest (their true interests as rational beings) over and above their private interests.

Schematically, states can coordinate individuals' behaviors in either of two ways: through the use or threat of force; or through operations upon what, in the eighteenth century, was called "opinion" and today would more likely be called "consciousness." Rousseau's genius was to focus acutely on the latter. The political measures he proposes in *The Social Contract* and elsewhere – measures ranging from the institution of civil religion to the establishment of public sports and festivals – are all intended, by transforming opinion, to promote citizenship; to foster individuals who, in their deliberations and ultimately in the very ends they will, subordinate private interests to the interests of the whole community. The same intent underlies Rousseau's political economic prescriptions too. Rousseau was, of course, anti-feudal; but he was also an opponent of capitalisms that divided society into opposing classes. He advocated a yeoman society of simple commodity producers, where everyone owns his own means of production, and where products of labor, if they are not directly consumed, circulate on "free markets." However utopian this vision may be in the face of the emerging capitalist organization of Europe, its theoretical import is clear enough: the point is to establish a classless society in which there are no social divisions of a sort that might detract from or even undo that generality of the will the exercise of which, in Rousseau's view, *is* sovereignty. In other words, appropriate transformative measures are workable only if they are sustained by a suitable "economic base." But in the end, it is the transformative measures themselves that are politically decisive. The individual's will is, in Kant's expression, the *Kampfplatz*, the site of struggle, over which the fate of the just state is determined.

In a word, the alternative to rights Rousseau proposes is *education*; education, however, by no means confined to the schools, but rather education in the broadest sense – conceived as the effect of institutions upon the individuals living under them. To do the work rights are intended to do, what Rousseau suggests, in effect, is that we undo what rights are introduced to correct. The objective is to transform ourselves until we treat human beings, ourselves and others, as ends, as bearers of essential dignity – and never as means only.

As was remarked in discussing autonomy (in Chapter 1), of all the transformative institutions conceivable, of paramount importance, in Rousseau's view, are the institutions of direct democratic collective choice. It is by acting as citizens that individuals *become* citizens; that they *constitute* "the sovereignty of the general will." The social contract, in Rousseau's view, then, is not so much a founding event as it is an end towards which all the institutions of society – but, above all, the institutions said to be implied by the contract itself, the institutions of direct democratic rule – conspire. Democratic institutions comprise society's principal "school" for the formation of the general will.

There is a connection, therefore, between the case Rousseau proposes for direct democracy – and against representative government – and his alternative to rights. Viewed as transformative instruments, there is a profound difference between representative institutions that enjoin only minimal levels of political participation, leaving civil society free to work its effects upon "opinion," and direct democratic institutions that enjoin substantial levels of political participation and direct popular control. Representative institutions do nothing to counter the debilitating effects of capitalist market relations or, for that matter, state bureaucratic socialist administration. They are indeed expressly non-transformative. Therefore, both capitalist and (imaginable) state bureaucratic socialist societies, administered through representative institutions, need rights. But, in the end, so long as rights ascriptions remain without adequate grounding, they are too fragile a basis upon which to defend a notion of human dignity, and a corresponding distinction between ends and means, persons and things.[20] The Rousseauean strategy aims to dissipate the threat to humanity civil society poses, rather than to correct for it. Education, the alternative to rights, if successful, undoes what

151

rights are introduced to redress, rendering rights superfluous.

However, it is a long way from theory to practice. And it can hardly be assumed that well-intentioned attempts to transform persons will succeed. We have little historical experience upon which to justify speculations about the likely outcomes of imaginable institutional forms. I will suggest, accordingly, that to opt for democracy is, in the end, to wager, though to wager wisely. For now, it must suffice just to raise the democratic alternative. It is premature to assess it. But at least this much is clear: there is a plausible and longstanding theoretical alternative to the very doubtful strategy of ascribing rights to persons. It is wise, therefore, to consider taking democracy seriously. For the urgent need is not just to supply cosmetic solutions to the problems of actually existing societies, to supply these societies, capitalist or socialist, with a "human face." What is needed instead is genuinely to humanize society and politics.

Conclusion to Part One

In the preceding chapters, socialism and capitalism have been compared with respect to the principal valuational commitments of the dominant political culture. We have found that the position shared by libertarians and many mainstream philosophers – a view implicit also in "hyper-functionalist" versions of Marxism – that the dominant tradition favors capitalism over socialism, cannot be sustained. And we have found, on nearly every count, at least a tendential bias favoring socialism. The only likely exception, efficiency, is, I have argued, an inappropriate standard for assessing the relative merits of socialism and capitalism – at least where productive capacities are already well developed. And the one likely stand-off, respect for individuals' rights, is itself a deeply problematic standard for which it is possible, without straying from dominant tradition valuational standards, to intimate an alternative. We shall find in Part Two that the proposed alternative, radical democracy, is very likely both possible and desirable.

Nothing stronger than a tendential bias can be discerned at this level of abstraction. More determinate comparisons rest on empirical expectations about the likely consequences of particular institutional arrangements, and therefore require consideration of many more factors than the private or social (that is, non-private) ownership of society's principal means of production. Consideration of institutional arrangements is a crucial and largely uncharted task for socialists. All that can be concluded here is that *in so far as strictly philosophical considerations support comparative assessments of socialism and capitalism at this level of abstraction, they suggest conclusions in socialism's favor.*

The values against which socialism and capitalism have been

compared are, we have seen, values linked historically to the emergence of capitalism. If, following the dictates of historical materialism (see Chapter 5), we assign causal priority to political economic arrangements (the "economic base") over valuational commitments ("forms of consciousness"), we can conclude that capitalist societies have engendered values they are incapable, ultimately, of fulfilling, so long as they remain capitalist, and that socialism better fulfills these expectations. Important strains of socialist theory have expressly advanced the view that socialism effectively realizes capitalism's promise. The preceding chapters corroborate that contention, so long as capitalism's promise is conceived within the conceptual and valuational framework that has become dominant within capitalist societies and within which ongoing debates over the relative merits of socialism and capitalism are, in fact, conducted.

It does not follow, however, that the values of the dominant tradition tendentially support any socialism over any capitalism. Very likely, state bureaucratic socialism fares worse with respect to some of these values – freedom, democracy, respect for rights – and equally well (or badly) with respect to others – equality, justice, welfare – than does capitalism. The state bureaucratic model is, of course, approximated in actually existing socialist societies. Very likely, these societies fare worse with respect to all, or nearly all, of our standards for comparison than do some existing capitalist societies. However, the bearing of this situation on our question is, at best, indirect.

The point, again, has not been to compare actual social formations, but models of political economic arrangements – in light of values posed in the dominant political culture. Existing socialism is a manifest embarrassment for pro-socialists, but it does not undo the pro-socialist conclusions, tentative and indeterminate as they are, that we have been able to draw. However, existing socialism does raise a question of moment even for a defense of socialism in theory. We must address, finally, the *inevitability* of the state bureaucratic model or, what comes to the same thing, the *possibility* of alternative models. This question is a central theme of Part Two.

Part Two

Part Two

Introduction to Part Two

We have found that socialism fares better than capitalism with respect to the valuational standards constitutive of the dominant tradition of moral, social and political theory, but that this assessment does not carry over unambiguously to all forms of socialism. In particular, socialisms that approximate what I have called the state bureaucratic model have been found wanting, with respect to at least some of the values in question. I have suggested that these shortcomings are generally avoidable under democratic socialism, but nothing yet has been adduced to show that democratic socialism is more than a utopian fantasy. What follows aims, so far as is possible *in theory*, to defend the historical possibility and also the desirability of socialisms that accord with the democratic model; that is, of socialisms where direct popular control, not state bureaucratic domination, replaces the private ownership of society's principal means of production.

To this end, it will be necessary to appeal to theoretical considerations *outside* what I have been calling the dominant tradition. At the very least, we need an account of history sufficiently rich to indicate what is and is not on the historical agenda. About such matters, mainstream moral, social and political philosophy is characteristically silent. If dominant tradition theorists appeal to history at all, it is to widely known generalizations and commonsense beliefs. A substantive theory of history – of the nature and direction of historical change – is not part of moral, social and political philosophy, as these disciplines are presently conceived. The dominant theoretical culture is characteristically agnostic with respect to these matters and skeptical of bold historical theorizing.

Marxism, on the other hand, is anything but agnostic and

skeptical. Moreover, Marxism is indisputably the most important strain of socialist theory, historically and conceptually. For these reasons alone, it is worth investigating the historical possibility of democratic socialism from the standpoint of historical materialism, the Marxian theory of history. Orthodox formulations of historical materialism are deeply problematic and, in the end, indefensible (see Chapter 5). However, historical materialism does contain what we may call, borrowing a metaphor from Marx, a "rational kernel" that is of some bearing for our question. To grasp its bearing fully, it will be necessary (in Chapter 6) to examine aspects of Marxian political theory. With this theoretical apparatus, it will be possible, in the end, to argue plausibly for the democratic model. Of course it will not be possible to conclude anything *definitively*. There is, as we have come to expect, a limit to what can be said in behalf of socialism, including democratic socialism, *in theory*. But theoretical justifications can, at least, clearly exhibit what remains to be demonstrated in practice. It is with this objective in view that, in the chapters which follow, we leave the dominant tradition behind to investigate socialism in *Marxian* theory.

In current discourse "Marxism" designates nearly as wide a variety of views as does "socialism" itself. Apparently no particular substantive positions of any specificity count as sufficient or even necessary for describing a position as "Marxist." Marx's writings and the theoretical traditions they have inspired are sufficiently complex and multi-faceted to admit of quite divergent interpretations. A very wide range of positions, including some that are incompatible with others, can be traced back plausibly to Marx. And there is scarcely a position that some "Marxist" or other has not held. What then does "Marxism" mean? It is plainly impossible to define the term uncontroversially. However, I would advance the following reflections.

To be a Marxist is, above all, to identify with a certain political tradition – or family of traditions – growing out of the European socialist and labor movements, shaped by Marx's and Engels's decisive contributions to these movements, and developed in diverse organizational and social forms by millions of militants throughout the world. Related to this political identification is a theoretical tradition – or family of traditions – originating in Marx's own investigations of capitalism and world history, and continued by a host of philosophers and social scientists who have identified, theoretically as well as politically, with the tradition Marx inaugurated. Though there are no criteria for counting a position as Marxian, some substantive theoretical positions are, as it were, more Marxian than others: more joined to the Marxian tradition in theory and politics and more linked conceptually with Marx's express views. It is to Marxian theory in this sense that I appeal here.

In calling what follows Marxian, then, I do not mean to suggest that all Marxists would acknowledge the positions I will develop, nor even that these positions are accurate representations of Marx's own views. With regard to historical materialism particularly, it is clear that what will be defended here is a good deal less than Marx himself thought defensible. And what I will say of Marxian political theory would likely be denied by the overwhelming majority of declared Marxists. Still, I think the views developed here *are* legitimately "Marxian." As with other – and even opposing – Marxian positions, it is enough that their ancestry and inspiration can be traced back to Marx and to others who have identified with Marxism, and that they exhibit a plain affinity with the Marxian tradition in politics and theory. Accordingly, there will be very little appeal to textual authority in what follows, and very little concern with establishing the Marxian pedigree of the theses to be advanced. What Marx himself believed is, I think, largely of historical interest. However, a Marxian position on socialism and capitalism is of considerable philosophical and even political importance. What follows aims to support these contentions.

5
Historical materialism

The elaboration of a theory of endogenous, epochal historical change – historical materialism (according to the designation widely accepted among Marxists) – is surely among Marx's major theoretical achievements. However, relatively few of Marx's writings directly address history as such. It was mainly in unpublished writings (for example, *The German Ideology*) and texts not intended for publication (*The Grundrisse*) that we find express attempts to elaborate aspects of the theory. Elsewhere there are mainly intimations. The one explicit and general discussion of historical materialism in the Marxian corpus occurs in some very brief but celebrated passages of the *Preface* to *The Critique of Political Economy* (1859). Historical materialism, then, was not a principal focus of Marx's theoretical investigations. However, it is a presupposition of these investigations and a fundamental component of Marxian theory.

The 1859 *Preface* has come to enjoy a certain notoriety among Marxists. Its schematic assertions, while hardly transparent, seem disarmingly simple, lending themselves to easy adoption by the "orthodox" Marxisms of the Second and Third Internationals. In consequence, what is hardly more than a sketch of a theory became frozen into dogma, immune from the often facile but sometimes trenchant criticisms leveled against it, and impervious to theoretical elaboration and clarification. Sympathy for the positions advanced in the 1859 *Preface* goes very much against the grain of the best recent Marxist thought. The cutting edge of twentieth-century Western Marxism, as it has developed in more or less overt opposition to the official Marxisms of the Communist Parties, has tended to oppose the assertions of the *Preface*, though express opposition is seldom admitted. Western Marxists, including those most adamantly opposed to the substantive claims of Marx's theory of history, outdo even those they write against in professing allegiance to "historical materialism," even while they contest its fundamental positions.[1]

The reasons for opposition to historical materialism, or at least to its orthodox formulations, are readily apparent. There is, first of all, a rigidly determinist cast to the historical materialism of the 1859 *Preface* that accords poorly with the general tendency of Western Marxist thought. Western Marxists have focused upon the role of human (individual and collective) agency in social transformation – a theme that, at best, enters at a lower level of abstraction from that at which historical materialism is pitched. There are also more immediately political grounds for opposition. Indisputably, the *Preface* accords causal primacy (of a sort it does not clearly explain) to what Marx calls "productive forces" or "forces of production" (*Produktivkrafte*) over "relations of production" or "production relations" (*Produktionsverhältnisse*), thereby suggesting the kind of "evolutionary" or "economist" politics Western Marxists have opposed with virtual unanimity. If it is indeed the case, as Marx contends in the *Preface*, that "no social formation ever perishes before all the productive forces for which there is room in it have developed," and if "new, higher relations of production never appear before the material conditions of their existence have matured in the womb of the old society itself," then it would seem that socialist transformation depends less on revolutionizing production relations directly, as Western Marxists tend to maintain (in opposition to the principal line of the Second International and then the Communist Parties), than on the development of productive forces (as Soviet Communism, particularly, seems to have supposed).

A straightforward reading of Marx's injunctions in the *Preface* would suggest the folly of attempting to build socialism anywhere but in the most advanced capitalist centers, a position universally adhered to by the Marxists of the Second International – including, at first, even the Bolsheviks who, in overthrowing bourgeois rule in Europe's most backward capitalist country, sought to spark world revolution by attacking imperialism (the global system of the capitalist world order) at its "weakest link." The failure of the revolution elsewhere in Europe, however, complicated efforts to develop a politics – and a political theory – based on the orthodox position. Read sympathetically; Stalin's notion of "socialism in one country," though literally opposed to what all Marxists believed before the October Revolution, was an attempt to develop an appropriate political response to the situation precipitated by the failure of the revolution in Germany and elsewhere. So too was Trotsky's opposing theory of "permanent revolution." This is not the place to compare the success of these positions in translating the classical Marxian view of the primacy of productive forces into a politics appropriate for the world situation that developed after 1917. The point is just that, for both Stalin and Trotsky, what was crucially important in socialist transformation, and what must therefore have primacy in any socialist politics, are society's productive forces and their development.

The importance of developing productive forces has been emphasized by the Communist Parties, as by many others; and it has inspired a political program in the existing socialist countries (and, indeed, wherever Soviet Communism exercises ideological influence) from which most Western Marxists outside the Communist Parties, and many within, in varying degrees dissent. The litany of Soviet sins, committed for the sake of developing productive forces, is all too well known: the brutal collectivization of agricultural production; the hierarchical structure and "productivist" ideology that governs factories; the selective, technocratic and authoritarian structure of the educational system; the severe centralization of political power; and, most important – in view of our discussion to this point – the indefinite prolongation of police terror and the progressive (and, apparently, inexorable) growth of bureaucratic domination. Needless to say, commitment to the theoretical positions of the 1859 *Preface* does not entail support for the political programs adopted by the leaders of the Soviet Union. In any case, the best Marxian thought in the West, with very few exceptions, has sought to distance itself from the Soviet experience; and therefore, sometimes inadvertently, sometimes deliberately, from the theoretical positions advanced by Soviet leaders.

The Cultural Revolution in China (or, at least, Western perceptions of it) provided, for a time, an official Marxism at odds with the 1859 *Preface*. Proclaiming "politics in command," Maoism apparently aimed at the revolutionary transformation of relations of production while relegating the development of productive forces to second place. Maoism had a certain resonance too within Western Marxism, particularly among Althusserians. In very different ways, each led what appears in retrospect to have been a revolt against historical materialism. But these revolts have now collapsed, and historical materialism has returned, as it were, to reassert its authority.

This authority is reinforced from an unexpected quarter. The resurgence (or better "surgence," since it is without precedent) of interest in Marxism in the English-speaking world, particularly among philosophers trained in the analytic tradition, has kindled a new and generally sympathetic interest in the positions of the 1859 *Preface*. This emerging tendency, at odds both with earlier orthodoxies and also with some of the principal currents of Western Marxism, has been given important theoretical expression in a host of recent discussions of Marx and Marxism, of which the best known and most important for the present purpose is G.A. Cohen's *Karl Marx's Theory of History: A Defence*.[2] Cohen's book must be a point of departure for any discussion of historical materialism. There are, to be sure, differences between Cohen's position and Marx's – particularly on the extent to which historical materialism is held to assert an order and necessity for transformations among pre-capitalist "economic structures" (Cohen) or "modes of production" (Marx).[3] Cohen's intent is not quite to defend Marx's express views, but to defend what he takes to be defensible in Marx's view. The reconstruction of defensible positions requires, Cohen thinks, some modification of Marx's formulations, and also a diminished expectation of the explanatory range of the theory. The theory of history he presents and defends is nearly, but not quite literally, Marx's own. With this caution, and in view of its fidelity to orthodox understandings of historical materialism, it is fair to identify Cohen's with the *orthodox* or *standard* view, and to discuss Cohen's clearly elaborated positions rather than Marx's own diffuse intimations of a systematic theory.

Western Marxism's stance on the kind of position Marx and Cohen advance is, again, in large measure a reaction to the dogmatism of the official Marxisms of the Second and Third Internationals. By now, this stance has itself become, if not quite dogma, at least an automatic response. Views that accord primacy to productive forces over relations of production – and, in turn, over legal and political "superstructures" and forms of consciousness – are widely faulted by Marxists as "crude" and "vulgar," and for leading to a "mechanistic" politics that denies the effective historical role of individual and class agency, and even the theoretical importance of class struggle. Cohen's reconstruction and defense of the standard view shows, beyond any question, that this kind of response is facile and inadequate. The standard view, whatever we finally make of it, is eminently worth taking seriously. We cannot grasp socialism in (Marxian) theory apart from historical materialism, or more exactly its "rational kernel."

Basic tenets

Orthodox historical materialism advances the following two, very general claims:

(a) that the level of development of productive forces accounts for (explains) epochal transformations in social relations of production; and therefore, since social relations of production define discrete "economic structures" or "modes of production," that the level of development of productive forces accounts for (explains) the economic structures or modes of production in place in societies; and
(b) that economic structures or modes of production (the "economic base," according to the widely accepted metaphor) account for (explain) legal and juridical "superstructures" and forms of consciousness.

Both (a) and (b) figure in the orthodox, historical materialist case for socialism. Here the principal focus will be on (a), what Cohen calls the *Primacy Thesis*. It may be noted, however, that the explanations offered in Part One to account for the genesis of the valuational standards of the dominant tradition provide, if correct, some corroboration for (b). In each case, what was decisive was the emergence of capitalist social relations, constituting a new "economic base" which, in turn, as (b) asserts, accounts for new valuational standards (forms of consciousness). We have found, though, that these valuational standards nevertheless support pro-socialist positions. There is indeed a functional relation between forms of consciousness and modes of production, but it is plainly not so constraining as some (hyper-functionalist) Marxists suppose.

The case for the Primacy Thesis, in Cohen's reconstruction, may be decomposed into a number of distinct theses. In outline, the argument goes as follows: A given level of development of productive forces is compatible with only a limited range of social relations of production (Thesis 1). Since forces of production tend to develop over time (Thesis 2), these forces eventually reach a level at which they are no longer compatible with existing relations of production (Thesis 3). When this occurs, the relations are said to "fetter" the forces of production. Because human beings are at least partially rational (in the way the dominant tradition understands), because we are capable of adapting means to ends, and because there is a compelling, trans-historical need to impel the development of productive forces (as Thesis 2 maintains), human beings will transform the corresponding relations of production (Thesis 4), and substitute new relations of production that are optimal for the further development of productive forces (Thesis 5). Each of these claims, individually, is a tenet of the orthodox view. Together they constitute a case for the Primacy Thesis. They will be commented upon presently and subjected to critical scrutiny in the next section.

(1) *The Compatibility Thesis*: A given level of development of productive forces is compatible with only a limited range of relations of production.

"Compatibility" here has a precise sense: forces and relations of production are compatible whenever the relations of production allow for the further development of the productive forces, and whenever productive forces help to strengthen and reproduce existing relations of production. Relations of production comprise economic structures or modes of production. Therefore Thesis 1 claims that not all, but only certain, economic structures can be reproduced at a given level of development of productive forces, and that not all productive forces can be properly utilized and developed within particular economic structures.

If true, Thesis 1 is not true *a priori*. There is no reason in principle why some economic structure should not, in fact, be compatible with any level of development of productive forces. Thesis 1, if true, is a truth about the world, an empirical truth. However, within broad limits, its plausibility is obvious, even in the absence of historical investigation. We can agree, I think, that the social relations of production characterizing, say, early medieval feudalism are incompatible with contemporary production technologies. Thesis 1 is plausible and almost certainly true, but not necessarily true.

The Marxian tradition is unclear as to precisely what is incompatible with what. Cohen postulates a sparse typology of correspondences between economic structures and levels of development of productive forces.[4] Pre-class society corresponds to that level of development of productive forces where there is no surplus produced; pre-capitalist class society corresponds to levels of development generating small surpluses; capitalism corresponds to moderately high surpluses; and post-class society is compatible only with productive capacities producing massive surpluses. Cohen provides no criteria for distinguishing precisely the different levels of productive development he specifies – small, moderate, massive. And in his account, there is no attempt to identify correspondences between forms of pre-capitalist economic structures and levels of development of productive forces, correspondences Marx plainly intended to draw. Even so, this typology does specify enough in the way of incompatibilities to introduce epochal social divisions (though not so many as Marx intended) of the sort required for a substantive theory of epochal historical change.

The rationale for these correspondences is readily apparent. In the standard Marxian view, classes are determined by their relation to other classes in the social process of appropriating the economic surplus in non-subsistence economies. Whenever a surplus exists, therefore, class society becomes possible. Indeed, where there is surplus, class society is (instrumentally) necessary, because it is only under conditions of class domination that productive capacities can expand – through "investment" in technological innovations and in new productive facilities. Individual producers would not generally be willing to make the sacrifices required for further developing productive forces, unless effectively coerced. Typically innovation requires more than just incorporating new tools or methods. It requires radical social reorganization and massive social dislocations of a sort that rational, self-interested individuals would not voluntarily choose. Thus an exploiting class that appropriates the economic surplus and uses it – or allows it to be used – to spur development is essential for a rise in the level of development of productive forces. Pre-class society ("primitive communism," according to the standard terminology) is therefore incompatible with any level of development of productive forces capable of generating a small surplus. And a small surplus, in turn, is incompatible with capitalist class relations. Capitalism requires a moderately high surplus to allow for "repeated introduction of new productive forces and thus for regular capitalist investments."[5] When a moderately high level of surplus is achieved, pre-capitalist relations of production increasingly fetter the further development of productive forces and therefore give way, it is claimed, to capitalism. Likewise, a moderately high level of development of productive forces is incompatible with "post-class societies," characterized by public control of the economic surplus. Since the development of productive forces from moderate to massive levels requires considerable deprivation and toil, direct producers would never freely impose such sacrifices upon themselves. However, a production system dominated by market imperatives, forcing an accumulation dynamic on direct producers and owners of means of production, can accomplish that historic mission. But capitalism can impede the rational deployment of the massive surplus it generates, and is therefore incompatible with massive surpluses. For Marx, the economic structure compatible with highly de- veloped productive capacities capable of generating massive surpluses is, of course, socialism.

Thesis 1 only postulates a system of mutual exclusions. The Primacy Thesis asserts an asymmetry to the incompatibilities postulated by Thesis 1. That asymmetry is introduced by Thesis 2.

(2) *The Development Thesis*: Productive forces tend to develop throughout history.

The claim is that there is a tendency for forces of production to develop continuously, not that forces of production in fact develop continuously. Thesis 2 is not falsified, though it is surely infirmed, by historical examples of stagnation and regression. Likewise, it is corroborated, though not established definitively, by the many historical illustrations that can be adduced in its support.

In Cohen's reconstruction, and arguably also in Marx's view, the Development Thesis is supported by appeal to specific characteristics of the human condition, human capacities and human nature. These characteristics are conceived trans-historically (despite Marx's repeated injunctions against trans-historical characteriza-

167

tions) and closely parallel descriptions advanced in contractarian accounts of "the state of nature" (despite Marx's occasional, but always disparaging, allusions to the contractarian tradition).[6] Human beings, the argument goes, are at least somewhat rational; and "rational human beings who know how to satisfy compelling wants...will be disposed to seize and employ the means to satisfaction of those wants."[7] Under conditions of relative scarcity, where few if any wants can be satisfied immediately or without effort, the development of productive forces becomes a "compelling want." Then persons will seize the means for the satisfaction of this compelling want, and will develop productive forces continuously and progressively (assuming, of course, that no countervailing tendencies of greater strength or outside forces – like invasions or natural calamities – intervene). Thus there is a permanent, human impulse to try to improve humanity's abilities to transform nature to realize human wants. In consequence, there is a tendency for productive forces to develop, and indeed to develop continuously. For the development of productive forces could not fail to be cumulative. Inasmuch as human beings are rational, having once improved their situation by developing the productive forces they find at hand, they will not revert to less developed forces, except under extraordinary – and usually exogenous – circumstances beyond their control. In sum, then, in virtue of human nature and (rational) capacities, wherever (relative) scarcity pertains, as it always has, there is a general tendency for human beings to try to improve their means for transforming nature (in accordance with their wants), and therefore a tendency, as the Primacy Thesis asserts, for productive forces to develop continuously.

Theses 1 and 2, in conjunction, suggest a further claim, also crucial if the Primacy Thesis is ultimately to be sustained:

(3) *The Contradiction Thesis*: Given the reciprocal constraints that exist between forces and relations of production, and the tendency of the productive forces to develop, the productive forces will develop to a point where they are no longer compatible with – where they *contradict* – the relations of production under which they had previously developed.

What is claimed, in other words, is that with the development of productive forces, incompatibilities will intensify and develop into untenable, structural instabilities. Forces and relations of production come to oppose one another, so to speak, from within. They are internally opposed. The structural instabilities that emerge with the development of productive forces are therefore properly described as "contradictions" in roughly the sense in which Hegel understood that term. Externally related entities that are in conflict are not, in Hegel's view, in contradiction. Contradictions arise in internally developing systems that, as it were, generate their own structural instabilities.

In principle, the contradictions Thesis 3 declares inevitable might be resolved by a downward adaptation of the productive forces, by a regression sufficient to restore compatibility. But there is an historical dynamic, asserted in Thesis 2, that precludes any downward adaptation. Contradictions, as in Hegel's account of the development of "Spirit," cannot be dissipated; they can only be "superseded" (*aufgehoben*). The picture is of a new structural arrangement that in some sense "incorporates" the contradiction that generates it. The sort of supersession historical materialism postulates is hardly captured by the metaphor of incorporation, however. It is better described more prosaically as a simple "transformation" or reorganization of the social relations of production. Thus, as forces of production develop continuously, production relations change discontinuously, giving rise to discrete "economic structures." Or, in other words,

(4) *The Transformation Thesis*: When forces and relations of production are incompatible (as they are bound to become, so long as class society persists), the relations will change in a way that will re-establish compatibility between forces and relations of production.

The contradiction between forces and relations of production will always be resolved in favor of the forces, not the relations. It is the relations of production that give way. The reason why is just, once again, the pervasive human interest in augmenting the level of development of productive forces now in conjunction with the inevitability of contradictions between forces and relations of production. Thesis 4, in other words, follows from Theses 1 and 3 (which follows, in turn from Theses 1 and 2).

Thesis 4 foretells the doom of relations of production that fetter productive forces, but by itself it does not foretell what new relations will replace the old. It only specifies that, whatever these relations might be, they will be compatible with the level of

169

development of productive forces. However, for forces to *explain* relations, forces must account for *actual* production relations, and not just exclude (possible) production relations. We should be able, in other words, to specify the outcomes of the (necessary) transformations Thesis 4 postulates. The Primacy Thesis therefore requires the following claim:

(5) *The Optimality Thesis*: When a given set of relations of production become fetters on the further development of productive forces and are therefore transformed, they will be replaced by relations of production that are functionally optimal for the further development of the productive forces.

Unlikely as this thesis may at first appear, it does follow from the argument just reconstructed: specifically, from the Development Thesis and Thesis 4. If relations of production that fetter the development of productive forces are abandoned because they conflict with a universal, trans-historical desire for development, it would be irrational, for those who share this desire (and are capable of acting upon it), to replace what is abandoned with anything less than those social relations of production that, in the circumstances, are optimal for the further development of productive forces. The selection of optimal relations need not be, in this view, a direct consequence of intentional deliberation and choice. In actual history, such choices do not occur. To be sure, the class agent of socialist revolution, in the standard Marxian view, pursues its revolutionary objectives deliberately; but even in this instance, as we shall see, there are numerous mediations – irreducible to deliberate choices – separating the supposed universal desire for development from the choice of a post-capitalist economic structure. Orthodox historical materialism is, in any case, agnostic with respect to how relations of production are selected. What is claimed is just that the production relations selected are, in fact, those that are most suitable for the further development of the forces of production.

It is a tenet of the standard view that capitalism is the optimal and, therefore, necessary form of economic structure appropriate for the rapid development of modern industry, and is therefore a prerequisite for post-capitalism (socialism). These claims, once believed by all Marxists, are of course opposed to the now standard view, dominant within Marxian circles since the October Revolution, that socialism too can rapidly and systematically develop forces of production. However, the new orthodoxy on this issue coheres poorly with other tenets of the standard view. Orthodox historical materialism considers a high level of development of productive forces, a massive surplus, a necessary condition for socialism – not a task to be achieved under socialism. Classical Marxism therefore opposes "premature" attempts at socialist construction, and denies the possibility of non-capitalist roads to a massive surplus. The standard view, in other words, countenances only one future for pre-capitalist class society, capitalism; and only one future for capitalism, socialism. Historical materialism postulates a unique and necessary order of the epochal economic structures it recognizes.

The orthodox case for socialism

Were the orthodox view sustainable, a case for socialism over capitalism – wherever there is already a massive economic surplus – would be strictly unnecessary. For socialism, in the orthodox view, is the unique solution to the inevitably emerging contradictions of capitalism. Therefore socialism would not require justification, and the sorts of considerations marshalled in Part One would be beside the point. If socialism were indeed the inevitable outcome of inexorable historical processes, there would be nothing further to say. Socialism would prevail over capitalism, as many Marxists have claimed, on "scientific," not moral grounds. Moral argument, would be, at best, irrelevant. If a traditional "justification" were still insisted upon, proponents of the standard view might advert to the universal human interests that, according to Thesis 2, motivate the historical processes they postulate. Then socialism's justification would derive from the (unique) way it furthers universal human interests, whenever the historical preconditions for socialism have been attained. In the orthodox view, if socialism is possible, it is also – just in virtue of its possibility – desirable, and therefore, in the long run, since this desire is what moves history along, inevitable.

An immediate difficulty with this position is, of course, that it is in blatant contradiction with the evidence provided by contemporary capitalism. Whatever the failings of existing capitalist societies, a fettering of the development of productive forces does not seem to be among them. There are, to be sure, many conjunctural – and even structural – factors inhibiting investments in new technologies. But there do not appear to be any inexorable tendencies at work leading to permanent economic decline. Capitalism has generated the sort of massive economic surplus socialism requires, just as orthodox historical materialism claimed it would; but it also seems capable of continuing to do so indefinitely, in apparent violation of what historical materialism asserts. Moreover, as many social critics, including some Marxists, have come to realize, it is far from clear that the indefinite expansion of productive capacities in present circumstances is a response to any human interest – true or express. Ecological considerations, with important ramifications for human well-being, can militate against this end, as can a desire for community and "meaningful work" (see Chapter 3) – desires that may well conflict with a super-technological future. Yet the standard, historical materialist case for socialism depends upon just such an interest, and upon the claim that capitalism inevitably comes to fetter its realization. This objection plainly does have force, and will necessitate emendation of the standard position. But it is not nearly so fatal an objection to the orthodox view as may at first appear. More substantial difficulties lie elsewhere.

Many Marxists support the orthodox view that socialism requires no moral justification beyond an appeal to its accord with human interests. Sometimes it is even suggested that to seek specifically moral justification is wrong-headed and ideologically tendentious, a vestige of "forms of consciousness" inextricably linked to bourgeois society and inappropriate for socialists. I will suggest that this stance is wrong-headed and very likely incoherent. But in view of its influence among Marxists, it cannot be dismissed casually. It is, in fact, a position well worth considering. What is particularly instructive to investigate is how, for adherents of the orthodox view, the urgency of working for socialism – an urgency that defines Marxian politics and indeed Marxism itself – can be conceived. I think we can gain some purchase on what is wrong with the standard view if we consider the position of Marxian politics within the conceptual framework of orthodox historical materialism.

At the level of abstraction at which the Primacy Thesis is pitched, no account is taken of *how* epochal transformations of production relations occur. It is asserted only that these transformations do occur, in accordance with functional imperatives. Still, it is clear, if only in a very general way, how, in the orthodox view, these transformations come about. In class societies, the agents of social change are always, for Marxists, social classes. The universal human interest in augmenting the level of development of productive forces is expressed as an "objective" class interest.[8] Determined by differential access to and ownership of means of production, classes are engendered by prevailing production relations. In consequence, the contradictions that, according to Thesis 3, inevitably emerge between forces and relations of production become historically effective in so far as they are represented as class contradictions. Struggles between classes become, in Marx's expression, the "locomotive" of history. A moribund mode of production generates that social class that is to be the bearer of new social relations of production and, therefore, in an epochal sense, of a new social order. The new society is "born in the womb of the old."

Thus, as Marx and Engels declared in *The Communist Manifesto*, class struggle, not moral argument, advances historical processes. And class struggle is as ineluctable as the contradictions that engender it. But classes, in the end, are composed of individuals; and it is these individuals who must act to maintain or overthrow an existing order. Evidently, class position alone will not suffice to determine an individual's politics. Members of declining social classes do sometimes side with their historically progressive class antagonists (Marx and Engels themselves are examples); and members of historically progressive classes often side with their class enemies. Had workers "nothing to lose but their chains," as *The Communist Manifesto* also declares, it is likely that the vast majority of workers would declare themselves openly and boldly to be mortal enemies of the existing order. But where, as in all existing capitalist societies, workers have a good deal more than chains to lose, the situation is more complicated and vexing.

Still, however class identification and individual political motivation are, ultimately, determined, political choices are not, in the view of orthodox historical materialists, moral issues. There may be individuals who, in varying degrees, base their political commitments on moral considerations. But these individuals, even when they side with the working class, are caught up in a

173

pre-Marxian mentality. They have failed to understand the lessons of historical materialism. In the final analysis, according to the "scientific" view, one takes sides in the class struggle because it is there, and because one cannot avoid taking sides. Which side one chooses will depend on many factors. Among these factors, class position will generally be among the most important, though it can plainly be overcome. Some individuals may even be able to choose their class identifications freely, perhaps for expressly moral reasons. Others, doubtless the vast majority, will have class identifications thrust upon them. But, in neither case is there any moral imperative underlying such choices as might be made. Moral arguments are always derivative and largely epiphenomenal. They may sometimes be causally efficacious, but their causal efficacy derives from underlying social processes. But whatever the causal efficacy, in particular circumstances, of moral argument (or of other causally pertinent ideological mechanisms), class identification and politics have no moral grounding. Morality, in this view, is simply not the basis of politics.

What motivates political commitment does not matter, so far as the Primacy Thesis itself goes. This issue enters in at a lower level of abstraction. What the Primacy Thesis asserts is only that the class agent, the bearer of new social relations, comes into being and performs its historical mission *somehow*. Thus the Primacy Thesis implies:

(6) *The Capacity Thesis*: Where there is an "objective" interest in progressive social change, the capacity for bringing that change about will ultimately be brought into being.

Thesis 6 is not part of the derivation of the Primacy Thesis. It is an implication of it. That Thesis 6 is an implication of the Primacy Thesis is, I think, deeply revealing. For the Capacity Thesis indicates a flaw in orthodox historical materialism – a flaw that must be rectified if historical materialism's "rational kernel" is to be extracted and put to use.

Plainly, class capacities for struggle – the organizational, ideological and material resources available to class agents – are not *identical* to class interests in the *outcomes* of struggles. But in the orthodox historical materialist view, interests generate capacities, at least in the long run (Thesis 6). For ascending and progressive classes, class interests breed the capacities required for seizing and exercising class domination. For classes that are historically retrograde, class capacities for exercising domination correspondingly decline.

The Capacity Thesis, in its application to socialist revolution, reflects a similar optimism to that implied by Thesis 5. For the ascendant working class under capitalism, the emergence of revolutionary, transformative interests generates, according to Thesis 6, the capacity for revolutionizing society, for transforming capitalist into socialist production relations. However, even in this case, the standard Marxian position does not appeal to any general mechanism through which interests come to generate capacities. It is claimed instead that there is a coordination of interests and capacities in virtue of the mutual determination of interests and capacities by the development of forces of production. That development, at the same time, engenders an increasingly antagonistic contradiction between forces and relations of production (as proclaimed generally in Thesis 3) and also furthers working-class capacities – by bringing workers together in factories, by educating them technically and politically, and by instilling a propensity for discipline and organization of a sort necessary for defeating capitalism definitively, and for building a socialist order. If Thesis 6 were to be defended generally, a similar story would have to be told for each of the epochal historical transformations historical materialism postulates.

But it is far from clear that the Capacity Thesis holds even for the development of working-class capacities. Certainly many Marxists would nowadays deny what it asserts. Instead of seeing an inexorable growth in the capacity of the working class to struggle against capitalism, it is often argued that there are processes at work in capitalist society that disorganize the working class, and block its capacity to undo capitalist relations of production. These processes include, among others, labor market segmentation, the effects of racial, ethnic and sexual divisions of labor, the internationalization of capital, and the promotion of privatized consumerism. All of these processes, and others as well, contribute to the disorganization and incapacitation of the working class, not to the inexorable enhancement of its capacities for revolutionary transformation.

At the very least, it is clear that there is no automatic development of working-class capacities in consequence of the development of productive forces under capitalism. Orthodox historical materialism is doubtless correct in calling attention to processes that encourage the development of working-class capacities. But there are also processes that profoundly, perhaps overwhelmingly, discourage that development. There is no adequate general theory of the balance between these processes.

What holds for the emergence of working-class capacities under capitalism surely pertains more generally. There is no necessary connection between the development of an objective interest in epochal social change on the part of a class and the development of class capacities for bringing about epochal transformations. An objective interest in moving from one mode of production to another is not sufficient, even in the long run, for revolutionizing modes of production. But if class capacities do not, in the end, derive from the development of productive forces – if class capacities are radically irreducible to class interests – it is unwarranted, finally, to impute to these productive forces the kind of primacy orthodox historical materialism imputes to them.

Subordinating class capacities for action to class interests in the outcomes of actions is a consequence of the individualist style of argument Marx sometimes lapses into, despite his many disparaging allusions to contractarians and other "individualists." By abstracting human beings and their interests from the social and historical conditions in which these interests are formed and sustained, orthodox historical materialism (implicitly) maintains that structural conditions for the translation of interests into actions are derived from these interests themselves. However, this claim is almost certainly false. What the best Marxian social science of this century has shown repeatedly is that the major determinants of political action are irreducible, social determinations. Human beings may be generally interested in augmenting the level of development of productive forces, yet thwarted permanently from acting upon that interest. There may be insurmountable social constraints blocking epochal historical change. An abstracted, ahistorical account of human interests and rationality will not, it seems, provide a basis for explaining the historical efficacy of these constraints, nor even for acknowledging their existence.

This general reproach against the orthodox theory may be corroborated by looking more critically at each of the central tenets that together comprise the case for the Primacy Thesis.

The case for the Primacy Thesis criticized

(1) The Compatibility Thesis

Strictly speaking, the Compatibility Thesis makes two interconnected claims: (a) that for any given level of development of productive forces, there are limits on compatible relations of production; and (b) that for all pre-socialist production relations, there is an upper limit beyond which the further development of productive forces generates incompatibilities. I have already suggested that (a) is difficult to fault. So long as we can imagine (speculatively) production relations that would be incompatible with some specified level of development of the forces of production, that claim is sustainable. Claim (b), however, is more problematic. To repeat the question posed earlier: why must there be a ceiling to the level of development or the forces of production within capitalist production relations? Or, more generally: why can't there be production relations capable of developing productive forces indefinitely?

Orthodox historical materialists would support (b), in the case of capitalism, by invoking the inevitability of accumulation crises under capitalism. According to the view standard in Marxian political economy, a rising organic composition of capital – roughly, a rising proportion of constant to total capital, itself a consequence of capitalist investment in means of production – activates a general tendency for the rate of profit to fall,[9] creating disincentives for new investments in, among other things, technological innovations, and thereby "fettering" the further development of productive forces. The declining rate of profit, the argument goes, erodes the capacity for capitalism to generate advances in the level of development of the forces of production beyond a certain point. Endogenously, capitalism generates its own fetters. However, it is now clear that the standard argument for the inevitability of accumulation crises under capitalism, depending upon a falling rate of profit, cannot be sustained. The claim is empirically unfounded and conceptually defective.[10] Cohen's reconstruction of Marx's theory of history, accordingly, rejects any appeal to the inevitability of capitalist breakdown (as conceived in standard, Marxian political economy).[11] Cohen defends (b) in a way arguably consistent with the spirit of orthodox

177

historical materialism, though plainly at variance with its strict letter. If the defense of Thesis 1 which he launches cannot be sustained, then it is hard to see how (b), though not (a), can be maintained.

Cohen argues that capitalism, in promoting production for exchange rather than use, uses technological innovation to expand output, rather than to extend leisure time, where leisure is understood "as release from burdensome toil." Cohen writes:

> As long as production remains subject to the capitalist principle, the output increasing option will tend to be selected and implemented in one way or another . . . .Now the consequence of the increasing output which capitalism necessarily favors is increasing consumption. Hence the boundless pursuit of consumption goods is a result of a production process oriented to exchange-values rather than consumption-values. It is the Rockefellers who ensure that the Smiths need to keep up with the Jones's.

The boundless pursuit of consumer goods generates an incompatibility between forces and relations of production, not because productive power as such is fettered, but because it is irrationally deployed with respect to basic human interests.

> The productive technology of capitalism begets an unparalleled opportunity of lifting the curse of Adam and liberating men from toil, but the production relations of capitalist economic organization prevent the opportunity from being seized . . . .It brings society to the threshold of abundance and locks the door. For the promise of abundance is not an endless flow of goods, but a sufficiency produced with a minimum of unpleasant exertion.[12]

Capitalist production relations become irrational, in Cohen's view, with respect to a general notion of improving the human condition (through the development of the forces of production). They therefore do not quite "fetter" the *level* of development of these forces, but their rational deployment. Before advanced capitalism, human interests were advanced straightforwardly, by augmenting the level of development of the forces of production. In advanced capitalism, where the forces of production are already sufficiently developed to support socialist relations of production, human interests are furthered by the rational deployment of the forces of production that already exist. "Fettering," therefore, is ultimately a matter of impeding the furthering of human interests through forces of production. Orthodox historical materialism erred – slightly – in generalizing from special cases (the only cases historically extant, prior to the advent of advanced capitalism). Before advanced capitalism, augmenting the level of development of productive forces and rationally deploying the productive forces already in place came to the same thing. In advanced capitalism, however, they no longer come to the same thing; and so an emendation of the strict orthodox account is in order. If there are no endogenous processes at work leading to the general break-down of capitalism, if capitalism could continue to develop and even "revolutionize" productive forces indefinitely, there must be something other than the level of development of productive forces for capitalist social relations to "fetter." For (b) to hold, it is crucial, therefore, that there be trans-historical human interests specific enough to be fettered. Otherwise, (a) of Thesis 1 might survive, but (b) would not; and Thesis 1 would be diminished to the very weak and hardly controversial claim that not all conceivable sets of production relations are compatible with all levels of development of forces of production. A substantive theory of epochal historical change can hardly be founded on this truism.

(2) The Development Thesis

At first glance, there seems to be little to fault in the view that productive forces tend to develop over time, given the interests and (rational) capacities of human beings living in conditions of (relative) scarcity. The problem, however, as with Thesis 1, is that the Development Thesis requires that human interests – and, more fundamentally, the rationality and scarcity that condition human interests – bear a trans-historical sense that these notions likely cannot support. If there are no trans-historical human interests of sufficient specificity to account for development, if interests and also rationality are endogenous to social systems in the sense that they are irreducibly conditioned by social circumstances, then the Development Thesis will not serve the purpose it must, to make a case for the orthodox view. It will not establish an explanatory asymmetry between forces and relations of production.

Consider, first, scarcity. Of course there is a sense in which humanity always has, and likely always will, live in a milieu of scarcity. Nature is generally not so abundant or bountiful as to provide for the easy satisfaction of all the demands human beings might make of it. But this trans-historical scarcity is socially efficacious only in determinate forms. In so far as scarcity is socially efficacious, it is relative to expectations that are, in turn, relative to such specifically social factors as the availability and distribution of alternatives. Marx insisted that even a subsistence wage is historically conditioned: wine is a component of the subsistence wage of French workers; beer of English workers. A hut by itself might be perceived as an adequate shelter; but next to a palace, it becomes a hovel. To be sure, but for the pervasive miserliness of nature, scarcity would not be a fact of the human condition. But it is not pure scarcity that conditions our interests. The scarcity that moves us is irreducibly socially conditioned.

In the original state of nature, according to Rousseau's account in *The Discourse on the Origin of Inequality*,[13] scarcity was not a crucial determinant of human interests. The world the first hunters and gatherers confronted was sufficiently abundant to provide for their needs. There was no competition. Individuals were generally self-sufficient. However, with the introduction of private property – an epochal event that, in Rousseau's account, occurred by accident in the sense that no endogenous historical processes necessitated its occurrence – scarcity, as a determinant of human interests, was *introduced*. This change in human social relations precluded hunters and gatherers from moving freely about the countryside, appropriating from nature what their modest wants demanded. It made settled agricultural production inevitable, creating the "economic base" for population increases and further exacerbating the socially induced scarcity of natural resources. In time, everyone came to be in competition with everyone for everything, as Hobbes thought they always already were, and scarcity came to condition human interests. It was not that nature as such had become more miserly. Rather, scarcity came to condition human interests in consequence of social relations, structured, in the story Rousseau tells, by the institution of private property.

Many Marxists have made a similar case for the scarcity that conditions interests in late capitalism. This position is acknowledged by many non-Marxists too. It is widely believed, not only by Marxists, that the principal task of economic policy in advanced capitalism is to generate effective demand. The "need" for much of what capitalist firms produce must itself be produced. In so far as scarcity is socially efficacious, then, it seems more nearly imposed by social relations than confronted as a fact of nature. If this impression is right, advanced capitalism particularly illustrates perspicuously what is universally true for class societies: that the scarcity that spurs on the development of productive forces is not, strictly, a characteristic of the human condition as such, but a scarcity that production relations themselves induce.

Similar considerations pertain to rationality. If, as Cohen ultimately suggests, relief from burdensome toil is the prime component motivating the universal human impulse to develop forces of production, it is hard to see why there should have been an impulse to move, say, from feudalism to capitalism. There were at times in medieval Europe nearly as many holy days (in which burdensome toil was proscribed) as there were work days. Thus under feudalism, people were blessed with considerably more surplus time (though not surplus product) than people are even today. If relief from burdensome toil is in fact what impels social change, the transition from feudalism to capitalism would have been blatantly irrational. There undoubtedly was an impulse for technical change in feudal Europe, an impulse that feudal social relations did eventually come to fetter. But if this impulse was not the result of a trans-historical, socially efficacious interest (in gaining relief from burdensome toil), then what did motivate it? It does not seem that this question can be answered by appeal to trans-historical notions of scarcity and rationality. We need a more concrete account of class-specific scarcity and rationality. Scarcity for whom? Rationality in light of what (class) interests?

Under feudalism, there was scarcity for feudal lords engaged in military competition for control of territories. To wage war, lords needed revenues, retainers and military equipment. There was, therefore, an incentive for feudal ruling classes to attempt to exact ever greater surpluses from direct producers (peasants) and to encourage the development of improved means of waging war. Thus, under feudalism, the imperative for technological innovation apparently did not come from a universal, cross-class desire to augment the overall level of production in the face of a miserly nature, and certainly not from a desire to diminish burdensome toil, but from the socially efficacious, class-specific needs of feudal lords; from scarcity as the feudal ruling class confronted it. Technological innovation under feudalism was an effect of feudal social relations of production.

This claim may not, at first, seem inconsistent with the Primacy Thesis. For the Primacy Thesis requires only that relations of production be accounted for by the level of development of productive forces; that production relations change (discontinuously) to restore fundamental compatibility with (tendentially) developing forces of production. And it may seem fair to suppose historically specific circumstances condition what is required for functional compatibility. But recall that the explanatory asymmetry the Primacy Thesis requires be accorded to forces over relations of production depends upon an independent argument for the development of the forces of production, one that does not depend upon production relations. This is why Cohen appeals to trans-historical notions of scarcity and rationality, despite Marx's own – inconsistent – strictures against doing so. The Development Thesis cannot both follow from the Primacy Thesis and, at the same time, be a presupposition of it. But unless scarcity and rationality are accorded a trans-historical sense, as they are in Cohen's reconstruction, the Development Thesis lacks the required independence.

For reasons noted in Chapter 2, in discussing feudal exploitation, the rational peasant (and other subordinate direct producers) in feudal society probably would have preferred a society without feudal lords and military competition, a society where peasants could directly consume all of the surplus product. In view of the very slow rate of development of productive forces under feudalism, most peasants would probably have preferred even outright stagnation without feudal exploitation to slowly developing forces of production under feudal social relations. From their point of view, there was little, if anything, to be gained by the technological innovations lords might find it in their interest to introduce. But peasants, as a subordinate class, lacked the capacity to translate their interests into effective actions. Therefore, the class-specific rationality and scarcity of feudal lords was, so to speak, imposed on them – by those with the capacity to make their class interests efficacious. This result, I think, applies generally. Contrary to what would have to be the case for the Development Thesis to be sustained, relations of production condition the development of productive forces – not by allowing for the translation of universal, human interests into historically specific "moments," but by imposing class-specific rationalities and forms of scarcity.

(3) The Contradiction Thesis

If the Development Thesis is wrong for the reasons indicated, there can be class societies in which there are no endogenous tendencies for contradictions to develop between forces and relations of production. Societies can lack mechanisms for translating incompatibilities into contradictions.

Consider the "Asiatic mode of production," mentioned by Marx in the *Grundrisse* and elsewhere and much discussed by Marxists. If the Asiatic mode of production is a coherent concept with some possible applicability to concrete social formations, we have a counter-example, provided by Marx himself, to the Contradiction Thesis. According to Marx, in the Asiatic mode of production, the social form of production relations and the attendant form of the state generate a permanent tendency towards stagnation. The productive forces develop to a point, and then stop developing. In the Asiatic mode of production, there is a definite incompatibility between forces and relations of production. The relations fetter the further development of the forces. But there is no contradiction, and therefore no endogenous imperative for transformation. Therefore, the Asiatic mode of production can continue indefinitely (accompanied by stagnation of productive forces, not continuous development).

In the Marxian view, imperatives for change are represented as objective class interests. Thesis 3 asserts the development, within the "womb" of the old society, of a new class, capable of organizing the development of the forces of production under its rule. Thus if no revolutionary class is brought into being, there is no endogenous basis for change. This is precisely the situation where the Asiatic mode of production dominates in social formations. For example, in classical China, according to the traditional Marxian account, there was no class capable of advancing the level of development of productive forces. For many reasons – among others, the centralization of state power, the pattern of town/countryside relations, the absorption of merchants into the ruling class, and even the technical system of agricultural production – there was no proto-capitalist class, no bourgeoisie. And the peasantry was so fragmented and dispersed into organic peasant communities, having little contact with one another, that it too was unable to function as a revolutionary class, whatever its "objective" interests might be in eliminating the mandarin ruling class. It was only with the assault of Western capitalism upon the Chinese social structure, an exogenous intervention, that the power of the traditional ruling class was finally broken.

Incompatibility leads to contradiction if and only if there exist class actors capable of becoming bearers of a new social order, an order that would unfetter the forces of production. Whether or not such a new class exists, however, depends upon specific historical forms taken by prevailing social relations of production; and not, as the orthodox view maintains, upon a dynamic invested in the forces of production as such – a dynamic derived, ultimately, from trans-historical human interests and capacities.

It appears, in other words, that orthodox historical materialism takes the transition from feudalism to capitalism in Western Europe as paradigmatic of epochal social transformations generally. In European feudalism a new ruling class, the bourgeoisie, did develop in the womb of the old society. And this new class was, as the Primacy Thesis requires, interested in and capable of developing productive forces. But it does not follow, even for this special case, that an imperative to develop the forces of production was the principal cause for the rise of the bourgeoisie and the emergence of capitalism. Far more crucial, as some Marxists have suggested,[14] appear to be such particularities of European geopolitical conditions as the pattern of town/countryside relations (a quite different pattern from the Chinese), the fragmentation and decentralization of political authority (again, in contrast to the Chinese case), the discovery of the Americas, accidents of geographical location and so on. These and similar factors are either characteristics of the particular social structure of European feudalism or else exogenous factors. They are not reducible to the

184

level of development of the forces of production. But if the key elements of an account of the emergence of capitalism in Europe are indeed these historically very particular circumstances, then so far from being paradigmatic, the transition from European feudalism to capitalism is highly anomalous – and the Asiatic mode of production, or other non-developing economic structures, much more nearly what we might postulate as a norm.

Put differently: orthodox historical materialism proclaims a certain inevitability to the emergence of capitalism, in virtue of the inevitability of contradictions between forces and relations of production developing in pre-capitalist class societies. However, it is likely that there is no such necessity; that the emergence of capitalism, though possible, is hardly necessary nor even very likely. Had feudal Europe been obliterated, say, by some natural calamity, capitalism might never have developed anywhere on earth.

(4) The Transformation Thesis

Even were the case for the Primacy Thesis sustainable to this point, the Transformation Thesis would still be a very doubtful inference to draw. For there is no reason in general to hold that when contradictions exist between forces and relations of production – contradictions appropriately represented in class struggles – that the potential bearers of new relations of production will, even in the long run, prevail. Thesis 4 is vulnerable for a reason that has already been noted briefly: the irreducibility of class capacities for changing society to class interests in the outcomes of social change.

All Marxists agree that the working class under capitalism is in principle the bearer of an alternative social order. The working class can organize a socialist economy and progressively dismantle the vestiges of capitalism. But has the working class the capacity to do so? Or if it does not yet have this capacity, *must* it eventually develop the means for fulfilling this historical mission?

Marx himself was exuberantly, and naively, optimistic in this regard. Cohen, reconstructing Marx's position more than a century later, after so many failed hopes, is more cautious. Still, he does present a general argument in support of the view that class capacities for change follow from class interests in change; that is, from the intensification of contradictions between forces and relations of production. Specifically, he holds that ruling classes whose rule blocks the development of productive forces will lose support from outside their class; while ascending classes capable in principle of liberating the forces of production from the social relations that fetter their further development, will gain allies and support. Capacities arise along with interests, because (rational) people will cast their lot with classes that promise a better future.

Another argument, specific to the development of working-class capacities, is linked to an account of economic crises under capitalism. Cohen writes:

> In our view, Marx was not a breakdown theorist, but he did hold that once capitalism is fully formed, then each crisis it undergoes is worse than its predecessor. But the forces improve across periods which include crises in which they stagnate. Hence they are more powerful just before a given crisis than they were before any earlier one . . . . Therefore, socialism grows more and more feasible as crises get worse and worse (but not because they get worse and worse). There is no economically legislated final breakdown, but what is *de facto* the last depression occurs when there is a downturn in the cycle *and* the forces are ready to accept a socialist structure *and* the proletariat is sufficiently class conscious and organized.

This third, crucial condition, Cohen notes, "is not entirely independent. The maladies of capitalism and the development of the forces under it stimulate proletarian militancy."[15] The more general argument – that people will cast their lot with that class which promises the better future – is plausible only if we assume that people generally understand their situation and have reasonable expectations about the consequences, for themselves, of living under radically different social relations; and, above all, that people can translate their interests into the requisite organizational and material means for implementing them. None of these claims is self-evident; and the latter claim, of course, is just what is in contention.

The more specific argument for the development of working-class capacities confronts less evident difficulties. The claim that socialism becomes increasingly feasible as productive forces grow seems unproblematic. However, the claim that crises become ever more intense is far from clear. In virtue of what processes do crises become ever more intense? If, like Cohen, we deny traditional Marxian accounts of capitalist breakdown, what is left to account for ever intensifying crises? At best, this claim stands in need of further argument. The related claim that the proletariat will become sufficiently class conscious and organized to implement new, socialist relations of production is hardly established by appeal to an "objective" interest in transforming capitalism into socialism. Disillusionment with bourgeois class rule is not sure to lead to the revolutionary formation of the proletariat. Disillusionment is, at most, a necessary condition for revolutionary class consciousness and organization; it is hardly sufficient. And if the inevitability of capitalist breakdown is denied, disillusionment is not even a very likely cause of revolutionary class consciousness. Were it the case that crisis tendencies inexorably lead to permanent stagnation, the case for the inevitability of the working class becoming capitalism's "gravediggers" would be at least more plausible. Given ever increasing impoverishment and a horizon of deteriorating conditions, revolutionary organization – and a revolutionary will – might be likely to develop, just as Marx, in his more optimistic moments, thought. But if we agree with Cohen that the distinctive contradiction of advanced capitalism is evident not in stagnation and immiseration, but in the irrational deployment of productive resources, then the automatic development of class consciousness seems a good deal less plausible. An increasingly irrational deployment of productive forces will not by itself lead workers to revolutionary opposition to capitalism. In a privatized consumer society, of the sort characteristic of advanced capitalism, workers plainly have much more to lose than their chains.

Claims for the inevitable development of working-class capacities arising out of the "fettering" of the forces of production under capitalism are doubly inadequate: first, because class capacities are determined by a variety of factors irreducible to the development of the forces of production; and second, because technological change itself can systematically undermine the capacities for struggle of the working class.

The capacity of the working class to forge effective organizations for struggle depends upon a wide range of economic, political and ideological factors. At the economic level, for example, labor market segmentation and the development of complex job hierarchies and internal labor markets can undermine the unity of the working class, at least in immediate, market-related issues. The economic fragmentation of the working class is further intensified when it coincides with – and reinforces – racial, ethnic and sexual divisions. While there are indeed tendencies favoring the homogenization and degradation of labor of the sort Marx investigated, and while these tendencies may contribute to the growth of working-class capacities, there are also important counter-tendencies promoting differentiation and segmentation that undermine these capacities.

It has been argued that the capitalist state also contributes to the erosion of working-class capacities, by disorganizing subordinate classes, undermining the class character of working-class parties, and deflecting political programs from revolutionary towards reformist objectives.[16] Finally, on the ideological level, the class capacities of the working class are undermined by mechanisms rooted in capitalist production and distribution itself, as Marx recognized long ago (capital and commodity fetishism); and in the multitude of ideological or broadly cultural institutions that impose individualist, privatist and consumerist values – values that militate against the formation of revolutionary class consciousness and contribute towards the disorganization of the working class and its integration into the prevailing order.

Needless to say, there are tendencies counteracting each of the incapacitating tendencies just noted. But unless it can be shown that the development of the forces of production *necessarily* defeats each of these disorganizing processes (in the long run), there is no reason to hold that the fettering of the forces of production under capitalism – manifest, as Cohen would have it, in their increasingly irrational deployment – will inevitably lead to a growth in the revolutionary capacity of the working class, and therefore to socialism.

It might even be doubted whether the development of the forces of production under capitalism increases the class capacities of the working class *at all*. While it is likely, as Marx stressed, that the factory system, the distinctively capitalist form of organization of the production process, does improve communications among workers by drawing large numbers of workers together and breaking down (some) forms of craft and skill divisions within the working class, it is also evident that technical change – especially in advanced capitalism – can weaken working-class capacities. The global telecommunications revolution, combined with dramatic improvements in transportation systems, has made it easier for the bourgeoisie to organize production globally – in "world market factories." This phenomenon, so far from bringing workers together, exacerbates national and regional divisions within the working class and isolates technical coordination from direct production. The virtual monopolization of technical knowledge within managerial strata closely linked to the bourgeoisie materially and ideologically has undermined the capacity of the direct producers to organize production. These and similar aspects of modern capitalism may not have quite the debilitating effect on working-class capacities sometimes ascribed to them. But it is clear that there is no unequivocal and automatic connection, even of a tendential character, between technical change and development under capitalism and the growth of working-class capacities for the revolutionary transformation of capitalism into socialism.

(5) The Optimality Thesis

Thesis 5 completes the case for the Primacy Thesis. The claim is that the mode of production that supersedes a transformed contradiction between forces and relations of production is one which is optimal for further developing the forces of production. Thus the Optimality Thesis makes two related claims: first, that there is in fact an optimal economic structure ready, as it were, to supersede contradictions between forces and relations of production; and second, that this optimal structure will, in fact, be selected. To the degree either of these claims is doubtful, the Optimality Thesis is doubtful; and the explanatory force of the Primacy thesis is diminished accordingly.

There is, needless to say, a certain superfluity in questioning the Optimality Thesis at this point. For if Thesis 4 cannot be sustained, if contradictions between forces and relations of production do not always engender their own "supersessions," then the Optimality Thesis, even were it plausible, would be otiose. We have seen that this is in fact the case; the Transformation Thesis is deeply flawed. Still, it is worthwhile to examine Thesis 5 in its own right. It is in virtue of this claim, after all, that the Primary Thesis derives its explanatory force. If the forces of production did not *select* production relations, but only excluded incompatibilities, the forces would hardly *explain* the relations. It would be as if it were claimed that the climate of ancient Greece explains the development of Greek architecture, because that climate is incompatible with certain architectural forms (for example, the construction of igloos). To explain production relations *adequately*, the forces of production must do more than limit or exclude possible production relations; they must select particular ones. Finally, it is through Thesis 5 that historical materialism conceives an "end" (*telos*) of human history, a goal of the historical process, without recourse to specifically teleological views of history of the Hegelian sort – views that helped form Marx's thinking about history, but from which he also broke.

For Hegel, history is the career of a subject, Spirit, that exhibits (indeed, is ultimately identical with) an internal and dynamic principle, Reason, through which Spirit works out its destiny, culminating in the recovery of an original unity that incorporates through supersession (*Aufhebung*) all the contradictions that have propelled its "becoming," its process of development. Historical materialism breaks from this view of history as the career of a subject and its "monadic" development. Historical change is propelled by a trans-historical and ever urgent need to develop forces of production (Thesis 2), and not in virtue of an imminent and inexorably unfolding logic. The contradictions that develop endogenously (Thesis 3) are not analogues of the internal divisions of Spirit, but consequences of the (empirical) incompatibility of (some) production relations with (some) levels of development of forces of production. Still, in the orthodox view, there is an end to history: communism, the end but also the "culmination" of class society. If not quite a goal in the Hegelian sense, communism is still an inevitable destination. It is because the Optimality Thesis postulates a unique succession of epochal historical transformations that this result – communism as the end-point of the historical trajectory, the culmination of the process of historical change – is conceivable.

For Darwin too, the evolution of species is intelligible through an optimizing selection mechanism, not through the discovery of an imminent principle of transformation. Variation occurs by chance. (This is not to say that chance variation is literally random, but only that its causes – barely understood even today – are logically independent of evolutionary change.) Then, through natural selection, those chance variations most conducive to reproductive success under particular environmental conditions prevail. Natural selection, then, is an optimizing *mechanism*. Neither Marx nor Cohen specifies an analogous selection mechanism for economic structures. But they do claim, in parallel fashion, that optimal selection occurs. Historical materialism, then, is a less developed evolutionary theory than Darwin's. It is an evolutionary theory in a pre-Darwinian stage: asserting optimal functional correspondences, without specifying the mechanism(s) through which optimality is achieved. The comparison with Darwinian theory is therefore to historical materialism's detriment.[17] But it does underscore the radical departure historical materialism undertakes from its immediate ancestor, Hegelian philosophy of history. For historical materialism, as for Darwinian evolutionary theory, there is no subject of history and no notion, therefore, of an imminent logic of development. But there is a theory of historical transformation and its direction. Inasmuch as the epochal divisions Marx conceives are so few, in comparison with the very large number of species recognized by evolutionary theorists, the outcome of the process Marx envisions, unlike the outcome of biological evolution, is foreseeable. In fact, though for non-Hegelian reasons, there is, in Marx's view as in Hegel's, only one possible outcome. Then history does, in effect, have a *telos* – communism – though it is intelligible non-teleologically.

The first claim – that there is always an optimal set of production relations – is far from sure. Even Cohen, *pace* Marx, admits that among pre-capitalist economic structures, there is no universal and necessary sequencing of discrete economic structures. Presumably, there are, in Cohen's view, no optimal forms of pre-capitalist economic structures for particular levels of development of productive forces capable of producing some surplus, but still incapable of generating the level of surplus capitalism requires. In Cohen's account, the Optimality Thesis figures only in the selections of capitalism and socialism at the appropriate levels of development of productive forces. But even in these cases there is, as already noted, ample reason for skepticism. However matters may have appeared in Marx's day, historical evidence now plainly inclines against what the Optimality Thesis implies. Though

191

classical Marxism never imagined the possibility, contemporary Marxists know that "primitive socialist accumulation" is possible; that at the level of development of productive forces where capitalism is traditionally deemed optimal, productive forces can be developed too – perhaps with even greater rapidity – without private ownership and substantial reliance on markets, but instead with public ownership of productive capacities and central planning. The Soviet Union and other socialist countries contradict the view that capitalism alone can develop productive forces once a moderate level of economic surplus is attained.[18] What the Optimality Thesis asserts is therefore contradicted by the evidence at hand.

Socialism is defined here so generally that it is hard to imagine an *alternative* candidate for capitalism's future, assuming capitalism cannot continue indefinitely. But, as noted, it is far from clear that capitalism cannot continue indefinitely. Therefore, just as we should not conclude that the contradictions of pre-capitalist society can only admit of one "solution," capitalism, neither should we automatically assume that socialism will emerge inevitably from the contradictions of capitalism.

The rational kernel

It might seem, after all its indefensible pretensions are removed, that there is nothing left to Marx's theory of history; that there is no rational kernel. This conclusion would be mistaken. The theory does not account for epochal historical change. But it is an indispensable component of any adequate account, for it is a defensible theory of the most fundamental determination regulating epochal change. There is much to fault orthodox historical materialism for; but, in the end, the core theory is sound.

Orthodox historical materialism is a doctrine that asserts the inevitability of progress – in the development of productive capacities and therefore, ultimately, in what that development is for: the general human capacity for self-actualization. There is a necessary and progressive order of economic structures. In consequence, allowing for time lags and the turbulence that arises from efforts to restore or maintain compatibility between forces and relations of production, the actual is as good as can be. In the end, ours is the best of all possible worlds.[19]

This optimistic vision is, we have noted, remarkably Eurocentric. European feudalism was indeed transformed into capitalism through endogenously developing imperatives for change. And that transformation was plainly progressive. This epochal change is then deemed necessary – at least in the long run – and projected spatially, to apply to all extant pre-capitalist societies, and temporally, into the future, to an inevitable and progressive transformation of capitalism into socialism. Socialism is justified, then, for that level of development of productive forces where it alone can maintain compatibility between forces and relations of production. It is justified because no other economic structure, including capitalism, can do what is required to further human interests. At that level of development, capitalism, once the optimal solution to the all-powerful human need for development, ceases to be adequate. Socialism *ought* to be, at the appropriate historical moment, just because it is possible and therefore, ultimately, inevitable.

But we have seen that claims for the inevitability of socialism cannot be sustained. Neither, therefore, can the orthodox "justification" for socialism be maintained. It will hardly do to defend socialism by pointing to inexorable "laws of development." The orthodox view that socialism can be defended "scientifically" – that it requires no "moral" justification at all – is plainly indefensible. However, we can deny historical inevitability and the flawed tenets of the orthodox view – and even the Primacy Thesis these tenets imply – without relinquishing the core, the "rational kernel," of Marx's theory of history. To grasp that core, it is well to recall the general form of Marx's view of historical change.

Marx's break from the Hegelian philosophy of history, from the view that history is the career of a subject working out its always implicit destiny, is decisive. Even in the orthodox view there is no imminent logic of historical change and development, and therefore no *telos* or end of history in light of which all that comes before is retrospectively intelligible. In the orthodox account, the end of history, communism (the "final stage" of socialism) is realized not because it is the "principle" of all preceding economic structures, but in virtue of its best satisfying the functional relation that holds throughout history between forces and relations of production. Communist production relations are optimal for deploying the forces of production that make it possible. It is only in virtue of this relation that communism is the "end" of history.

Like Darwin's account of biological evolution and unlike Hegel's philosophy of history, historical materialism is a non-teleological evolutionary theory. There is no Providence, no "cunning of Reason," guiding the course of historical change. History is intelligible, but not in virtue of any superintending agency that directs it, nor in virtue of any imminent logic of development. The rejection of teleological accounts of history is an element of historical materialism's rational kernel.

But it is not the whole of it. For Marx, there plainly is a *theory* of history. There are intelligible, endogenous processes promoting epochal historical transformations. Thus historical materialism retrieves some of what is intended by the Hegelian view of history – in opposition, say, to more mainstream views, according to which particular historical changes are explicable, at least in principle, but history itself admits of no comprehensive account.[20] Reduced to its rational kernel, historical materialism is a theory of *possible* production relations; an account of what can be placed on the historical agenda, *in view of the level of development of productive forces*.

Put differently: historical materialism, stripped of its indefensible pretensions, provides a theory of what is *economically possible*. For Marxism, this determination is fundamental. Economic structures account for the forms and limits of class structure, formation and struggle – the fundamental categories of Marxian *explanations*. And, as noted, in the historical materialist vision economic structures account as well for legal and juridical "superstructures" and for forms of consciousness. For better or worse, there is no theory of what is necessary or inevitable. What is economically possible may be *politically* difficult or even impossible to realize and sustain. What is explained by the functional requirements of material production are historical agendas, not historical actualities.

To reduce historical materialism to its rational kernel is of course to deflate its self-representations. A defensible historical materialism *shows* much less than it *claims*. But it still shows a great deal. What it shows is just that the historical conditions under which economic structures become *possible* are determined, in the end, by the level of development of productive forces and the correspondences that pertain between forces and relations of production. Even in the long run and at the level of abstraction at which historical materialism is pitched, epochal transformations cannot be explained just by reference to the processes historical materialism recognizes. But neither can they be explained adequately without reference to these processes.

The progress historical materialism describes can be overwhelmed by class incapacities – brought about, at least in part, by particular forms of social relations of production. But the structure historical materialism imputes to history is at least tendentially efficacious. The endogenous processes historical materialism identifies are real processes. What is historically possible is determined, ultimately, by the functional correspondence of forces and relations of production, and the contradictions these correspondences engender. The orthodox theory, reduced to its rational kernel, will not by itself explain historical change; nor will it predict the outcomes of class struggles. But it does give an account of the conditions for the possibility of change and of the options available to classes in struggle. This is enough, it seems, to motivate Marxian theoretical practice, and to support Marxian politics.

In view of what historical materialism shows, we know that capitalism need not continue indefinitely; that a genuinely *post*-capitalist future is possible. We therefore have theoretical warrant for juxtaposing capitalism and socialism (post-capitalism), not just as alternative models of political-economic organization, but as alternative historical possibilities. This may seem a slight achievement. Existing socialism already proves socialism possible. But we know from Part One that to defend socialism – even in theory – we need to establish the historical possibility of the democratic model, of that model which avoids the shortcomings of the sort of socialism that is historically extant. The historical materialist case for socialism's possibility contributes substantially to this end, as we shall go on to see.

6
Socialism and democracy

We know from the arguments marshalled in Part One that to the extent conclusions can be drawn at this degree of remove from concrete institutional specifications, socialism (post-capitalism) fares better than capitalism, with respect to central values constitutive of the dominant tradition in moral, social and political philosophy. And we have concluded in Chapter 5 that with the level of development of productive forces capitalism brings about, socialism (post-capitalism), though hardly inevitable, does come *onto* the historical agenda. What is generally preferable to capitalism in light of dominant tradition values is also historically possible.

However, this conclusion requires qualification. For state bureaucratic socialism does not unequivocally fare better than capitalism, and even fares worse with respect to some of the values in contention. Existing socialisms, however, all approximate the state bureaucratic model. Nowhere, to date, is the theoretical alternative to state bureaucratic socialism – democratic socialism – historically realized. This fact cannot fail to raise a doubt about the case for socialism developed to this point. The problem is not just that we have only considered socialism *in theory*. Rather, the problem is that a defense of socialism in theory is philosophically interesting only if what is defended is in some pertinent sense *feasible*. Our task is not to compare a utopian fantasy with a feasible model, but to compare feasible models. Had we reason to think socialism realizable only in the state bureaucratic form, there would hardly be a case for socialism even in theory. We would have to conclude, in that event, that with even this modest institutional specification, this very slight descent from the level of abstraction supposed when socialism and capitalism are compared in general, socialism's advantages vanish. To conclude that socialism is defensible in theory we must therefore provide reasons for thinking the democratic model realizable in practice.

What is defensible in Marx's theory of history will not by itself suffice to establish this result, though it does provide more support than may at first appear. Indeed, the feasibility of the democratic model cannot finally be established by theory at all. Democratic socialism will be shown definitively possible only when it is realized in practice. There is some risk, therefore, in adopting pro-socialist positions. But reasons can be provided for taking this risk. To elaborate these reasons, we must add to our repertoire of Marxian theoretical positions. To this point, we have examined socialism in light of Marx's theory of history or, more precisely, its defensible aspect. Now it is appropriate to appeal as well to a certain strain of Marxian political theory, based largely on Marx's reflections on the revolutions of 1848 and the Paris Commune, and developed incisively by Lenin in *The State and Revolution*.

In doing so, we will find ourselves at some distance from the political theory of the dominant political culture. The roots of Marxian political theory are, we shall see, in the idealist tradition in democratic theory. What follows, therefore, does not so much add to the conceptual apparatus supposed throughout Part One – as our use of Marx's theory of history does – as depart from it. This departure is necessary, however, to defend democratic socialism – and therefore, ultimately, socialism in general – in theory.

The state

The Communist Manifesto, always a suitable point of departure for explicating Marx's principal positions, offers a number of characterizations of the state. In the first section of that text, in discussing the rise of the bourgeoisie as a class and its distinctive form of economic domination, Marx and Engels, in a well-known passage, describe "the executive of the modern State" as "a committee for managing the common affairs of the whole bourgeoisie."[1] The bourgeois state is, in other words, the organization of the bourgeoisie – its organization to realize and insure its domination, its role as a ruling class. Then in the following section, where Marx and Engels focus on the proletariat, we are told that with the conquest of political power, "the proletariat will use its political supremacy to wrest, by degrees, all capital from the bourgeoisie, to centralize all instruments of production in the hands of the state, i.e. of the proletariat organized as a ruling class."[2] There is, in short, a striking similarity in the *Manifesto*'s characterizations of the bourgeois and proletarian states.[3] These formulations suggest a tentative, general definition of the state: the state, in the *Manifesto*'s view, is *the organization of the ruling class*, its organization to realize its domination.

This theme persists throughout virtually all of Marx's writings on the state, and is the basis for Lenin's contribution to Marxian political theory. According to this view, the state rests on, intensifies and reproduces a relation of forces between classes. It is the organization of the dominant class, the "device" through which class domination is achieved and maintained.

This position of both Marx and Lenin bears a striking affinity – and a correspondingly striking difference – to the position of Hobbes and other "founding fathers" of the dominant tradition. We have noted how the Hobbesian state of nature may be described as a generalized Prisoners' Dilemma situation where – in virtue of what is supposed about human nature and the human condition – the payoffs awaiting individual utility maximizers are radically sub-optimal. In the state of nature the schedule of payoffs is such that individuals, by pursuing their own interests, will not always do as well for themselves as they otherwise might. Agreement will not suffice to put an end to the state of war because individuals, in so far as they are rational, have an interest in disobeying whatever agreement is reached. The only way out of the war of all against all, in Hobbes's view, is to alter the payoff structure, making agreement of a sort that would avoid sub-optimal outcomes possible (for self-interested rational agents). The institution of sovereignty is Hobbes's device for achieving this end. In making rules and enforcing them (or in having them enforced), the Hobbesian sovereign achieves – through the use or threat of force – what individuals by themselves cannot achieve. Under the yoke of sovereignty we escape the war of all against all that renders our lives so miserable. The Hobbesian sovereign solves the Prisoners' Dilemma problem individuals in a state of nature confront.

Needless to say, in the Marxian view, Hobbes's social "ongy" is wrong: the fundamental unit which social and political theory should countenance is not the atomic individual, the individual whose interests are radically independent of those of other atomic individuals, but the social classes whose struggles, in the historical materialist view, move history from one epochal structure to another. Classes are, of course, comprised of individuals; but they are radically irreducible to the individuals that comprise them. Generated by the modes of production that constitute epochal social divisions, it is classes, not individuals, that act upon the stage of history; and class struggle, not individuals' conflicts, that is of historical moment. But *within* classes there are coordination problems analogous to those faced by individuals in the Hobbesian state of nature. Within classes there are antagonistic interests that threaten to undo what historical materialism – conceived just as a theory of historical possibility – claims is the overriding class interest: insurance of ruling class domination over subordinate classes. Within the bourgeoisie, each bourgeois is, as it were, in mortal competition with all others. But as an owner of means of production – and therefore, in actual circumstances, as an employer of labor (since, where capitalism exists, direct producers generally do not own their own means of production) – each bourgeois has an overriding class interest in the maintenance and reproduction of capitalist social relations, and therefore in the reproduction of bourgeois class domination. The state is the means by which this end is achieved, the means through which the ruling class succeeds in establishing and maintaining an overriding framework of cooperation, within which different intra-class interests can compete without devolving into a "war of all against all." The state does for the ruling class what, for Hobbes, it does for individuals as such. It overcomes Prisoners' Dilemma situations. The state is the means through which the ruling class coordinates itself – in order to dominate subordinate classes. It is, as the *Manifesto* would have it, the organization of the ruling class – its organization for the purpose of exercising its domination.

State power

It is for this reason that, in Lenin's view, the question of state power is the fundamental question, the pivot, upon which his central focus, the question of revolutionary strategy, turns. In Lenin's view, consonant with what historical materialism suggests, state power is always the power of a single, dominant class; for the state is, again, the organization through which the dominant class exercises its domination. State power can never, therefore, be held by an individual or group of individuals, by a social stratum nor even by a particular class fraction. State power, for Lenin, is always the power of a class, of bearers of social relations of production. The state is the arena in which the power of the dominant class is concentrated and exerted.[4]

From 1848 on, but particularly after the defeat of the Paris Commune in 1871, Marx insisted that the state is always a *class dictatorship*. Why a "dictatorship"? Were the word intended in its contemporary sense, to refer to a form of government (in contrast to a democratic form), its use would be both misleading and incorrect. The bourgeoisie, we know, is capable of exercising class domination in non-dictatorial ways; indeed, the representative state (the antithesis of dictatorship, according to contemporary usage) is, according to Marx and Engels in *The Communist Manifesto*, the pre-eminently bourgeois form of the state. Marx and Lenin after him plainly do not intend "dictatorship" in its contemporary sense. Rather, for Marx and Lenin, the term derives its sense from earlier strains of political theory, and refers not to the government but to the state and to the nature of political power. A dictatorship, Lenin says, is "rule based directly upon force and unrestricted by laws."[5] It is absolute political power, power that is indivisible and unlimited (whatever the institutional means through which it is exercised). To say that the state is always a class dictatorship, then, is to hold that the political power of a class rests, ultimately, upon force unrestricted by law. This claim is certainly controversial. It is patently non-liberal, where liberal political philosophy would restrict the competence of states to infringe on individuals' lives and behaviors (see the Introduction to Part One). But it is by no means peculiar to Marxism. That political power is always exercised through a *dictatorship* is a common principle of political theory from Bodin and Machiavelli to Weber and beyond. Both Hobbes and Rousseau would agree. What is distinctively Marxian is the assertion that this dictatorship is always the dictatorship of a *class*.

In bourgeois society, the dictatorial character of state power reveals itself only occasionally and briefly – in moments of crisis when order is threatened. And the class character of that violence is even less transparent, for it contradicts what juridical and other societal institutions promote – a sense of *classlessness*, where the law and the state through the law, address not classes, but individuals. It required the breakdown of order in major revolutionary upheavals (1848, the Paris Commune, the Russian Revolution of 1905, the October Revolution) and sustained theoretical investigation of these experiences to elaborate this position fully and to recognize its implications. In non-revolutionary situations, it remains fundamentally counter-intuitive; and for that reason difficult, once acquired, to retain.

State power, then, is always exercised through a class dictatorship. Under capitalism, state power is exercised by the dominant, capitalist class; capitalist societies are dictatorships of the bourgeoisie. Under socialism (post-capitalism) state power is exercised by a different ruling class. For classical Marxists, that class can only be the proletariat. The dictatorship of the bourgeoisie and the dictatorship of the proletariat exhaust the historical possibilities. However, that view is plainly wrong. It derives, we now can see, from the optimistic vision orthodox historical materialism postulates of capitalism's demise and replacement. In the orthodox historical materialist view, socialism is the inevitable resolution of the contradictions of capitalism. The working class becomes a revolutionary class agent in the womb of bourgeois society, just as the bourgeoisie had become a revolutionary class in the womb of European feudalism. The working class ultimately seizes power, establishes its class dictatorship and initiates the task of socialist reconstruction. Progressively, the abundance capitalism has made possible is rationally deployed. In consequence, distributional conflicts pale in importance and politics itself withers away. Forms of domination diminish. Ultimately, in the "final stage" of socialism, communism, a society without classes, is realized. In this way, orthodox historical materialism deems inevitable what is, in fact, only a possible, best-case scenario. All we can defensibly assert, at this point, is the economic possibility of this outcome. Post-capitalism, we know, is a possible outcome of the contradictions of capitalism. We can now add that post-capitalism is incompatible with political forms, class dictatorships, that assure the rule of capital or the reproduction of pre-capitalist economic structures. Beyond this very weak constraint, however, the political character of post-capitalist regimes is open. A dictatorship of the proletariat is a possible political form of socialist (post-capitalist) society. But it is hardly an inevitable form – unless the proletariat were, as some classical Marxists believed, the only possible successor to a deposed bourgeoisie. We now know the classical Marxian account of post-capitalist class structure was overly simple and politically naive: new forms of domination, new class dictatorships, can replace the dictatorship of the bourgeoisie. The dictatorship of the proletariat is possible, but not inevitable even under socialism.

The state apparatus

The state rests on, intensifies and reproduces a relation of forces between classes. But the state is plainly not identical with this relation of forces. Strictly speaking, the state is a collection of institutions, a complex *apparatus*. State power is realized in the development of a state apparatus.

As is well known, Lenin fought a long and largely unsuccessful battle against those Marxists who thought it sufficient simply to seize the existing state apparatus and use it to advance proletarian class positions. A ruling class cannot make use of just any state apparatus, but only of one appropriate to the exercise of its domination. And what is appropriate for the bourgeoisie is not, Lenin insisted, appropriate for the proletariat. This is why it is not enough for communists to seize the apparatus developed by the bourgeoisie. Nor would it be enough to seize the apparatus developed by other ruling classes in socialisms where the proletariat is, again, a dominated class. The dictatorship of the proletariat must undo the state apparatus it seizes – "smash" it, as Lenin would have it – and replace it by alternate forms of the state.

What is crucial, Lenin insists, is destroying the inherited *repressive* state apparatus, the "forces of order" that, in the final analysis, compel compliance through the use or threat of force. The repressive state apparatus, Lenin held, remains largely invariant in all the many forms of bourgeois class rule: a standing army hierarchically organized, a paramilitary police, a system of courts and prisons for "the administration of justice." The destruction of these institutional forms and their replacement by new forms proper for proletarian class domination is the crucial political task, in Lenin's view, of the dictatorship of the proletariat.

Alone among class dictatorships, the dictatorship of the proletariat does not aim at its indefinite reproduction. Rather, proletarian class rule aims precisely to undo the conditions for its "social necessity." Its end is communism, a society without any state. The form of the state apparatus appropriate to proletarian class rule must always be, in Lenin's view, subordinate to this objective.

Although Lenin and other classical Marxists would not have acknowledged the possibility, it is clear that there can be socialist states – states in socialist societies – that are not in transition towards communism. This possibility is, however, recognized implicitly in the strain of political theory Lenin develops. Thus Marx and Engels, reflecting upon the experience of the Paris Commune, concluded that political struggle *over* the state continues to be fundamental, even after the state is in proletarian hands. The Commune failed, they thought, in part because the proletariat, having seized state power, did not proceed to revolutionize the state it had seized. This task, the revolutionary transformation of the state apparatus, is the paramount political task under socialism.

The immensity of this world-historical project is difficult to overestimate. Changes in institutions, though necessary, are not sufficient. Still less is the achievement of socialism a matter of directing repressive measures against "counter-revolutionary" individuals or recalcitrant social strata. Resistance to communism is not reducible to the resistance of particular individuals or social strata, nor to the revanchist aspirations of the overthrown bourgeoisie. The dictatorship of the proletariat, in Lenin's view, requires nothing less than the radical transformation of social relations and therefore of the masses themselves – the "human material" that is the support of these social relations. In the end, the dictatorship of the proletariat requires new masses. A successful *communist* assault on the bourgeois state must be guided by this objective. The point is to transform people; to form bearers of new, communist social relation.[6]

Thus this strain of Marxian political theory effectively joins the

Rousseauean tradition of political philosophy according to which, in the end, politics is a matter of *education*, of transforming individuals' wills to the rigors of citizenship. This is not the place to reflect on the sad fate of Russian revolutionary institutions in the face of economic backwardness and world hostility; but we should recall how these institutions were conceived by Lenin and his co-thinkers, when the Russian Revolution was still considered just the first rupture, at its "weakest link," of the world capitalist system. The revolutionary institution *par excellence*, the workers' councils (soviets), were of course instruments for the administration of public affairs – and therefore, in Lenin's sense, part of the repressive state apparatus. But they were also, above all, schools for the formation of the proletariat, for their education in communism. It is this express educational role that distinguishes the state apparatus characteristic of the dictatorship of the proletariat from other forms of class rule, including those that might develop in socialist societies that are not proletarian class dictatorships. For the strain of Marxian political theory the Lenin of *The State and Revolution* epitomizes – Bolshevik political theory, we might say – all reflections on institutional arrangements, all questions of organization and administration are posed with this end in view – the creation of communist men and women.

Democracy

This end cannot be achieved, however, without the widest possible mass participation in the institutions that direct society, without an overwhelming democratization of the state apparatus. It will not do for a "workers' state" to act on behalf of the working class, nor even to act with its express consent (registered, as in representative democracies, in periodic elections, and reaffirmed by a general habit of obedience to authorities). In the dictatorship of the proletariat, the working class and its allies must control the state; for, as Rousseau insisted, only real popular control educates. Therefore the dictatorship of the proletariat *cannot* be dictatorial in the contemporary sense of the term – except perhaps in emergencies, in dire and extraordinary circumstances. Proletarian class dictatorship cannot be exercised by a minority of the population; nor can it be exercised non-democratically. The proletarian revolution cannot be a minority revolution, even where the working class is a minority of the population. In the very dire and extraordinary circumstances of Russia in the 1920s, Bolshevik practice failed to live up to these requirements. But the teaching of Bolshevism is clear, even if the practice (partially) based upon it is not. The key problem of revolutionary strategy, in Bolshevik theory, is always the problem of class alliances; and the chief political task therefore throughout the entire revolutionary process, is the formation of an overwhelming revolutionary bloc. The proletarian revolution must become a *popular* revolution, a revolution of the vast majority – for the proletariat to exercise its class dictatorship.

We know that unlike other class dictatorships, including non-proletarian class dictatorships under socialism, the dictatorship of the proletariat does not reproduce relations of domination indefinitely. It is rather an expression – in institutions – of a politics that aims at undoing what, for both dominant tradition theorists and Marxists, makes states necessary: the certainty of a war of all against all – within society generally or within classes – unless behavior is suitably constrained. This politics must be radically democratic. The democratic institutions of proletarian class rule transform individuals – ultimately to the point where the coordination of behavior no longer requires a repressive state apparatus at all: to the point where, as Marx would have it, the free development of each (individual) becomes the condition for the free development of all.

Thus the state apparatus through which the proletariat overcomes its internal divisions, realizes its class power and organizes its domination is of a radically different order from any other extant or even imaginable form of the state. The state apparatus of the proletarian state consists of institutions of radical and direct democratic control. In place of a standing army, there are the armed workers; in place of "independent" courts, popular tribunals; and in place of parliaments, the soviets. But the dictatorship of the proletariat is not defined by these characteristic institutional forms. Rather, the dictatorship of the proletariat, for Lenin and the strain of Marxian political theory he develops, is the institutionalization, as it were, of a tendency of the state apparatus to supersede itself, to render itself obsolete. Proletarian class rule, the dictatorship of the proletariat, is distinguished, ultimately, by

the historical tendency it furthers; by the tendency to make actual
the historical possibility Marx's theory of history demonstrates –
the possibility of communism – and thereby, the end of the state
itself.

Socialism and communism

Orthodox historical materialism erred both in thinking socialism
the inevitable outcome of the contradictions of capitalism and also
in thinking communism the inevitable "final stage" of socialism.
Socialism is only a possible alternative future for capitalism; and
communism is only one possible outcome of socialism. In each
case, what is crucial for making the possible actual is the
cultivation of class capacities. The key element is therefore always
political. For communists, before and particularly *after* the
revolutionary overthrow of capitalism, politics must be in command.

This position is consonant with the spirit, but not the letter, of
Lenin's strictures in *The State and Revolution*. For Lenin was still
too much of an historical materialist. There is in consequence a
tension deeply inscribed in Bolshevik theory, focusing particularly
around the concept of socialism. "Socialism" bears, at the same
time, two distinct senses. On the one hand, "socialism" means
roughly what it has meant here: a political economic system with
formal equality and without private ownership of society's
principal means of production. According to this understanding,
we can speak appropriately of a "socialist mode of production."
But sometimes, particularly in contexts where explicitly political
motifs are elaborated, the concept of a socialist mode of
production is denied. Then communism, not socialism, is proposed as capitalism's historical rival. In those contexts, "socialism"
and "the dictatorship of the proletariat" effectively designate the
same ensemble of institutions, though from different perspectives.
"Socialism" comes to stand for the period of transition to
communism. It is not, strictly, a rival to capitalism, but the way out
of capitalism.

This ambiguity is, again, a consequence of Lenin's continuing
commitment to orthodox historical materialism – an indefensible
commitment and one at odds with the crucial determining role his

political theory accords to politics. But it is an ambiguity that is easily avoided. We need only acknowledge what Bolshevik political theory suggests, even if it does not quite acknowledge: that communism is a possible outcome of particular – democratic – socialisms, but not an inevitable consequence of socialism as such. Socialism, we know from historical materialism's rational kernel, represents an epochal advance over capitalism, and is preferable to its rival in light of dominant tradition values. But Marxian political commitments are not, after all, for socialism as such. Marxists, or, more strictly, Marxists who identify with Bolshevik political theory, want communism.

Lenin's repeated insistence, after the collapse of the Second International, that the political formations he sought to build be designated "communist," rather than "socialist" or "social democratic" (as Marxian political groupings had been called) was motivated in part by conjunctural political considerations. Lenin wanted to distinguish these nascent political movements from those "socialist" and even "Marxist" parties that had collaborated with their respective governments in the First World War, and that were, in the war's aftermath, working to rebuild their national capitalisms and to block the contagion of socialist revolution. But there is a deeper, still political point underlying this insistence. It literally is communism, not socialism, that Bolsheviks want.

Orthodox historical materialists would not concede that political consequences turn on the distinction. For them, communism is just the final stage of socialism. Lenin, on the other hand, drew important political consequences from the distinction, but expressed them along with a still orthodox view of history. From this fidelity to orthodoxy comes an unfortunate and deeply misleading inclination, too often evident in Bolshevik practice and theory, to counterpose capitalism and communism as exhaustive historical alternatives.

Communism is conceivable as the outcome of historical processes developing endogenously within capitalist social relations, just as other forms of socialism (post-capitalism) are. This is what historical materialism, reduced to its rational kernel, shows. Capitalism renders communism possible. But it does not make communism necessary. Political practice alone can have that effect. Thus there is a "rational kernel" to Bolshevik theory too. The very basic, indeed determining, role of politics in socialism is

207

what Bolshevism contributes to understanding socialism in theory, once it is severed from orthodox historical materialism. Socialism is not, as Bolsheviks sometimes claim, the dictatorship of the proletariat. The dictatorship of the proletariat is one possible political form of socialist society – the form Marxian politics enjoins.

There is, finally, an optimism in this strain of political theory that remains even when its rational kernel has been extracted. In view of the historical record, this optimism is inappropriate. It is well, therefore, to caution against it.

For societies genuinely in transition towards communism, there is no guarantee of staying on course. The dictatorship of the proletariat is a contradictory and inherently unstable configuration. It is reversible. Bolshevik political theory, however, has little of consequence to say of this possibility. Classical Marxists were, we now can see, deeply and naively optimistic in supposing that societies once embarked upon the road to communism would never retreat, except in consequence of a victorious counter-revolution. Trotsky extended the classical view somewhat, maintaining that – as in the French Thermidor (when the Revolutionary Government of Robespierre was overthrown and replaced by the Directoire) or in its supposed Soviet analogue, the victory of Stalin over the Left Opposition – counter-revolution can insinuate itself in the mantle of revolutionary legitimacy. But neither Trotsky nor any other Marxist of the classical period imagined socialist societies deviating from the road to communism without internal subversion, betrayal or outside intervention.

The obverse view, implicit in the work of the best conservative thinkers, maintains that socialism, once inaugurated, cannot but evolve towards something far worse than what it replaces; that the road to communism is impassable. We shall consider this claim in the Conclusion to Part Two.

For Marxists, however, communism is possible and desirable. But among Marxists, it has only been the Maoists who have recognized the possibility of the dictatorship of the proletariat turning into something less than communism, for reasons other than its clear or mystified (but still real) defeat. Borrowing a term from pre-World War I intra-Marxian polemics, Maoists have misleadingly labeled this possibility "revisionism," thereby suggesting what is, on the face of it, exceedingly implausible: that what accounts for proletarian class dictatorships straying from course is retreat from Marxian orthodoxy. But at least the Maoists have given this possibility a name. No Marxian tendency, however, has contributed much to the rectification in theory or practice of classical Marxism's plainly inordinate optimism. The possible futures of proletarian class rule remain an urgent subject for investigation.

The democratic model

Where the dictatorship of the proletariat exists, the democratic model of socialism pertains. The dictatorship of the proletariat *is* radical democracy: direct popular control of the institutions – social, political and economic – that coordinate behaviors and shape individuals' lives.

No other form of class dictatorship is systemically democratic. Forms of class rule that produce socialisms according with the state bureaucratic model are systemically non-democratic, just as capitalism is – though (despite the practice of existing socialist countries) they surely *can* support representative institutions, just as capitalist states often do. It is important for socialists to investigate possible forms of post-capitalist class domination. It may be unrealistic and even misleading to distinguish only democratic and state bureaucratic models of socialism, as we have to this point. Other socialist forms of the state, other models, may be conceivable, and worth considering. However that may be, it is unlikely that any variety of socialism would be so directly, systemically, democratic as the dictatorship of the proletariat.

It follows, then, that in so far as the dictatorship of the proletariat is feasible, the democratic model is realizable in practice. This result largely removes the hesitation that haunted our discussion throughout Part One. Not only is it clear that socialism in general, post-capitalism, is historically possible, but there is reason also to admit the possibility of that model of socialism which, unlike the state bureaucratic model, does seem to realize the general advantages socialism enjoys over capitalism. If we grant that Marxian views of history and politics do establish the possibility of communism and therefore of socialisms leading to communism, then so far as theory can dissipate such hesitations, our worry that we have defended a utopian fantasy is addressed.

But in dissipating this worry, a new fear may with some justice arise: a fear of radical democracy itself. Even if the democratic model is on the historical agenda, is it desirable, in the end, to risk what liberal social philosophy would deem "the tyranny of the majority"? Will radically democratic institutions respect individuals and accord proper due to human dignity? These are pertinent and vexing questions.

However, I would venture that we can answer these questions affirmatively, though hardly uncontroversially or definitively. To develop an appropriate response, it will be necessary to explore some of the implications for moral philosophy of the rational kernels of Marx's theories of history and politics; and to ask, finally, from a specifically Marxian point of view, why socialism – or, more precisely, since Marxian politics aims not just at socialism but at communism, why communism – is a proper goal of political practice.

Why communism?

Communism, like socialism generally, requires moral justification, despite orthodox historical materialist protestations to the contrary. The arguments marshalled in Part One are relevant in this regard, particularly now that we have warrant for identifying communism or, more strictly, socialisms *en route* to communism, with the democratic model of socialism. It may be surprising, but is nevertheless so, that in light of standards proffered in the dominant tradition of moral, social and political philosophy, there is a case to be made for communism (with a small "c," for what Bolshevism aims towards, as opposed to what it actually achieved).

However, it is not at all clear to what extent, if at all, Marxism should endorse dominant tradition standards. For Marxists, these standards are ultimately determined by the real-world conditions – indeed, the "social relations of production" – in which they arose and continue to be sustained. Their historical relativity has been noted repeatedly throughout Part One. Marxists would therefore do well to be cautious in justifying communism by appeal to these standards – even if, for reasons evident to historical materialists, there likely cannot now be developed alternatives.

Be that as it may, a case for socialism generally and even for communism that appeals to dominant views of freedom, distributive, aggregative and political values will not by itself contribute to an understanding of socialism in *Marxian* theory. A characteristic Marxian concern with real property relations is crucial, we have seen, for making a case for socialism with respect to some distributive values; but this concern can be shared even by those who are not at all sympathetic either to Marx's theory of history or to Marxian political theory. Were we to leave matters at this point, we should have to conclude that Marxism's distinctive contribution to the defense of socialism in theory is less than we might have supposed. Marxian theory would provide reasons for thinking a desirable kind of socialism, communism, possible. But it would not contribute anything distinctive to a case for its desirability.

I think this conclusion can be avoided. There is a distinctively Marxian case to made for socialism in general and for communism in particular. The rational kernel of historical materialism is crucial for making this case. In effect, what follows is a successor claim to the orthodox view that socialism (with communism as its "final stage") may be justified, should justification be deemed necessary in the face of historical inevitability, by appeal to its rationality.

We know from Chapter 5 that notions of rationality, in so far as they figure in accounts of endogenous historical processes and transformations, are class-specific and therefore historically relative. We know too that, for Marxists, legal and juridical superstructures and also "forms of consciousness" (including, presumably, the standards by which social and political arrangements are assessed) are accounted for by prevailing economic structures, and are therefore also historically relative. Would it not follow, then, that assessments of institutional arrangements that appeal to their rationality must also be historically relative; and that, in general, we cannot affirm the moral superiority of some institutional arrangements over others – of communism over rival socialisms and over capitalism? Historical materialism, even reduced to its rational kernel, seems incompatible with unqualified, comparative assessments.

Much of this argument is beyond dispute. However, the

relativism it conjures up is largely avoidable. Comparative assessments of political economic systems *are* possible in the Marxian view, and of course redound overwhelmingly in socialism's – and particularly communism's – favor. To see how, it is necessary to say something of the nature of moral argument in Marxian theory. Thanks in large part to the orthodox historical materialist denial of the need for moral justification and the suspicion with which Marxists have viewed moral discourse, the question of the nature of moral argument in Marxism is a largely neglected issue, where confusion abounds. Still, by reflecting on Marx's theory of history we can confidently find our bearings.

Marx's moral argument has deep roots in Western moral philosophy. But the character of Marx's position goes against what has plainly become the prevailing view, according to which external, indeed sometimes even transcendent, standards may be postulated and used for assessing social and political arrangements. Marx is Aristotelian, not Kantian, in assessing forms of life.[7] Moral assessments, for Aristotle, so far from being grounded in standards external to the (political) communities that would apply them, depend radically on the communities in which they emerge and function. Of course, Aristotle conceived the *polis*, the city-state, as the only proper political community; and this cultural myopia damages his express judgments. But the moral philosophical position Aristotle articulates survives the anachronism of his particular views and the provincialism of his outlook. Marx, in effect, appropriates Aristotle and generalizes his insight by integrating his style of moral discourse into an historical materialist perspective. For Marx, as for Aristotle, standards of assessment are communally grounded. But there are many sorts of communities than Aristotle – or even Marx – was prepared to admit. Still, if socialism is to be compared favorably to capitalism, and if communism is to be justified, it will not be with respect to independently specifiable ideals. The comparison will have to be with respect to standards specific to particular communities or sorts of communities.

For Aristotle, happiness is an intrinsic good; and social and political arrangements are justified to the extent that they foster happiness. Happiness consists essentially in the fulfillment of individuals' plans of life.[8] Plans of life are, of course, individually chosen; but individuals' choices are constrained by circumstances, by the historically variable conditions in which individuals live and make choices. Just as we make history not as we please – under circumstances of our choosing – but under conditions history itself imposes, so too our plans of life are constrained by historical circumstance. We are constrained in what we are able to do and, more importantly, in what we want. The ends of our actions and ultimately our plans of life depend both on where we are (in ongoing political communities) and at what point we are (in the course of historical development and change). Happiness, the intrinsic good, does indeed consist in the fulfillment of individuals' ends and in the cultivation of "powers" for achieving ends. Happiness is *self-actualization*. But our ends are in large measure historically conditioned.[9] Like societies, individuals can set for themselves only those tasks that are already on the historical agenda. Precisely what "self-actualization" means in particular circumstances is therefore always historically relative. This is why self-actualization is not an external standard against which social and political arrangements may be assessed. Strictly speaking, self-actualization has no trans-historical status at all, except as a regulative ideal: a formal goal, so to speak, of individual and collective life.

In so far as productive forces develop continuously, human history is progressive with respect to material progress. But it is not just for furthering humanity's capacity to produce – for augmenting means for achieving satisfaction of human interests – that the general course of history is, in the Marxian view, progressive. All Marxists, including the most orthodox historical materialists, believe in moral progress as well. The overall succession of discrete modes of production, corresponding, as Marx claims they do, to different levels of development of productive forces, is progressive. Moral progress, however, is not measured according to some external standard. It is, rather, the ever expanding possibility for forming and realizing plans of life, for developing "powers" and shaping ends, that Marxists applaud, as the forces of production develop. As we ascend the historical trajectory, we augment, it is believed, our capacity for individual and collective self-actualization.

There is plainly an affinity between self-actualization, the formal goal of an historicized Aristotelianism, and autonomy (see

213

Chapter 1). In furthering our capacities to realize historically expanding ends, we further our capacities to set ends before ourselves, to determine our own ends free from the domination of others and also the domination of circumstance. Autonomy, itself a formal ideal, is a component, perhaps the most important component, of moral progress.

We have already noted (in Chapter 1) the role of democratic control in fostering autonomy. The politicization of civil society and its radical democratization are, it seems, the best way, under any likely historical conditions, to develop individuals capable of seizing control of their lives and destinies. We therefore concluded that, to the extent autonomy is valued, socialism in general and the democratic model of socialism in particular are preferable to capitalism. We can now add that socialisms in transition to communism, socialisms governed by proletarian class dictatorships, necessarily implement the democratic model. For communism requires precisely what radical democratization fosters: autonomous individuals capable of coordinating behavior without coercive restraint. Communism is a social order without a state. It is the realization – in consequence of the exercise of proletarian class rule – of the anarchists' ideal of uncoerced harmony. Communism is that social order where, in Engels's expression (taken over from Saint-Simon), "the governance of men" gives way to "the administration of things."

For Hobbes and his successors within the dominant tradition, coercive states are necessary to coordinate behavior in order to avoid the drastically sub-optimal outcomes that can result from unconstrained individual utility maximizing in "the state of nature." Marxian political theory takes issue with Hobbes on many points, but it does not alter the Hobbesian view of the role of coercion in coordinating behavior. Within a dictatorship of the proletariat, as within a Hobbesian commonwealth, it is still, in the end, the use or threat of force that is the basis of social order. The dictatorship of the proletariat, like its historical antecedents and rival forms of class domination, is still a state. What distinguishes the dictatorship of the proletariat, in the Marxian view, from other forms of the state, is again, its tendency to supersede itself, to diminish progressively the need for coercive coordination and thereby to undermine its very necessity. The dictatorship of the proletariat aims, we now can say, at making people autonomous.

We know, following Rousseau, that a community of autonomous agents is possible only if the "private interests" that necessitate coercive domination are overcome. For autonomy to be realized, individuals must be moved not by egoistic concerns, but by more solidary, communal or, as Rousseau would have it, "general" interests. The dictatorship of the proletariat is, in a word, the historically realizable form of what Rousseauean political philosophy enjoins: a state that aims at making individuals capable of acting in their own best interests as free beings, without binding themselves, by subjecting themselves to political domination; a state that implements and carries to completion "the sovereignty of the general will."

Marxian political theory directly joins Rousseauean political philosophy both in its insistence on the importance of autonomy, and in its view of the means by which autonomy is to be achieved. It is in virtue of the politicization of civil society and the radical democratization of institutions of social control that we are transformed from brute creatures, moved by "private interests," to autonomous citizens, directed by a general will. Rousseau calls for a politics of autonomy, a politics that aims at fostering capacities for autonomous choice. So too do Marxists. In each case, the means proposed is the same: the radical democratization of social and political life.

However, we should be wary of overstating the affinity. Rousseauean autonomy is conceived within an idealist framework according to which practical reason rules on the content of our ends. We are autonomous, in Rousseau's view, to the degree we are rational; to the degree our actions are determined by "objective" moral laws – laws of our own legislation, to be sure – but laws that are none the less binding on rational agents as such. It is unnecessary and misleading to impute this conceptual structure to Marxism. For all the reasons Marxists should hesitate to endorse dominant tradition positions, it is unwise for Marxists to endorse positions conceived by the dominant tradition's idealist rival. When humanity has finally overcome the conceptual and valuational horizons of bourgeois society, idealist autonomy will, in all likelihood, appear anachronistic. But there is no reason to doubt that autonomy in some recognizable sense will continue to be a viable and attractive ideal, or that its evident connections with democracy will cease to hold. It is this belief that informs Marxian politics. Marxian politics is a politics of autonomy, just as Rousseau's politics was – a politics, however, informed by a theory of history of which Rousseau had no inkling.

In this one instance, the dominant tradition concept, freedom (F3), just because it is so lacking in precise conceptual specification, may prove a good approximation of how, if the historical materialist view of the relativity of valuational standards is right, the moral philosophy of the future will conceive autonomy. Autonomy, as the dominant tradition already conceives it, is surely part – indeed, a principal part – of any likely, future notion of self-actualization; of what, in the Marxian view, ultimately justifies communism.

Conclusion to Part Two

A number of distinctively Marxian reasons have been marshalled to show the historical possibility and moral desirability of socialism in general and socialisms in transition towards communism – radically democratic socialisms – in particular. However, we are still far from a full-fledged defense even of democratic socialism. For the path from theory to practice may be fraught with perils that no account of socialism in theory, including Marxian theory, can fully address.

Existing socialism raises the spectre of such perils. For nowhere has the attempt to establish proletarian class rule, the dictatorship of the proletariat, worked out well. We might therefore wonder whether, for such beings as we are, attempts at establishing genuinely and radically democratic socialisms can succeed. Even if the democratic model is on the historical agenda, might it be *politically* unfeasible? Can radically democratic socialisms of the sort Lenin envisioned in *The State and Revolution* avoid devolution into systems of state bureaucratic domination? These questions are plainly of considerable moment for Marxists and indeed for socialists of all sorts, including those who advocate more benign forms of state bureaucratic socialism than have so far existed.

I have already suggested that blame for the shortcomings of existing socialist societies cannot be ascribed in the main to their socialist economic organization. Fault lies with the absence of sustained democratic traditions; and, above all, with the extraordinary historical circumstances – the economic backwardness and overt hostility – with which socialist polities, from their inception, have had to contend. If these suggestions are right, the view that existing socialism is the only form politically feasible, and

217

therefore the best form of socialism attainable, cannot be maintained.

To conclude that more desirable forms of socialism than now exist are unfeasible would imply that we would do well to leave capitalism in place, whatever socialism's advantages in theory may be. This position parallels an important conservative response to the revolutionary upheavals that, two centuries ago, brought capitalism into predominance in Western Europe. A classical statement of this position is Edmund Burke's *Reflections on the Revolution in France*. For Burke, the French revolutionaries, however worthy their aspirations, were bound to go disastrously wrong. In their attempt to improve inherited situations by revolutionizing prevailing institutions, rather than by gradually reforming them, they set in motion a process culminating in the despotic usurpation of the revolutionary movement, leading to an outcome worse, in Burke's view, than the *ancien régime* against which the French people were in revolt. Burke saw ample evidence of this outcome in the revolutionary measures that followed, wave upon wave, the modest challenge initially posed to the institutions of the French monarchy. The aspirations of the French revolutionaries, Burke insisted, would be better served by the rigorous avoidance of revolutionary challenges to received institutions. We are likely to do ourselves considerable harm, Burke thought, should we try to do much good. We are well advised, therefore, to be modest in our aspirations and conservative in our practice.

Writers after Burke – from de Tocqueville through Pareto and Michels to some contemporary political scientists – have gone on to insist that the formation of elites is somehow unavoidable in large-scale human associations, and that despotic domination can only be avoided by rigorous adherence to the rule of law and by significant legal restrictions on the scope of governmental activity. Democratic institutions *are* vulnerable to despotic usurpation. Elites *can* manipulate popular assemblies and rule in the guise of the majority. It is not despotic majorities – that constant worry of the early liberals – that are to be feared, but plain despotism, despotism of the few, exercised through popular institutions. Caution in democratization is therefore advised, if the *demos* is to avoid being ruled, while appearing to rule. The dictatorship of the proletariat, then, cannot fail to become a dictatorship *over* the proletariat, whatever the intentions of socialist revolutionaries and whatever the institutional forms they construct.

It follows, in this view, that Marxian politics is at fault both because it is revolutionary and also because it is democratic. On both counts, in so far as Marxists succeed, things are sure to end badly. Severing the tie with received institutions by unleashing popular energies is unconscionably risky. A revolutionary politics is deeply and dangerously unwise. And democratization – no matter how desirable in theory – is sure to have unfortunate, unintended consequences. It is hardly surprising therefore that the Russian Revolution took the turn it did. The backwardness of Russian capitalism, the devastation of the First World War and ensuing civil war, and the unrelenting hostility of world capitalism were not, after all, the decisive factors. Of even less importance were the political mistakes and "crimes" of the Bolshevik leadership. In the end, the degeneration of the Russian Revolution was unavoidable, in this view. It was a simple consequence of the foolhardy attempt to improve human life through revolutionary means, and, worse still, through the democratization of institutions of administration and control.

These contentions cannot be taken on directly in an account of socialism in theory. But it is appropriate to counterpose an alternative perspective. Nowadays hardly anyone, including even the ideological descendants of Burke and de Tocqueville, would deny the enormous historical advance registered by the French Revolution, despite its excesses and the extravagantly naive claims of many of its militants and ardent defenders. The French revolutionaries did not usher in an era of human perfectibility; but they did advance human history. This advance is discernible in terms of "superstructural" changes, registered plainly in the theoretical pretensions of anti-feudal revolutionaries – for liberty, equality and fraternity. I would hazard that in the distant future, should humanity survive and progress, our descendants will view the anti-capitalist revolutionaries of this century in a similar light. They have hardly ushered in heaven on earth, despite the best efforts and sacrifices of so many. Existing socialism is deficient even in comparison with some existing capitalisms. Still, in the long run, anti-capitalist, socialist revolution will be seen to represent an enormous historical advance – just as the anti-feudal revolutions of the past are now understood to have done. This advance too will be discernible, I think, in terms of the theoretical pretensions socialists advance; pretensions that continue to be promoted and acknowledged even in the countries of actually existing socialism.

This expectation, if conceded, would not by itself undo the claim that communism is an unattainable and even dangerous ideal. Only communist practice can refute that charge definitively. At this point, in theory, all that can be said is what has been said already – following Rousseau, Marx and Lenin on the transformative role of democratic institutions – the institutions proper for proletarian class rule, for socialisms in transition towards communism. Democracy is the prescribed antidote for the tendency, such as it might be, for elites to form and dominate large-scale organizations. If we fear despotic usurpation of democratic institutions, the remedy is more democracy, not less. Of course, there is no guarantee this remedy will work. In the end, the question of the possibility of communism remains open. There is ample cause for suspicion, but no good reason for despair. Quite the contrary. That we lack conclusive reasons for thinking Rousseau, Marx and Lenin right is no reason for thinking them wrong. Nor is existing socialism a reason for thinking them wrong, so long as the shortcomings of existing socialism can be otherwise explained. In the absence of pertinent and unequivocal historical evidence, the question must remain open.

To the degree it is not supported by incontestable considerations, Marxian politics, aiming at communism, rests on a kind of faith: faith in democracy and its transformative effects. There is consensus, we know, on the value of democratic collective choice, among pro-capitalists and pro-socialists of virtually all persuasions (see Chapter 4). Disagreement, however, is rife over how democratic our institutions should be; over the extent and scope of the commitment to democratic choice. Marxian politics represents an extreme valorization of democratic values. It is radical democratic politics, inscribed in the framework of the Marxian theory of history.

Marxian theory can demonstrate the possibility of a communist political economy. And it can provide reasons supporting the desirability of what it deems possible. But it can only *assert* the *political* feasibility of developing socialisms genuinely in transition towards communism. Marxian politics is a wager on that possibility.

Conclusion

It was argued in Part One that, despite (sometimes considerable) indeterminacy, socialism fares better than capitalism with respect to values widely shared throughout our political culture – values constitutive of a dominant tradition in moral, social and political theory. In Part Two, distinctively Marxian claims were introduced both to address hesitations raised in Part One, and also for their own sake: to investigate socialism in Marxian theory. Socialism does represent an advance over capitalism, from a Marxian point of view. It is both materially and morally progressive. But Marxian politics, or at least that version of it elaborated perspicuously by Lenin in *The State and Revolution*, does not aim merely at establishing and maintaining socialism. It aims at a particular kind of socialism – socialism in transition towards communism. Despite what orthodox historical materialists (including Lenin) believe, socialism with communism as its "final stage" is by no means the only possible socialism, the inevitable resolution to the contradictions of capitalism. But in light of what is defensible in Marx's theory of history, we can conclude that communism is one of capitalism's *possible* futures. This possible future instantiates the democratic model. It represents the kind of socialism most plainly in accord with both Marxian and dominant tradition values.

To be for this kind of socialism – and, indeed, to be for socialism in general – is a sound choice, so far as the theoretical considerations adduced here support political commitments. But it is not an indisputable choice. For even those who are persuaded by arguments for socialism – and communism – in theory, may still have doubts. Existing socialism, socialism in practice, does not look nearly so appealing as socialism in theory. And we cannot be sure, in theory, that better socialisms, democratic socialisms, are

222

in fact feasible. Marxian political theory addresses this fear, but cannot lay it to rest. In the end, we are left with a faith in democracy; a faith in the capacity of the *demos* to exercise power in its own best interest. A commitment to socialism is therefore always, to some degree, a wager. Can we justify joining that wager?

Pascal thought that faith in the Christian God was a wager.[1] God's existence, Pascal maintained, can neither be proven nor disproven conclusively. But God either does or does not exist *and we must choose* whether or not to believe in Him. (In Pascal's view, we cannot directly force ourselves to believe, but there are actions we can take that can elicit belief; and we can choose whether or not to undertake these actions.) This God, if He exists, sends believers to Heaven and non-believers to Hell. Therefore, Pascal concludes that non-belief is irrational, no matter how unlikely God's existence may be.

No matter what one's attitude towards risk, it is rational to wager on God's existence. The disadvantage (disutility) in not believing in God when God in fact exists is far greater than the disadvantage (disutility) in believing in God when God does *not* exist. The disutility in the former case is infinite, and very minor in the latter. Likewise, the reward of belief in God if God exists is very much greater (it too is infinite) than the reward of non-belief should God not exist. Indeed, the payoff for an atheist who is right will hardly be greater than the payoff for a theist who is wrong. Therefore, Pascal concludes, so long as it is *possible* that God exists, the rational waverer will opt for God, and act accordingly.

Needless to say, Pascal's partition of the possibilities is tendentious (there might well be a God who doesn't favor Christians or who casts into Hell those who come to believe in Him out of calculation of self-interest); and so the conclusion – that it is rational to wager on God's existence – cannot be sustained. But Pascal *would* be right were the choice situation as he describes. In conditions of uncertainty, where we cannot fail to choose, it is wise, as Rawls would have it, to maximize the minimal payoff; to cut our possible losses.[2] But even if we are unwise enough to seek to maximize possible gains, we still ought to opt for God; since the rewards of belief *may* be infinite, while the rewards of disbelief can only be slight.

History, in so far as Marx has captured its developmental

structure, places us in something like the position of Pascal's waverer, who must opt for one choice or the other and act accordingly. In the orthodox view, we must choose between capitalism and socialism. In fact, the choice is more complex, for socialism is more varied than orthodox historical materialism acknowledges. Socialisms developing towards communism, the only socialism orthodox historical materialism recognized, are only one possible choice. But, as Marxists do, we can, in effect, partition alternatives with respect to it. Is it wise to wager on communism? Since communism is the most extreme instantiation of the democratic model, and since the democratic model alone, unequivocally, fares better than capitalism with respect to the theoretical standards of both the dominant tradition and Marxism, this question is a fair approximation of the following question, even if it is not strictly identical with it: is it wise to opt for socialism *in practice*, to bet on the socialist alternative?

I have tried to make a case for socialism in theory. This case, however, is of little help in assessing probable outcomes; for there is little that can be said – in theory – to recommend the *political*, as opposed to the strictly economic, feasibility of genuinely democratic socialisms, of socialisms in transition towards communism. We know, like Pascal's waverer, that we are embarked and must choose and we know something of the distribution of payoffs; but since we do not know the odds, we cannot conclusively infer what is to be done.

Pascal's waverer was in similar darkness about the likelihood of God's existence. But this uncertainty did not impugn the possibility of rational choice, since, by hypothesis, the rewards and punishments are infinite. Given the payoffs, it is eminently reasonable to opt for God, so long as there is any chance at all that God exists. But we are plainly not in that situation with respect to the choice we must make for or against socialism and capitalism. The advantages of socialism in theory, though significant, are not infinite; nor are the shortcomings of capitalism. We are left, therefore, with a theoretical case for socialism generally and particularly for socialisms in transition to communism, but with no practical guide to action.

This conclusion may be disappointing, but it is hardly surprising. After all, it is seldom theory that motivates political commitments, that accounts for taking sides. Political commitment is much more a consequence of circumstance and experience; much more nearly a response to actual conditions than to theoretical concerns. In politics, theory is typically retrospective.

We cannot be certain that we would be better off under socialism; nor can we be sure that a democratic faith of the sort communism requires is warranted. A case for socialism in theory cannot provide these assurances. Capitalism is not Hell on earth; and socialism, even in its most radically democratic forms, would not be Heaven. We therefore cannot *infer* what we ought to do, as Pascal would have us do for belief in God. But, as in Pascal's wager, *we must choose.* I think the choice is clear, even if it is not incontrovertible. The wise choice is our best hope and possible future. There is, after all, a world to win.

Afterword: 1988

My principal objective in *Arguing for Socialism* was to assess socialism and capitalism in light of standards around which, I maintain, there is substantial consensus in our political culture: freedom, equality, justice, welfare, efficiency, democracy and respect for rights. I also had some subsidiary aims: to assess these standards themselves by considering them in light of the support they provide or withhold for socialism and capitalism; and also to determine the relevance of distinctively Marxian positions in arguing for socialism. Another subsidiary aim was to investigate the plausibility of these Marxian claims. In retrospect, it is not surprising that the subsidiary aims came to overwhelm the principal objective. At the level of abstraction at which the choice between socialism and capitalism can be investigated philosophically, no sure answers are forthcoming. A more determinate conclusion would require specification of particular institutional arrangements, a task I did not undertake, in part for principled reasons.[1] It is clear, in any case, that *Arguing for Socialism* has more to say about standards for assessment prevalent in mainstream moral, social and political theory and also about Marxian theoretical claims than it does about the choice between socialism and capitalism.

Nevertheless, what I have written does contribute to the question I set out to address. Even at the level of abstraction at which a philosophical comparison of socialism and capitalism must be pitched, there is a weak case for socialism over capitalism in general – and a stronger case for democratic socialism. If nothing else, this result supports the faith of generations of socialist militants: that socialism is indeed a

227

desirable political ideal. However, there are more specific political lessons to draw from the arguments presented here; though again nothing definitive can be concluded. The theoretical considerations adduced in the preceding chapters have implications for intra-socialist disputes about strategy and for debates between socialists and others on the Left who are indifferent or even hostile to socialist objectives. In the Preface to this paperback edition, I suggest that these debates have taken on a particular urgency. Consideration of these issues is therefore appropriate and timely.

1

The problem I posed supposes that pro-capitalists and pro-socialists agree in general on standards for assessing socialism and capitalism. This position is controversial. Thus I contrasted my view with the "hyper-orthodox" historical materialist contention that the standards in question must favor capitalism, since they have all been developed or transformed under capitalism; but that this result is of no interest, in as much as standards for assessment are always only "functional" for reproducing the economic systems in which they arise or flourish.[2] I think it plain that this position rests on a misunderstanding of what historical materialism can plausibly be said to claim about the relation between economic structures and forms of consciousness.[3] In any case, hyper-orthodox historical materialism is demonstrably false – as the preceding chapters attest. The same evidence counts against any socialist who would insist on a "their morals or ours" position, according to which evaluative standards appropriate for socialists and capitalists are somehow incommensurable. In so far as I have succeeded in reaching determinate conclusions favoring socialism over capitalism, there is vindication for that tradition of socialist thought that holds that socialism is better than capitalism in respect to standards on which socialists and capitalists agree. To put this point in a more historicized form: under capitalism (and perhaps in pre-capitalist societies too), values and expectations are generated that socialism can realize better than capitalism. Thus capitalists' own values ultimately support socialism.

This conclusion is implicit in the question I asked. But it is corroborated by the answers I have been able to provide. If my arguments are sound, there is therefore a lesson to be drawn: that socialists would do well to eschew practices and attitudes that deny the role of values in motivating social change, and instead confront pro-capitalists as defenders of values which socialists and capitalists share. If both sides indeed suppose the same valuational standards, defenders of socialism can press their case on grounds even capitalists must accept.

However social movements – including those that today energize the left – do not form around expressly philosophical standards. It might therefore seem that a case for socialism based on these ideas simply fails to address what is important in actual politics; or at least that it would be more pertinent to compare socialism and capitalism with respect to concerns actually motivating political struggles. I do not disagree. I do think it would be worthwhile to compare socialism and capitalism with respect, say, to their prospects for furthering peace and avoiding nuclear annihilation, or for eliminating racial or gender-based oppressions, or for impeding environmental degradation. Nevertheless, there is political justification for adopting a philosophical focus too. The standards in question actually are important to real world politics even when they do not directly inspire political commitments. More importantly (in the present conjuncture), there are lessons to be drawn from the theoretical considerations advanced here that bear on what is becoming the central political question facing a Left divided between "reds" and "greens": the connection between new social movements, on the one hand, and "old-fashioned" socialist politics, on the other.

2

What is the connection between the ideas that comprise moral, social and political philosophy and the interests that motivate political commitments? This question points in two directions: towards a "metaphilosophical" examination of the status of moral claims and their applications in social and political philosophy, and towards an account of human nature and moral psychology. Plainly, it is not possible here to pursue either line of inquiry. I shall instead propose a position, with only scant supporting argument, that I think a more sustained discussion would support. The account I shall sketch underwrites the conclusion that freedom, equality, justice et al. matter more for real world politics than may sometimes appear. However this conclusion does not hinge on the particular view I shall advance. A similar conclusion could be defended in other ways.

The position I endorse, arguably the dominant view in Western moral philosophy since Aristotle, holds very generally that philosophical ideas track values that enter into causal accounts of human behavior and that articulate general human interests. There may be considerable variability in how these interests are expressed. Throughout *Arguing for Socialism*, I emphasize the historical particularity of the standards in consideration and of the values they articulate. Here I would stress the complementary claim: that there are powerful, trans-historical constraints, arising out of general features of human psychology, that pose limits on the variability of human values.[4] Moral philosophy provides an account of these values in their historically particular manifestations and, so far as possible, in their essential, trans-historical dimensions. There is no very satisfactory way of conveying a sense of these values, apart from particular attempts at giving them theoretical expression. Here I can only gesture in the direction of two arguably universal human interests that seem to motivate the values invoked here and, I would venture, any likely alternatives.

For assessing social and political arrangements, the most important of these interests is, I believe, a need to acknowledge the *dignity* of persons in contrast to the mere instrumentality of things. This expressive interest is represented perspicuously in Kant's insistence on the intrinsic value of humanity as such, in Feuerbach's and Marx's notion of "species-being," and in liberals' claims for an area of individuals' lives and behaviors in which (non-consensual) intrusions are illegitimate. It is this interest that motivates appeals to freedom in the historically particular forms traced in chapter 1. We have come to value freedom because the idea expresses what marks us off from the rest of nature: our capacity to choose among alternatives and to lay ends before ourselves – in short, our autonomy. At bottom, the same interest motivates the notions of equality and justice considered in chapter 2. These values articulate what Kant called "the moral equality of persons," grounded in the autonomy of the will. It is because we are equal precisely in the respect that matters for expressing our dignity that we are impelled to seek equality of condition or, where material equality is impossible or undesirable, to insist that we be treated fairly. The specifically political values considered in chapter 4 articulate a similar concern from the standpoint of individuals banded together in political associations. Democracy and the protection of rights, in so far as the latter idea is coherent, express respect for persons *qua* citizens – that is, as members of political communities. From within a specifically political framework, these values articulate the same underlying human interest as do freedom, equality, and justice. In different ways and from different vantage points, all of these standards represent a trans-historical disposition to attach value to humanity itself.

To account for this disposition, it is not necessary to suppose that humanity actually has value apart from the interest human beings have in acknowledging it. Values can be causally efficacious but still mind-dependent. My claim is just that regardless of circumstances of time and place, this interest will somehow be expressed; and that its expression is relevant, among other things, for political life. Standards expressing this interest will vary. In other times and places, values quite different from those invoked here would likely predominate. Even so, if I am right, the standards that would arise in place of the standards that now prevail would, in one way or another, articulate the same underlying human concern.

In his early writings, Marx used the idea of alienation to impugn the existing order and to account for its imminent revolutionary transformation. This use of alienation exemplifies the kind of value realism I have in mind. Alienation, for Marx (following Feuerbach), is a form of unfreedom – roughly, a denial of autonomy.[5] Where alienation flourishes, autonomy is blocked and even unacknowledged. But the interest it expresses is nevertheless real: it affects how people live, how they view themselves and each other, and their prospects for transforming their own condition. The end of alienation – the leap from the realm of necessity into the realm of freedom – is a move away from a deformed expression of this trans-historical human interest to its authentic realization. But whether autonomy is realized or not, the expressive interest that underlies freedom –

and its alienated "inversion" – remains efficacious and ineluctable.

The aggregative values of welfare and efficiency considered in chapter 3, like the valorization of development that, in the historical materialist scheme, provides human history with its structure and direction, articulates an interest more in common with the principle that motivates the behaviors of other species. Roughly, the interest we have trans-historically is to do well for ourselves – by increasing mastery of nature and diminishing burdensome toil. Historical materialism is, in effect, an account of the efficacy of this instrumental interest. Like autonomy, it may be blocked; the tendency for productive forces to develop may be countervailed. But an interest in development would nevertheless remain in force. For, like autonomy, development is rooted in human nature. It can fail to be realized, but it cannot fail to exact a toll.

If this view of the historical efficacy of the interests represented by the standards appealed to here is sound, there is reason to suspect that these values play a crucial role in forming and sustaining political movements – particularly those that address deep contemporary concerns – even when they are not directly implicated in the programmes or remonstrances of militants in these movements. This supposition is unproblematic, even trivial, in the case of the peace movement. World peace, or at least the avoidance of nuclear war, has become a condition for the continuation of human life on earth, and therefore for the realization of all human interests, including those that motivate the standards employed here. In movements for racial, ethnic and sexual equality it is also unproblematic that philosophical standards matter. These movements aim precisely at the fuller realization of equality and justice and democratic citizenship. Social movements that focus on environmental concerns are more problematic because, in some cases, militants active in environmental struggles appear to endorse values at odds with these standards and perhaps even with the interests they express. It should be noted, though, that even in this case there is a way to impute a causal role to each of the interests I have identified. Environmental politics can be seen as an attempt to implement justice across generations – by insuring a fair distribution of resources over time. It can also be construed as an attempt to further the instrumental interest that underlies our concern for welfare and efficiency, and that motivates the development of productive forces. Environmentalists sometimes appear to oppose development. It could be argued, however, that they are only taking a longer-run view, proposing development that does not sacrifice the future for the present. In so far as this depiction is fair, environmentalists do not at all oppose the mastery of nature and the diminution of toil, but only the unenlightened pursuit of these ends.

I will not say more here in support of the idea that values represent, in varying ways, underlying, trans-historical human interests. I would venture that this position is crucial for making sense, among other things, of political endeavors. But the claim that the standards invoked here for assessing socialism and capitalism are important even in political movements organized around more immediate concerns does not strictly depend on the truth of value realism. Values might be historically efficacious but unconstrained by trans-historical human interests or indeed by anything at all. Values might even be purely epiphenomenal on underlying social relations, as hyper-orthodox historical materialists would suppose. Even so, the point would remain: that for green concerns as much as for red, freedom, equality, and the rest matter.

3

However, there are currents on the Left that do not fit neatly into the account I have sketched, and some that do not fit at all. Expectations to the contrary, the ideas environmentalists advance are actually less problematic in this respect than are some views promoted by militants engaged in struggles against group oppressions and for national or sexual liberation.

We are told by environmentalists that it is wrong to think of nature strictly as a means for our own ends; that we are not the masters of nature, but its stewards. However, it is unclear how we could be part of nature without remaking it for human ends; without exercising mastery over it.[6] In this respect, we differ from other living things only in the means at our disposal. What then could stewardship be, other than enlightened mastery – the fusion of (immediate) human interests with the interests of the

233

rest of nature (as human beings understand it) – the better to accommodate the interests we have in our own well being? As stewards, we forbear from unconstrained exploitation, which depletes the environment from which we draw sustenance. Perhaps in doing so we would come to enjoy a less intrusive presence alongside the rest of nature. Perhaps, in other words, our conception of welfare would change. Our commitment to welfare as an ideal would nevertheless remain unchanged and apparently unchangeable.

Within the ecological movement of the past several decades a neo-Malthusian belief in (rapidly approaching) material limits to economic growth has been voiced from time to time. If such limits are indeed in sight, and if the human population continues to grow (as seems inevitable), economic expansion will become increasingly difficult to sustain. Individuals will therefore have to be satisfied with less; perhaps even to a point where the historical trajectory sketched in chapter 5, culminating in a level of abundance that makes communism possible and desirable, will become unachievable. I do not think that socialists have any cause for worry from this quarter. If I am wrong, many of the conclusions I draw in this book and in *The End of the State* would have to be rethought. But the valuational standards upon which these conclusions are based would remain intact. Even if they sometimes appear to make a virtue of necessity, neo-Malthusians are hardly committed to the view that the limits they identify are in themselves desirable; that less really is better. Their point is just that individuals ought to limit their expectations to what is, in fact, achievable.

More troubling for the claim that prevailing views of freedom, equality, justice and the rest actually motivate ongoing political struggles on the Left are positions sometimes advanced by nationalists or their feminist counterparts. Within these movements there are currents that insist on particularity, on the distinctiveness of group identifications – in apparent opposition to the moral equality of persons. It is important, however, to distinguish strategic positions from ultimate objectives. In particular circumstances, recognition of particularity – and separation from other groupings and from the dominant culture – may be crucial for achieving equality. In real world politics, some group identifications, even some nationalisms, are progressive.

234

Perhaps the most vexing problem the Left has faced has been to distinguish group identifications that are, as it were, part of the solution from those that are part of the problem. But this way of framing the question supposes – correctly, I believe – that in the final analysis all group identifications are part of the problem.

However, differences among persons sometimes are valued as ends in themselves rather than as means for achieving states of affairs in which these differences are inconsequential for social and political life. Thus some proponents of "identity politics" support separation not just as a strategy but as an ultimate aim. If their point is only the familiar pluralist idea that a universal, cosmopolitan culture is intrinsically less desirable than a mosaic of cultural differences – or that pluralism is instrumentally desirable, say, for realizing democratic ends – it is consistent with the position I have taken, and probably also sound. Or if the idea is that universalism is utopian and therefore dangerous because now and for the foreseeable future there can be no genuinely human identifications – that what appears to be universal is in fact insidiously particularist (perhaps in consequence of cultural imperialism or the persistence of patriarchal attitudes) – this point too, though often exaggerated, is well taken. It is, in any case, consistent with the position I have advanced. But there is a way of conceiving particularity as an end in itself that genuinely does oppose what I have called the consensus view.

The idea would be that group identifications are the proper locus of human beings' expressive interests: that we are first of all members of ethnic groups or races or genders, and only derivatively of humankind. I have claimed that there is a universal human need to acknowledge the dignity of humanity as such. The particularists I have in mind would oppose this contention. For them, if there is indeed an expressive interest in self-identification, it is group-centered rather than species-centered. However I am not at all sure that, if pressed, even ardent separatists would defend this position. It is more nearly consonant with racialism and other rightist ideologies than with longstanding traditions of the Left. Indeed, it is out of line with virtually all modern moral and social theory. But it is an idea towards which some separatist practices – and the rhetorical claims that support it – do appear to tend.

I suspect that the tension between universalists and parti-

235

cularists that runs throughout our culture, even into left-wing social movements, is largely, if not entirely, based on confusion; that a particularism genuinely at odds with universalism cannot be maintained, except perhaps by those whose sentiments remain obdurately pre-modern. But it is a coherent position, and nothing that I have said in the course of arguing for socialism decisively refutes it. However, support for the universalist view is suggested by the positions I have taken. In so far as there is a coherent body of philosophical doctrine that does in fact track values grounded in human nature, and in so far as a core idea expressed by the values that comprise this doctrine is the moral equality of persons, separateness can be, at best, only a strategic programme or a (pluralist) complement to an essentially universalistic vision. It cannot be an end in its own right.

4

In sum, the standards against which I have compared socialism and capitalism are pertinent to political movements organized around more immediate objectives – for world peace, for ending racial and sexual oppression, for preventing environmental harm. However the relevance of socialism and capitalism to these movements remains to be explored. To what extent, if at all, should socialism or capitalism matter to militants struggling for these concerns?

It is sometimes maintained that capitalism aggravates situations that lead to war by fostering international animosities through competition for markets and raw materials, while socialism supports a more cooperative allocation of the world's resources. Or it is argued that since capitalists have incentives to utilize the inequalities they find at hand in order to divide workers from each other, driving down wage rates and demobilizing challenges to their power, capitalism tends to exacerbate racial and sexual oppression – while socialism, in contrast, carries no similar imperative. Finally, it is held, again in contrast to socialism, that capitalism provides incentives for producers to plunder rather than protect the natural environment.

These considerations are familiar and, I think, sound. But they are hardly decisive. Good opposing arguments can be offered to each of them. Thus capitalism can be said to encourage peace as a condition for the proper functioning of its markets on a world scale; or to break down received inequalities and oppressions because of its structural indifference to the identities of the persons it joins in capitalist relations; or even to support environmental protection as a consequence of long-range, rational economic policy. On the other hand, socialism could be held to be indifferent to progress in all of these domains. It need not support peace at a world level nor does it require the demise of historically inherited oppressions. Some feminists have even insisted that socialism is compatible with the persistence of patriarchy and have expressed indifference or outright hostility towards it in consequence. Presumably, similar considerations apply to racial and ethnic oppressions. Finally, with regard to preventing environmental degradation, what is needed apparently is sound planning. But the deprivatization of ownership of alienable productive assets hardly guarantees that planning will be sound.

As in all the comparative assessments undertaken throughout this book, definitive conclusions can be drawn only after fuller specifications are provided of the institutional arrangements of particular socialisms and capitalisms. In addition, attention must be paid to the historical circumstances in which particular institutions figure. It is clear, for example, that the United States, still the premier capitalist state, is a greater threat to world peace than any existing socialist state; and it is fair to ascribe to capitalism itself a large part of the blame. But in other imaginable contexts, American capitalism could have different implications for world peace. Similar indeterminacies undo attempts at decisive judgments on any of the dimensions of concern to contemporary social movements. As I have noted repeatedly, it is one thing to argue that, as a matter of fact, existing socialisms or capitalisms perform more or less well according to one or another standard, and something else again to hold that these achievements or shortcomings count as arguments for or against socialism or capitalism.

However the theoretical considerations marshalled here, especially those of Marxian provenance, do have at least general pertinence for contemporary debates about the relevance of socialism for progressive social movements. Allowing for the indeterminacy that necessarily afflicts comparisons at this level of abstraction, I have concluded that *democratic* socialism is both possible and desirable – in comparison with capitalism, but also in comparison with non-democratic socialisms. I have argued too that democratic socialism, properly conceived, is socialism in transition to communism; and that this form of socialism is a dictatorship of the proletariat – not in the commonly accepted (and widely despised) sense of the term, but in the classical Marxian sense elaborated by Lenin in *The State and Revolution*. Finally, I have maintained that the dictatorship of the proletariat is a form of the state, a global organization of the social order that solves or at least mitigates what would otherwise be intractable coordination problems in societies fundamentally divided into social classes. These latter claims – advanced here in chapter 6 and developed further in *The End of the State* – are elements of a political theory implicit in a strain of Marxian thought but largely neglected in the Marxian theoretical tradition. Taken together, these considerations, tentative and inconclusive as they may be, suggest a definite political lesson: that progressive social change ultimately requires struggle in and over the state – for its radical democratization.

But this paramount political task, the democratization of the state, is the general democratization of the social order. Democracy – not the pale facsimile enshrined in the self-justifications of pro-capitalist liberal democrats, but the rule of the *demos*, the people in power – is the means but also the end of progressive social change. This is not to say that in every political struggle popular empowerment need be an express objective. Conjunctural circumstances may dictate otherwise. Struggles for world peace, for the end of racial and sexual oppression, and for the prevention of environmental degradation are some among many other likely progressive aims. The conclusion towards which we are led by the theoretical considerations adduced here is just that these struggles, in so far as they genuinely are progressive, become so in the final analysis because they further the global transformation of the social order through the radical transformation of the state – by and towards the empowerment of the people.

A strictly philosophical inquiry such as this cannot possibly provide an answer to the most vexing and urgent question of all: What is to be done? But, at least in this instance, a general perspective on that question has emerged. It follows from what has been claimed here, not strictly but tendentially, that we ought not to ignore the global objective that gives more particular concerns their progressive aspect. The wise course, in other words, is to be for socialism and for the greatest feasible democratization – and therefore for the dictatorship of the proletariat, the radical democratization of the (post-capitalist) social order, and communism.

"Old-fashioned" revolutionary socialists were encumbered with theoretical commitments that now seem naive and simplistic. After the New Left and the political forces that have succeeded it, it is clear as well that revolutionary socialists focussed too narrowly on economic objectives. They cared too little about the environment, and when they fought for peace or against racial, ethnic and gender-based oppressions, they failed to acknowledge the specificity and (relative) independence of these concerns. The political styles that have come to predominate on the Left have largely overcome these shortcomings. But in losing sight of the perspective of old-fashioned revolutionary socialism – its view of the relation between immediate struggles and ultimate objectives, the unity of its vision and its steadfastness of purpose – this advance has been won at great and unnecessary cost. In the end, it is unclear which style – the "postmodern" or the (now) "ancient" – has been more debilitating.

Again, no very precise guidelines follow from this general observation. In actual politics, conjunctural factors are always decisive. Perhaps for now the wisest policy for militants on the Left is to continue to pursue a diffuse, decentered politics, in disregard to ultimate socialist aims – a politics, in short, more green than red. I doubt the wisdom of this course, in part for the reason just indicated, though I concede that this reason vastly underdetermines my doubt.

In any case, it is beyond serious dispute that reversion to the political styles that dominated the Left decades ago would be folly. What I would suggest, however, is that this old-fashioned, unabashedly red politics did mask a "rational kernel" that is crucial to recover and build upon. For the foreseeable future, the fortunes of the Left will vary with its courage and ingenuity and with the vicissitudes of circumstance. But so long as capitalism survives, it is bound to generate fundamental opposition. There will always be a Left, therefore; and if the theoretical considerations provided here are even approximately on track, socialism, capitalism's unique historical rival, will continue to be a pole of attraction for it. The received tradition, whatever its shortcomings, never failed to acknowledge the centrality of socialism and its role in forging a communist future. Even as they pursued more immediate aims, traditional socialists kept a theoretically well-motivated final objective in sight. It would be well to retrieve this core dimension of their otherwise superseded political style. This is the immediately political lesson implicit in these remote theoretical considerations; and indeed the point of *Arguing for Socialism*.

Notes

Introduction

1 The expression "actually existing socialism" is taken from Rudolf Bahro, *The Alternative in Eastern Europe* (London: New Left Books, 1978), David Fernback, trans. It will be used in what follows to refer to the officially Communist countries: the Soviet Union, its Eastern European allies, China, Cuba, Vietnam and wherever else the "Soviet model" is in effect.

2 The equivalent terms "means of production" and "productive capacities" will be used here to denote non-labor factors of production. These terms are important, of course, in Marxian political economy; but their use here is simply descriptive.

3 This is a plausible use for the much invoked term "state capitalism." It is worth noting, in this regard, that capitalism can exist under juridical forms very different from those of traditional capitalist societies; that, as some who use this term intend, capitalism can exist in the (juridical) guise of state ownership. Capitalism exists wherever assets are privately owned – that is, wherever individuals or groups (less than the state, representing the public) have rights to income derived from particular assets (minimal capitalism) or in addition enjoy rights over the disposition of these assets (full capitalism, according to our definition), regardless of how these rights are represented juridically.

4 The term "post-capitalism" suggests a view of the direction of human history of a distinctively Marxian character. However, nothing in what follows, before Chapter 5 (where some aspects of the Marxian theory of history, historical materialism, are presented and defended), depends substantively on specifically Marxian claims about the nature and direction of human history. This term too is used here descriptively and for want of a theoretically neutral alternative.

5 Thus it would be reasonable to designate the Soviet Union or Eastern European Communist countries "state capitalist" if it could be shown that in these societies, despite the appearance of social control (through central planning), there are in fact capital markets. This is the position of, among others, Charles Bettelheim (see, for example, his *Calcul economique et formes de propriete* (Paris: Maspero, 1971)). Whatever its merits as an account of Soviet reality, Bettelheim's contention is conceptually apt. If social ownership of the means of production in the Soviet Union were only a juridical fiction, then the Soviet Union would not in fact be a socialist country.

Introduction to Part One

1 For a fuller elaboration of these claims, see my *Liberal Democracy: A Critique of Its Theory* (New York: Columbia University Press, 1981).
2 *Ibid.*
3 See my *The Politics of Autonomy: A Kantian Reading of Rousseau's Social Contract* (Amherst: University of Massachusetts Press, 1976).
4 See Chapter 6 below.

1 Freedom

1 For a discussion of this phenomenon, see Sheldon S. Wolin, *Politics and Vision: Continuity and Innovation in Western Political Thought* (Boston: Little, Brown, 1960), Chapters 9 and 10.
2 See my *Liberal Democracy: A Critique of Its Theory* (New York: Columbia University Press, 1981), Chapter 1.
3 A case in point is the discussion of negative and positive freedom in Isaiah Berlin's celebrated essay "Two Concepts of Liberty." See Isaiah Berlin, *Four Essays on Liberty* (Oxford University Press, 1969).
4 The expression is, of course, Rousseau's. See *The Social Contract*, Book 1, Chapter 7. For a fuller discussion of this difference, see my *The Politics of Autonomy: A Kantian Reading of Rousseau's Social Contract* (Amherst: University of Massachusetts Press, 1976), Chapters 1 and 2.
5 Cf. C.B. Macpherson, *The Political Theory of Possessive Individualism: Hobbes to Locke* (Oxford: The Clarendon Press, 1961), Chapters 1 and 2.
6 The expression is Robert Nozick's. See *Anarchy, State, and Utopia* (New York: Basic Books, 1974), p. 163.
7 It is also true that under socialism we are free (F1) to do some things we are not free (F1) to do under capitalism. In general, there is no algorithm for determining how free (F1) we are under one or another arrangement. As pointed out above, it certainly will not do to count up restrictions. For it is the *value* of the restrictions to those they restrict, not the sheer quantity of restrictions, that matters in assessing how free we are. See my *Liberal Democracy*, *op. cit.*, Chapter 9.
8 For data on wage differentials and degrees of inequality in actually existing capitalist and socialist societies, see Peter Wiles, *Distribution of Income: East and West* (Amsterdam: North Holland Publishing Company, 1974). Some capitalist countries, for example, Denmark, Sweden and Norway, fare better, by Wiles's measure, than do any of the countries of actually existing socialism in promoting material equality. Of course, the connection between equality and capacity-freedom has yet to be explored (see below and Chapter 2). But the fact that some actual capitalisms may fare better than any

actual socialisms in realizing equality should, at the very least, speak against facile assumptions about socialism and capitalism.

9 Isaiah Berlin, "Two Concepts of Liberty" in *Four Essays on Liberty*, *op. cit.*

10 The liberal tradition is insistent on this point. See, for example, John Stuart Mill, *On Liberty*.

11 See my *Liberal Democracy*, *op. cit.*, Chapters 2 and 9 for a fuller account of this characteristic, but strictly unnecessary, stipulation of many liberal democratic positions.

12 This position is cogently argued by Isaiah Berlin in the *Introduction* to *Four Essays on Liberty*, *op. cit.* Berlin argues that to count institutional impediments as restrictions on liberty is to confuse liberty with the conditions for its exercise.

2 Distributional values

1 See John Rawls, *A Theory of Justice* (Cambridge, Mass.: The Belknap Press of Harvard University Press, 1971). Rawls's position is developed further in a number of articles. Among the latter, see particularly, "The Basic Structure as Subject," in A.I. Goldman and J. Kim (eds), *Values and Morals* (Dordrecht, Holland: D. Reidel, 1978), pp. 47–71; "A Kantian Conception of Equality," *The Cambridge Review*, February 1975; and "Reply to Alexander and Musgrave," *Quarterly Journal of Economics*, November 1974.

2 Cf. *A Theory of Justice*, *op. cit.*, pp. 258–73. What Rawls argues is that the principles of justice he elaborates (see below) can in theory be satisfied by both capitalist and socialist political economic arrangements. This view is strictly compatible, of course, with the contention that these principles are more *likely* to be satisfied under one or another system of political economy. I will argue, contrary to what Rawls *seems* to think, that justice is indeed more likely to be realized under socialism than under capitalism.

3 Rousseau, for example, advocated equality (not strict equality, to be sure, but limits on permissible inequalities, according to which "no citizen should be rich enough to be able to buy another, and none poor enough to be forced to sell himself") not for its own sake, but because "liberty cannot subsist without it." See *The Social Contract*, Book 2, Chapter 1.

4 It will be necessary, in Chapter 6, to qualify this statement somewhat in as much as the key concept of Marxian political theory, the dictatorship of the proletariat, a concept crucial for the case I will advance for the historical possibility of democratic socialism, can be taken to imply political *inequality* along class lines. We will see, however, that this qualification does not in any way vitiate the point made here. It should also be noted that wherever social choices are made through representatives (as in parliamentary democracies), and where representative districts are not strictly proportional (as is

typically the case), formal political equality is, strictly speaking, also violated. But this situation is, I think, a shortcoming of institutional implementations of generally acknowledged theoretical commitments, not an expression of these theoretical commitments. Actual formal inequalities endured by women or members of racial or ethnic minorities similarly do not impugn the general, theoretical commitment. This is why it is easy to argue against these inequalities, though it is often very difficult to rectify them.

5 A useful selection of de Maistre's writings can be found in *The Works of Joseph de Maistre*, trans. Jack Lively (New York: Macmillan, 1965). Bonald's most important work is *Théorie du pouvoir politique et religieux*, 3 vols (Paris: Bloud & Barral, 1880).

6 See, for example, E.R. Rawson, *The Spartan Tradition in European Thought* (Oxford University Press, 1969). On the notion of virtue in the eighteenth century, particularly in French political thought, see the magisterial study of Robert Mauzi, *L'Idée de bonheur dans la littérature et la pensée française au 18e siècle* (Paris: A. Colin, 1960).

7 See n. 2 above.

8 See my *The Politics of Autonomy: A Kantian Reading of Rousseau's Social Contract* (Amherst: University of Massachusetts Press, 1976), Chapter 5.

9 Cf. *The Nicomachean Ethics*, Book 5; and for a more systematic and contemporary treatment, see Chaim Perelman, *The Idea of Justice and the Problem of Argument*, John Petrie, trans. (New York: Humanities Press, 1963), pp. 1–88.

10 Universal egalitarian humanism is an explicit objective and even an end-in-itself for some socialists. See, for example, George Bernard Shaw, *The Intelligent Woman's Guide to Socialism and Capitalism* (New York: Brentano's, 1928).

11 Cf. Karl Marx, "The Critique of the Gotha Program: Marginal Notes to the Program of the German Workers' Party," in K. Marx, F. Engels, *Selected Works* (Moscow: Foreign Language Publishing House, 1962), vol. 2.

12 "To each according to productive contribution" is, according to Marx in "The Critique of the Gotha Program," to govern distributions under socialism (that is, before the full realization of communism, where distributions will be made according to need). However, with a qualification to be noted presently, it does not appear that, in Marx's view, productive contribution constitutes a moral claim on benefits. Rather, I think Marx proposes that distributions be made according to productive contribution under socialism because, in his view, if talents and skills are not rewarded, they will not be cultivated and deployed, impeding development and ultimately, therefore, communism (where morally warranted distributions are finally possible). In other words, distribution according to productive contribution is a concession to the capitalist mentality that socialism inherits and ultimately seeks to overcome.

There is, however, a sense in which productive contribution may generate a claim on benefits, that even Marx would acknowledge. Thus we might think it proper to reward effort; to give more to those who work harder than others (by working longer hours or by doing more in the same time or perhaps even by performing more onerous tasks). It would not automatically follow, then, that in an advanced socialism, where the capitalist mentality that makes talent-pooling difficult to achieve is largely overcome, strictly egalitarian distribution would be appropriate. Indeed, it would seem that so long as there is scarcity such that not everyone can have everything they might reasonably want or need – the more industrious *should* get more. My suggestion is not contradicted by Marx's insistence that, under communism, distributions will be according to need. Under communism, in Marx's view, there is sufficient abundance that distribution is no longer problematic; and justice is therefore unimportant. Then there is, as it were, no particular point in rewarding effort. In such circumstances, distributions would be made according to need in the sense that wherever there is a need, one may take, as it were, from the common stock. Then "to each according to need," is not, strictly, a substantive principle of justice at all, but rather a *description* of how abundant resources will in fact be distributed under communism. Be that as it may, so long as distributional questions remain pertinent, it is well to distinguish *deserving* more from being in a position to extort more (which is, I have just suggested, the situation, even under socialism, of those who have scarce and vital skills).

13 See Bernard Williams, "The Idea of Equality" in Peter Laslett and W.G. Runciman (eds), *Philosophy, Politics and Society*, second series (New York: Barnes & Noble, 1962). What follows in this section draws upon Williams's analysis.

14 Cf. John Roemer, *A General Theory of Exploitation and Class* (Cambridge, Mass.: Harvard University Press, 1982), Chapters 7 and 8.

15 In *Anarchy, State, and Utopia, op. cit.*, Robert Nozick argues that egalitarianism, or indeed any theory of justice according to which justice consists in conformity to "patterns," is incompatible with liberty. See, particularly, pp. 160–4. This is indeed a challenge egalitarians – and socialists, in so far as they are also egalitarians – must confront. See G.A. Cohen, "Robert Nozick and Wilt Chamberlain: How Patterns Preserve Liberty," *Erkenntnis* II (1973), pp. 5–23.

16 See my *Liberal Democracy: A Critique of Its Theory* (New York: Columbia University Press, 1981), Chapter 9, especially pp. 159–61.

17 Cf. Roemer, *op. cit.*; and "New Directions In the Marxian Theory of Exploitation and Class," *Politics and Society*, vol. 11, no. 3 (1982), pp. 253–88.

18 The concept of exploitation Roemer develops is, I think, Marxian in the sense that it captures the spirit of the Marxian concept, even as it

takes direct issue with Marx's express formulations. For some reservations about Marx's own account of exploitation, see Roemer, *A General Theory of Exploitation and Class*, *op. cit.*, pp. 1–24. The use here of an essentially Marxian notion of exploitation is strictly descriptive. No commitment to distinctively Marxian views about history is intended, at this stage of the argument.

19 Strictly speaking, the exploited coalition need not be the proletariat. In Roemer's analysis, capitalist exploitation can exist even without labor markets. It is enough that there be differential distributions of owned assets, where "ownership" need imply no more than rights to income generated by assets (as in the proposed definition, in the Introduction, of "minimal capitalism"). It is therefore not strictly necessary for capitalist exploitation that capitalists exploit workers, nor even that there be a class of capitalists and workers. See Roemer, *A General Theory of Exploitation and Class*, *op. cit.*, Part 1.

20 Or, in other words, the concept of exploitation is invariant to the difference between coercive and non-coercive labor markets. What Marx showed in arguing for capitalist exploitation (not, to be sure, in the way just sketched, but with reference instead to the expropriation of "surplus value") is that the concept of exploitation, regarded as unproblematic for feudalism, can be *generalized* – to apply to societies with voluntary labor markets.

21 Cf. Roemer, *A General Theory of Exploitation and Class*, *op. cit.*, Chapter 7. In the main, Roemer uses the term "alienable assets" to designate what I have been calling "means of production" – that is, non-labor inputs to the production process. "Inalienable assets," in Roemer's terms, designate labor inputs. Skills, therefore, are inalienable assets.

22 Socialist exploitation is, in Roemer's account, the exploitation of the less skilled by the more skilled. It is exploitation in consequence of the private ownership of "inalienable assets" (such as skills). In this case, the exploited coalition, the unskilled, could improve its position by withdrawing with its per capita share of *all* assets, alienable and inalienable. The less skilled, in other words, would do better with talent pooling and without differential rewards to productive inputs, than they would under a system that rewards skills (or other productive contributions) differentially.

Status exploitation exists wherever there are differential rewards attached to incumbency of positions, irrespective of skills. A coalition will be said to be status exploited if it could improve the lot of its members by withdrawing with its own assets, but exempting itself from the dues accorded to status.

Both socialist and status exploitation are undoubtedly, to some extent, socially necessary, and will continue to be so for an indefinite future. None the less, they are forms of exploitation; and their elimination, wherever possible, should be a priority for socialists.

23 See, for example, Arthur M. Okun, *Equality and Efficiency: The Big Tradeoff* (Washington, D.C.: The Brookings Institution, 1975). Okun's position is plainly pro-capitalist, but also egalitarian.

24 What is remarkable, in the countries of actually existing socialism, is the paucity of attempts at motivating people ideologically without reliance on the carrot (material incentives) and stick (coercion). In the Soviet Union, just after the October Revolution and again, briefly, in the 1930s; in China during the Cultural Revolution; in Cuba for a few years in the mid-1960s; and sporadically elsewhere, there were some abortive attempts at motivating production "ideologically"; but all failed dismally. The motivational structure of individuals in the Communist countries today is, by all accounts, a mirror image – some say even a caricature – of the motivational structure dominant in the capitalist countries.

25 Also see my *The Politics of Autonomy, op. cit.*, especially Chapters 4 and 5.

26 For example, Marx, whose account of exploitation is unrivaled in historical and conceptual importance, was loath to compare socialism and capitalism with respect to justice. It is sometimes held, therefore, that, in Marx's view, justice is not a "critical" concept; a concept that can be used to compare discrete modes of production. The case for this interpretation of Marx is argued incisively by Allen Wood in "The Marxian Critique of Justice," *Philosophy and Public Affairs*, vol. 1, no. 3 (1972), pp. 246ff. This essay has elicited many replies. For a comprehensive review of the literature and also an important contribution to the discussion, see Allen E. Buchanan, *Marx and Justice: The Radical Critique of Liberalism* (Totowa, New Jersey: Rowman & Littlefield, 1982), Chapter 4.

27 There are a number of alternative formulations of Rawls's principles of justice throughout his writings. The summary here borrows from two of these formulations. See Rawls, *A Theory of Justice, op. cit.*, pp. 60 and 83.

28 See n. 2.

29 Cf. Rawls, *op. cit.*, p. 62.

30 See my *Liberal Democracy, op. cit.*, for an extended argument in support of this contention. I argue there that the "core theory" of liberal democracy need not exhibit the unfortunate abstractness that actual liberal democratic theory characteristically does. Strictly, that argument applies only to the dominant tradition's notions of freedom and interest; that is, to those components of the dominant tradition that apply, strictly, to political theory. but I would hazard that an analogous claim can be sustained for other components of the dominant tradition, including "social" (as opposed to strictly "political") categories.

31 Rawls, *A Theory of Justice, op. cit.*, pp. 136–8.

32 See David Schweickart, *Capitalism or Worker Control?: An Ethical and Economic Appraisal* (New York: Praeger, 1980), Chapter 1.

33 Cf. Alfred Marshall, *Principles of Economics*, 8th edn (New York: Macmillan, 1948); and Schweickart, *op. cit.*, pp.20–7.
34 For what follows in this paragraph and the next, see Schweickart, *op. cit.*, pp. 26–7.
35 Cf. John Locke, *Second Treatise of Government*, Chapter 5.
36 Robert Nozick, *Anarchy, State and Utopia* (New York: Basic Books, 1974).
37 In Nozick's account, entitlement theories of justice have a third component as well: a theory of justice in *restitution*, an account of how past rights violations can rightfully be corrected.

3   Aggregative values

1 See my *Liberal Democracy: A Critique of Its Theory* (New York: Columbia University Press, 1981), Chapters 1 and 3.
2 This characterization of utilitarianism encompasses, but is not limited to, the classical utilitarian view that the point, both in acting and in arranging social and political institutions, is to maximize the occurrence of certain states of mind (happiness) or even feelings (pleasure). For the present, it is not necessary to be as precise as classical utilitarians were, in characterizing individuals' interests. It is enough to say that utilitarianism accords central importance to individuals' interests by maximizing over them.
3 Thus "interest" is used here in only one of the many senses the term enjoys in contemporary political discourse. There are uses of "interest" that make essential reference to human needs; or to ideals or standards of what is good for persons, independent of their wants. In *Liberal Democracy: A Critique of Its Theory*, I suggest that "ideal-regarding" uses of "interest" very likely cannot be integrated conceptually into liberal democratic theory (the specifically *political* theory of the dominant tradition), and that they are introduced *ad hoc* to fulfill a number of tasks that cannot be fulfilled with the conceptual apparatus the dominant tradition provides. See my *Liberal Democracy*, *op. cit.*, Chapter 1.
4 Typically, however, liberal democrats also support representative legislatures and other institutions that effectively contradict this theoretical commitment. I discuss this contradiction and its implications for liberal democratic theory in *Liberal Democracy*, *op. cit.*, Chapter 5; and in Chapter 4 below.
5 It has been known since the early 1950s, when Kenneth Arrow published his seminal *Social Choice and Individual Values* (New Haven, Yale University Press, 1951; sec. edn 1963), that if reasonable conditions are stipulated as constraints on this "device," conditions intended to reconstruct in very minimal fashion what apparently must be true of any collective choice procedure that counts as democratic, contradictions are generated; or, equivalently, that the device is

"impossible" or self-contradictory. The stipulated conditions cannot all be simultaneously true. This result may have far-reaching implications for the political theory of the dominant tradition. See my *Liberal Democracy*, *op. cit.*, Chapter 3.

6 See my *Liberal Democracy*, *op. cit.*, Chapter 4.

7 What follows draws upon Charles E. Lindbloom, *Politics and Markets: The World's Political-Economic Systems* (New York: Basic Books, 1977), Chapter 6.

8 For what follows, see Lindbloom, *op. cit.*, Chapter 5.

9 A characteristic example of this sort of argument from *The Wealth of Nations* (New York: Random House, 1937), p. 423, goes as follows:

> As every individual...endeavours as much as he can both to employ his capital in the support of domestic industry, and so to direct that industry that its produce may be of the greatest value; every individual necessarily labours to render the annual revenue of the society as great as he can. He generally, indeed, neither intends to promote the public interest, nor knows how much he is promoting it. By preferring the support of domestic to that of foreign industry, he intends only his own security; and by directing that industry in such a manner as its produce may be of the greatest value, he intends only his own gain, and he is in this, as in many other cases, led by an invisible hand to promote an end which was no part of his intention. Nor is it always the worse for the society that it was no part of it. By pursuing his own interest he frequently promotes that of the society more effectually than when he really intends to promote it. I have never known much good done by those who affected to trade for the public good. It is an affectation, indeed, not very common among merchants, and very few words need be employed in dissuading them of it.

4 Political values

1 See *The Social Contract*, Book 3, Chapter 4.

2 See C.B. Macpherson, *The Real World of Democracy* (Oxford University Press, 1966).

3 For what follows in this paragraph and the next, see Robert Paul Wolff, "Beyond Tolerance" in Wolff, Herbert Marcuse and Barrington Moore, Jr., *A Critique of Pure Tolerance* (Boston: Beacon Press, 1965).

4 Cf. my *Liberal Democracy: A Critique of Its Theory* (New York: Columbia University Press, 1981), Chapter 3.

5 Cf. my *The Politics of Autonomy: A Kantian Reading of Rousseau's Social Contract* (Amherst: University of Massachusetts Press, 1976), pp. 59–72.

6 This reproach is consistent with, but not identical to, the claim, sometimes advanced by Marxists investigating differential forms of

the state and their relation to specific "modes of production," that the capitalist state itself works to promote the interests of capital, even when capitalists do not directly exercise control over it. If that claim can be sustained, it would follow directly that the political process is weighted in favor of the interests of some individuals (owners of capital) at the expense of others (everyone else). However, the claim advanced here is independent of any particularly Marxian views of the capitalist state. The contention is just that states in capitalist societies generally fail to live up to the democratic ideals they characteristically profess, in virtue of the inequality that pervades capitalist societies. The specifically Marxian view of the capitalist state will be broached, again, in Chapter 6 – where a number of themes of Marxian political theory will be considered.

7 What might make other things not equal is the likelihood that, in democratic collective choice, individuals' rights are jeopardized. The concept of rights and its relation to democratic values will be discussed below.

8 This conclusion would be resisted by those for whom some or, at the limit, all matters pertaining to the acquisition and use of (private) property are protected by inviolable individual rights. The prototype for this sort of position is, of course, John Locke's argument for the inviolability of property rights in *The Second Treatise of Government*. As already noted (in the Appendix to Chapter 2), an important contemporary neo-Lockean argument is to be found in Robert Nozick's *Anarchy, State and Utopia* (New York: Basic Books, 1974). For Locke, in the end, it is God who justifies the ascription of property rights. Nozick's account is virtually bereft of any attempt at justifying the rights ascriptions upon which his arguments rest.

9 See my *Liberal Democracy*, *op. cit.*, Chapter 8.

10 Rousseau's most celebrated attack on representative government occurs in *The Social Contract*, Book 3, Chapter 15. However, it is not clear how consistently Rousseau maintained this hostility, especially in his reflections on actual political arrangements. It has even been argued that, on balance, despite some very pronounced remarks to the contrary, Rousseau can be seen as a *defender* of representative government! See, for example, Richard Fralin, *Rousseau and Representation: A Study of the Development of His Concept of Political Institutions* (New York: Columbia University Press, 1978).

11 The marking off an area of individuals' activities that is immune from societal and, particularly, state interference is definitive of the liberal strain of modern political philosophy. See the Introduction and also my *Liberal Democracy*, *op. cit.*, Chapter 1.

12 See *The Second Treatise of Government*, particularly Chapters 5, 7 and 8.

13 See my *Liberal Democracy*, *op. cit.*, Chapter 1; and Sheldon S. Wolin, *Politics and Vision: Continuity and Innovation in Western Political Thought* (Boston: Little, Brown, 1960), Chapter 9.

14 For a fuller discussion of many of these issues, see my *Liberal Democracy*, *op. cit.*, Chapter 7.

15 It is for reversing the ideal, Kantian order – for transforming persons (workers) into things and things (capital) into persons (in the sense that the requirements of capital accumulation and therefore capital itself determine, as would a human agent's will, the disposition of things) that Marx, in his early writings, faults capitalism for generating alienation. See Karl Marx, Frederick Engels, *Collected Works*, vols 3 and 4 (New York: International Publishers, 1975). I have discussed these issues in my "Alienation as Heteronomy," *Philosophical Forum*, vol. 8, nos 2–4.

16 Rights function as *correctives* in the way that, for Aristotle, considerations of *equity* (by which Aristotle intends something of what we might understand today by "mercy") should be introduced to mitigate and *correct* the rigorous requirements of strict justice. See his *The Nicomachean Ethics*, Book 5, Chapter 10.

17 See H.L.A. Hart, "Are There Any Natural Rights?", *Philosophical Review*, 64 (1955), pp. 175–91.

18 Strictly speaking, only some rights claims specify "liberties" in this sense. Thus, in Hohfeld's well-known classification of rights claims, there are also "demand rights," "powers" and "immunities." See Wesley N. Hohfeld, *Fundamental Legal Conceptions*, 2nd edn (New Haven: Yale University Press, 1964).

19 For a fuller account of what follows, see my *The Politics of Autonomy*, *op. cit.*, especially Chapters 4 and 5.

20 It might be held that even though rights lack foundations, their attribution to persons is still not arbitrary so long as there is some consensus within political communities as to what rights individuals hold. Very often, there is appreciable consensus on rights ascriptions. But, again, what is needed is a justification for rights claims, not a report on people's beliefs. For these beliefs are themselves part of what is to be evaluated when different social arrangements are compared with respect to how well they protect individuals' rights.

5 Historical materialism

1 A very striking case in point is the work of Louis Althusser and his colleagues. For Althusser, "historical materialism" is expressly endorsed, but the term is used to designate Marxian social science in general. In Althusser's view, historical materialism does not even include a substantive theory of epochal historical change of the sort Marx advanced in the 1859 *Preface*. This radically redefined "historical materialism" is elaborated extensively by Etienne Balibar, Althusser's principal collaborator, in "The Fundamental Concepts of Historical Materialism." See L. Althusser and E. Balibar, *Reading*

Capital (London: New Left Books, 1970). On the Althusserians' version of historical materialism, see my "Althusser's Marxism," *Economy and Society*, vol. 10, no. 3 (August 1981), pp. 243–83.

2 Cf. G.A. Cohen, *Karl Marx's Theory of History: A Defence* (Oxford University Press and Princeton University Press, 1978). A similar position is advanced by Allen Wood in *Karl Marx* (Boston: Routledge & Kegan Paul, 1981), Chapters 5–8.

3 Cohen argues persuasively against using the term "mode of production," insisting that a more apt designation for the epochal units into which historical materialism divides history is "economic structure." See *Karl Marx's Theory of History*, *op. cit.*, pp. 79–84. However, in view of the widespread and continuing use by Marxists of Marx's own term, it seems inappropriate to abandon it, even for the very good reasons Cohen advances, particularly when the point is to reconstruct the orthodox position. In what follows, accordingly, the terms "economic structure" and "mode of production" will be used interchangeably, despite Cohen's recommendations. It has been argued, however, that Cohen's choice of terms is not at all apt; and that how we designate epochal historical divisions is of considerable theoretical consequence. See Richard Miller, "Productive Forces and the Forces of Change: A Review of G.A. Cohen, *Karl Marx's Theory of History: A Defence*," *Philosophical Review*, vol. 90, no. 1 (January 1981). Miller insists that, for Marx, stable social structures and also epochal social transformations are based on and explainable by reference to *modes of production* – that is, "the activities, facilities and relationships, material *and* social, through which material goods are produced" (*ibid.* p. 106). Thus defined, the term "mode of production" is more inclusive than "economic structure," which comprises social relations of production only. The "mode of production" interpretation Miller goes on to sketch implies among its consequences a severe diminution of the technological determinism of Cohen's – and I think also Marx's – view of history. In substance, what follows largely agrees with Miller against Cohen on what is and is not defensible. However, I disagree with the suggestion that a more defensible Marxian position was, in fact, already developed by Marx. I think, in other words, that Cohen has reconstructed Marx's view correctly. However, this is not the place to debate points of interpretation. In what follows, I take it for granted that Cohen's is the orthodox view. But even if Cohen has not gotten Marx right – a point I am not at all prepared to concede – his position is still sufficiently "orthodox" to provide a point of departure for the elaboration and criticism of historical materialism, and for the search for its "rational kernel." In what follows, then, it is "economic structure" in Cohen's sense that will be intended even when the traditional term "mode of production" is used. Economic structures or modes of production are, in this usage, discrete sorts of social relations of production. They do not include, as Miller's "modes of production" do, *material* forces of production.

4 Cf. Cohen, *op. cit.*, p. 198.
5 *Ibid*.
6 Marx's most celebrated disparaging allusion to the contractarian tradition occurs in the opening sentences of the 1857 *Introduction* to the *Grundrisse*, a text that also serves as the *Introduction* to *The Critique of Political Economy*, the text whose *Preface* provides the most direct formulation of historical materialism. Probably the clearest account of the human condition in the absence of specifically political institutions – in a "state of nature" – and of human nature, as conceived in the contractarian tradition, is provided by David Hume in *A Treatise of Human Nature*, Book 3, part 2, section 2; and *An Enquiry Concerning the Principles of Morals*, section 3, part 1. A similar account can be gleaned from Thomas Hobbes's *Leviathan*, Book 1, Chapter 13. For a more recent statement, see H.L.A. Hart, *The Concept of Law* (Oxford: Clarendon Press, 1961), pp. 189–95; and John Rawls, *A Theory of Justice*, *op. cit.*, pp. 126–30. The salient features of the state of nature are, among others, the relative equality among human beings in the distribution of mental and physical endowments; the geographical proximity of human beings one to another; and the relative scarcity of most of what nature provides for the satisfaction of human wants. Human nature is, at the very least, self-interested, in the sense taken over by liberal democratic theory and considered above in Chapter 3. For Hobbes, more vividly, but still characteristically, human beings are, by nature, acquisitive and diffident (fearful) and given to dominate one another.
7 Cohen, *op. cit.*, p. 152.
8 The sorts of class interests in contention here are long-range interests: interests in maintaining existing economic structures (sets of production relations) or in overthrowing them and replacing them by new sets of production relations. "Objective" class interests may then be construed as a subset of the "true wants" proposed in Chapter 3. They are what the long-range class interests of individual members of classes would be, given full knowledge and adequate reflection. Historical materialism, then, claims to provide an account of these long-range objective class interests. Of course the interests of individual members of classes, their "subjective" interests, may deviate substantially from their objective interests. A fundamental task of Marxian politics, then, is to bring the subjective interests of the working class, the (potential) agent of socialist revolution, in line with long-range objective working-class interests.
9 In standard accounts, the organic composition of capital q is defined as the ratio of constant capital c, the labor "embodied" in means of production, over the sum of constant and variable capital v, the capital required to reproduce labor power. Thus $q=c/c+v$; or, in other words, the organic composition of capital is a measure of the extent to which labor is furnished with means of production in the production process. The rate of profit p is defined as the ratio of surplus value s to total capital outlay. Thus $p=s/c+v$. Finally the rate of surplus value

s' is defined as the ration of surplus value to variable capital; $s'=s/v$. Combining these definitions, it follows that $p=s'(l-q)$; and accordingly, that as the value of q, the organic composition of capital, rises, the value of p, the rate of profit, declines. See Paul M. Sweezy, *The Theory of Capitalist Development: Principles of Marxian Political Economy* (New York: Monthly Review Press, 1942).

10 See Geoff Hodgson, "The Theory of the Falling Rate of Profit," *New Left Review*, 84, March/April 1974; and Ian Steedman, *Marx After Sraffa* (London: New Left Books, 1977), Chapter 9. A more sustained and technical account of these issues can be found in John Roemer, *Analytical Foundations of Marxian Economic Theory* (Cambridge University Press, 1981), Chapters 3–6.

11 In *Karl Marx's Theory of History*, *op. cit.*, Cohen insists that none of his arguments depends upon any "specifically labor-theoretical account of value"; and in a later essay, "The Labor Theory of Value and the Concept of Exploitation," *Philosophy and Public Affairs*, vol. 8, no. 2 (1979), pp. 338–60, Cohen argues for the incoherence of the labor theory of value, thereby underscoring the independence of his account of historical materialism from traditional Marxian crisis theory.

12 Cohen, *Karl Marx's Theory of History*, *op. cit.*, pp. 306–7.

13 Cf. Jean-Jacques Rousseau, *The First and Second Discourses*, Roger D. Masters, ed. (New York: St Martin's Press, 1964).

14 On this point, even widely divergent tendencies in recent Marxian historiography agree. See, for example, Perry Anderson, *Lineages of the Absolutist State* (London: New Left Books, 1974); and Immanuel Wallerstein, *The Modern World-System: Capitalist Agriculture and the Origins of the European World-Economy in the Sixteenth Century* (New York and London: Academic Press, 1974).

15 Cohen, *Karl Marx's Theory of History*, *op. cit.*, pp. 203–4 and p. 204, n. 2.

16 See, for example, Nicos Poulantzos, *Political Power and Social Classes* (London: New Left Books, 1973); and Adam Przeworski, "Social Democracy as an Historical Phenomenon," *New Left Review*, no. 122, 1980.

17 Cf. Jon Elster, "Cohen on Marx's Theory of History," *Political Studies*, vol. 28, no. 1 (1980), and Cohen's reply "Functional Explanation: Reply to Elster," *ibid*.

18 To declare the Soviet Union capitalist would, of course, avoid the problem; but it would also beg the question – for in the Soviet Union capitalist property relations have indeed been abandoned. Defenders of the orthodox view who want also to acknowledge the socialist character of Soviet society could argue that the emergence of capitalism *elsewhere* – in Western Europe and then in North America – transformed the world context sufficiently to permit non-capitalist forms of development. But it is unclear how the existence of capitalism elsewhere can function as an exogenous pressure promoting development in ways distinct from the endogenous

tendencies historical materialism postulates – unless underdeveloped socialist countries are somehow integrated into the world capitalist system (as the Soviet Union, at the outset particularly, was not).

19 Cf. Joshua Cohen, "Review of *Karl Marx's Theory of History: A Defence*," *Journal of Philosophy*, vol. 79, no. 5 (May 1982), p. 255.

20 The prototype of this mainstream contention is the view of history propounded by Rousseau in *The Discourse on the Origin of Inequality*, *op. cit.* (see n. 13).

6 Socialism and democracy

1 K. Marx and F. Engels, *Selected Works in Two Volumes*, vol. 1 (Moscow: Foreign Languages Publishing House, 1962), p. 36.

2 *Ibid.*, p. 53.

3 Cf. Etienne Balibar, "La rectification du *manifeste communiste*," in *Cinq etudes du materialisme historique* (Paris: Maspero, 1974), p. 78.

4 For what follows, see Etienne Balibar, *On the Dictatorship of the Proletariat* (London: New Left Books, 1977); and my review essay "Balibar on the Dictatorship of the Proletariat," *Politics and Society*, vol. 7, no. 1 (1977).

5 V.I. Lenin, "Proletarian Revolution and the Renegade Kautsky," *Collected Works*, vol. 28, p. 236.

6 These ideas of Lenin's have been developed perspicuously by Antonio Gramsci and Louis Althusser, particularly. Cf. Antonio Gramsci, *Selections from the Prison Notebooks* (New York: International Publishers, 1971); and Louis Althusser in "Ideology and Ideological State Apparatuses (Notes Towards an Investigation)" in *Lenin and Philosophy and Other Essays* (London: New Left Books, 1971).

7 Cf. Richard W. Miller, "Marx and Aristotle," *Canadian Journal of Philosophy*, suppl. vol. 7(1981): *Marx and Morality*, pp. 323–52; and Alan Gilbert, "Historical Theory and the Structure of Moral Argument in Marx," *Political Theory*, vol. 9, no. 2 (May 1981), pp. 173–206. However, Marx's early philosophical writings – for example, *The Critique of Hegel's Philosophy of Right* (1843) and *The Economic and Philosophic Manuscripts* (1844) – are Kantian in their conceptual structure. See my "Alienation as Heteronomy," *Philosophical Forum*, vol. 8, nos 2–4 (1978).

8 See Aristotle, *Politics*, Ernest Baker, ed. (Oxford University Press, 1946), pp. 35–6 (126a, 5–20). Neither Aristotle nor Marx sees happiness as a commodity to be consumed, as in traditional utilitarianism, but rather as an active concomitant of self-realization and self-expression.

9 An objective of Marxian social science is to discover the possible scope of individual choice, of unconstrained individual self-determination, within historically developing social constraints. In different historical periods, under different historical conditions, the scope for individual choice will be more or less substantial, just as is the scope for individual choice and action in making history.

Conclusion

1 Cf. Blaise Pascal, *Pensées* (New York: Dutton, 1958), sections 3 and 4 (pp. 184–290).
2 The affinity between Rawls's account of the selection of principles of justice and Pascal's wager has been noted by Bernard Williams in "Rawls and Pascal's Wager," in *Moral Luck: Philosophical Papers 1973–1980* (Cambridge University Press, 1981).

Afterword: 1988

1 See *The End of the State* (London: Verso, 1987), especially chapter 4, for elements of a case against attempting detailed specifications of future social, political and economic arrangements in isolation from conjunctural analyses of particular situations.
2 See the Preface to the original edition of this book.
3 The discussion of historical materialism in chapter 5 herein indirectly supports this suggestion. See also *The End of the State*, *op. cit.*, chapter 5.
4 I believe, in addition, that there has been moral *progress* in human history; that the historical materialist trajectory of economic structures tracks not just increasing levels of development but also successively greater realizations of the interests that underlie valuational claims. Nothing that I say here, however, depends upon this additionally controversial contention. I shall therefore say nothing further in its defense except to refer the reader back to the discussion of exploitation in chapter 2, where some elements of an argument in defense of moral progress may be found.
5 See chapter 6, note 7.
6 The idea that the nature human beings confront is not purely given, but is necessarily a "humanized nature," a nature transformed by human purposes, is a central theme of Marx's early writings and of Hegelian social philosophy generally.